SPIRITUAL DEPRESSION

ITS CAUSES AND CURE

D. MARTYN LLOYD-JONES

Wm. B. Eerdmans Publishing Company
Grand Rapids, Michigan

PHOTOLITHOPRINTED BY GRAND RAPIDS BOOK MANUFACTURERS, INC.
GRAND RAPIDS, MICHIGAN
1965

To
ANN

FOREWORD

These sermons were preached on consecutive Sunday mornings at Westminster Chapel and are here reproduced virtually as they were delivered.

The need for them arose as the result of pastoral experience, and they are now published in book form largely as the result of repeated requests that they might be issued in this form.

Believing as I do that the greatest need of the hour is a revived and joyful Church the subject dealt with in these sermons is to me of the greatest possible importance. Unhappy Christians are, to say the least, a poor recommendation for the Christian Faith; and there can be little doubt but that the exuberant joy of the early Christians was one of the most potent factors in the spread of Christianity.

The treatment of the subject is by no means exhaustive. I have tried to deal with what I have found to be the commonest causes of trouble. In several instances (e.g., the relationship between the physical, the psychic, and the spiritual) I would have liked to deal with the problem more thoroughly, but that was hardly possible in a sermon. In any case sermons are not intended for the 'experts' but for the 'common people' and those who are in need of help.

I pray that God will bless them to all such.

All who may derive some help from them will want to join with me in thanking Mrs. Hutchings who originally took down the sermons in shorthand, and my wife who looked after corrections, proof-reading, etc.

WESTMINSTER CHAPEL,   D. M. LLOYD-JONES
September, 1964

CONTENTS

Why art thou cast down, O my soul? and why art thou disquieted in me? hope thou in God: for I shall yet praise Him for the help of His countenance.

Psalm 42. 5

Why art thou cast down, O my soul? and why art thou disquieted within me? hope thou in God: for I shall yet praise Him, who is the health of my countenance and my God.

Psalm 42. 11

I

GENERAL CONSIDERATION

'THE simplest description of the five books of Psalms is that they were the inspired prayer-and-praise book of Israel. They are revelations of truth, not abstractly, but in the terms of human experience. The truth revealed is wrought into the emotions, desires, and sufferings of the people of God by the circumstances through which they pass.'

It is because that is such a true description of them that the Psalms have always proved to be a great source of solace and encouragement to God's people throughout the centuries—both the children of Israel and the members of the Christian Church.

Here we are able to watch noble souls struggling with their problems and with themselves. They talk to themselves and to their souls, baring their hearts, analysing their problems, chiding and encouraging themselves. Sometimes they are elated, at other times depressed, but they are always honest with themselves. That is why they are of such real value to us if we also are honest with ourselves.

In this particular Psalm which we propose to consider the Psalmist is unhappy and in trouble. That is why he cries out in the dramatic words: 'Why art thou cast down, O my soul? and why art thou disquieted in me? hope thou in God; for I shall yet praise Him, who is the health of my countenance, and my God'.

This statement, which we have twice in this Psalm, is found also in the following Psalm. Some regard Psalm 43 as being part of the same statement and not a separate Psalm. It is a matter which cannot be decided, and it is quite immaterial, but in both these Psalms this statement is repeated, for we find it at the end of Psalm 43 as well.

The Psalmist is giving an account of his unhappiness, the unhappiness of his soul, the condition through which he was passing when he wrote these words. He tells us the cause of that unhappiness. Probably at that particular time he was prevented from joining with others in public worship in the House of God. But not only that, he was clearly being attacked by certain

9

enemies. There were those who were doing their utmost to depress him and he gave an account of that. We are interested chiefly, however, in the way in which he faces the situation, and the way in which he deals with himself.

Our subject, in other words, is that which we may describe as 'spiritual depression', its causes and the way in which it should be treated. It is interesting to notice the frequency with which this particular theme is dealt with in the Scriptures and the only conclusion to be drawn from that is that it is a very common condition. It seems to be a condition which has afflicted God's people right from the beginning, for you find it described and dealt with in the Old Testament and in the New. That in itself would be sufficient reason for drawing your attention to it, but I do so also because it seems in many ways to be the peculiar trouble with many of God's people and the special problem troubling them at this present time.

There are many reasons for that. One of the main ones being, undoubtedly, the terrible events which we have lived through in this generation, the two wars and the consequent upheavals. That is not by any means the sole reason, but I have no doubt it is partly responsible. But whatever the reason, the fact remains that there are large numbers of Christian people who give the impression of being unhappy. They are cast down, their souls are 'disquieted within them', and it is because of that that I am calling attention to the subject.

In making an extensive analysis of this subject we must proceed along two lines. First of all, we must deal with the Biblical teaching concerning this matter, and then we can go on to look at certain notable examples or illustrations of the condition in the Bible, and observe how the persons concerned behaved and how God dealt with them. That is a good way of facing any problem in the spiritual life. It is good, always, to start with the Bible, where there is explicit teaching on every condition and it is also good to look at examples and illustrations from the same source.

We can be greatly helped by the two methods; and I would enter a plea at this point for the importance of following both of them. There are some people who are only interested in the illustrations, in the stories; but if we are not careful to extract the principles which are illustrated by the stories, we shall probably end by aggravating our own condition, and though there is great profit to be gained by looking at examples and illustrations, it is very vital that we should take the teaching first. There are many people who seem to be in trouble because they are more or less living on other people's experiences, or are coveting other people's experiences; and it is because they are always looking at persons and their stories instead of first grasping the teaching, that they so often and so badly go astray. Our knowledge of the Bible should have forewarned and safeguarded us against that particular danger, because it invariably does both things, as we shall see in our discussions of this subject. There is this great doctrinal teaching, plain and clear, and then God in His grace has added also the illustrations in order that we may see the great principles being worked out in practice.

I need scarcely explain why I deem it important that we should face this particular question. I do so partly for the sake of those who are in this condition, in order that they may be delivered from this unhappiness, this disquiet, this lack of ease, this tension, this troubled state which is described so perfectly by the Psalmist in this particular Psalm. It is very sad to contemplate the fact that there are Christian people who live the greater part of their lives in this world in such a condition. It does not mean that they are not Christians, but it does mean that they are missing a great deal, missing so much that it is important that we should enquire into the whole condition of spiritual depression outlined so clearly in this psalm, if only for their sake.

But there is another and more important reason, which is that we must face this problem for the sake of the Kingdom of God and for the glory of God. In a sense a depressed Christian is a contradiction in terms, and he is a very poor recommendation for the gospel. We are living in a pragmatic age. People today are not primarily interested in Truth but they are interested in results. The one question they ask is: Does it work? They are frantically seeking and searching for something that can help them. Now we believe that God extends His Kingdom partly through His people, and we know that He has oftentimes done some of the most notable things in the history of the Church through the simple Christian living of some quite ordinary people. Nothing is more important, therefore, than that we should be delivered from a condition which gives other people, looking at us, the impression that to be a Christian means to be unhappy, to be sad, to be morbid, and that the Christian is one who 'scorns delights and lives laborious days'. There are many indeed who give this as a reason for not being Christian, and for giving up all interest they may ever have had in the Christian faith. They say: Look at Christian people, look at the impression they give! And they are very fond of contrasting us with people out in the world, people who seem to be so thrilled by the things they believe in, whatever they may be. They shout at their football matches, they talk about the films they have seen, they are full of excitement and want everybody to know it; but Christian people too often seem to be perpetually in the doldrums and too often give this appearance of unhappiness and of lack of freedom and of absence of joy. There is no question at all but that this is the main reason why large numbers of people have ceased to be interested in Christianity. And, let us be quite frank and admit it, there is a sense in which there is some justification for their attitude, and we have to confess that their criticism is a fair one. It behoves us, therefore, not only for our own sakes, but also for the sake of the Kingdom of God and the glory of the Christ in Whom we believe, to represent Him and His cause, His message and His power in such a way that men and women, far from being antagonized, will be drawn and attracted as they observe us, whatever our circumstances or condition. We must so live that they will be compelled to say: Would to God I could be like that, would to God I could live in this world and go through this world as that person does. Obviously, if we are cast down ourselves we are never going to be able to function in that way.

For the moment I want to direct attention to our subject in general. I want to survey and consider the causes in general, and also to look at the way in which we should treat the condition in general in ourselves if we are suffering from it. Having looked at it in general, we shall then be in a position to go into a more detailed consideration of the condition, and I would emphasize the importance of doing that. If you examine the works and the writings of those who are most famous in the history of the Church in this country for their work on this particular problem, you will find that they invariably dealt with it in this way. I know that that is not the fashion today. We are all in such a hurry, we want everything at once. We believe that all truth can be stated in a few minutes. The answer to that is that it cannot, and the reason why so many today are living superficial Christian lives is because they will not take time to examine themselves.

Let me use an illustration. So often you hear of people who are in difficulty about carrying out some treatment that has been prescribed by a doctor. They go to a doctor and he gives them instructions. They go home imagining that they know exactly what to do; but when they come to the carrying out of the treatment they find that the doctor did not give them sufficiently detailed instructions. He had made a general statement and had never come down to details. So they are at a loss, they do not know what they have to do, nor can they remember exactly how the treatment is to be applied. The same thing applies to teaching, and the wise teacher always lays down his general principles first, but never neglects to work them out in detail. General statements are not enough in and of themselves, we must also come down to the particular. For the moment, however, we are concerned with the general picture.

First of all, then, let us look at the condition. We can never find a better description of it than that which is given us here by this man. It is an extraordinarily accurate picture of spiritual depression. Read the words and you can almost see the man looking cast down and dejected. You can almost see it in his face. In this connection notice the difference between verse 5 and verse 11. Take verse 11: 'Why art thou cast down, O my soul? and why art thou disquieted within me? hope thou in God for I shall yet praise Him who is the health of my countenance and my God'. In verse 5 he puts it: 'Why art thou cast down, O my soul? and why art thou disquieted within me? hope thou in God, for I shall yet praise Him for the help of His countenance'. In verse 5 he declares that the sight of God's countenance is always helpful; but in verse 11 he speaks of 'my countenance'. In other words, the man who is dejected and disquieted and miserable, who is unhappy and depressed always shows it in his face. He looks troubled and he looks worried. You take one glance at him and you see his condition. Yes, says the Psalmist in effect, but when I really look at God, as I get better, my face gets better also—'He is the health of my countenance'. I lose that drawn, haggard, vexed, troubled, perplexed, introspective appearance and I begin to look composed and calm, balanced and bright. This is not the putting on of a mask, but something that is inevitable. If we are depressed or unhappy, whether we like it or not, we will show it in our face. On the other hand, if we are in the right relationship to God, and in a true spiritual condition, that again quite inevitably must express itself in our countenance, though I am not suggesting we should perpetually have that inane grin upon our faces that some people think is essential to the manifestation of true Christian joy. You need not put anything on, it will be there; it cannot help expressing itself—'He is the health of my countenance'.

But look again at the picture of this poor man. He looks as if he is carrying the whole universe, as it were, upon his back. He is borne down, sad, troubled, perplexed. Not only that, he tells us that he weeps: 'My tears have been my meat day and night'. He is weeping and tearful, and all because he is in this state of perplexity and of fear. He is worried about himself, he is worried about what is happening to him, he is troubled about these enemies who are attacking him and insinuating things about him and his God. Everything seems to be on top of him. He cannot control his feelings. He goes further and says that it is even affecting his very appetite. He says that his 'tears have been his meat'. We are all familiar with this phenomenon. If you are worried and anxious, you lose your appetite, you do not want food. Indeed, it seems almost repulsive to you. Now while this is an interesting condition even from the purely physical and medical standpoint, we must not stay with it except to stress the importance of recognizing the picture it presents. The trouble with this condition is that so often while we are suffering from it, we are not aware of the impression that is being made upon others, and because we should be concerned with this impression it is not a bad thing for us to look at the objective picture. If we but had the power to see ourselves as others see us, it would oftentimes be the main step to victory and release. It is good to look at ourselves and to try to conjure up this picture that we are presenting to others of a depressed person, tearful and weeping, who does not want to eat, or to see anybody, and who is so pre-occupied with all his miseries that the kind of picture and impression that he presents is one of gloom and depression.

Having thus described it in general we can now proceed to state some of the general causes of the condition. First and foremost I would not hesitate to put—temperament. There are, after all, certain different types of people. I wonder whether anyone is surprised that I put this first? I wonder whether anybody wants to say: When you are talking about Christians you must not introduce temperament or types. Surely Christianity does away with all that, and you must not bring that kind of consideration into a matter like this? Now that is a very important objection, and it must be answered. We begin by saying that temperament, psychology and make-up do not make the slightest difference in the matter of our salvation. That is, thank God, the very basis of our position as Christians. It does not matter what we are by temperament; we are all saved in the same way, by the same act of God in and through His Son, our Lord and Saviour Jesus Christ. That is our answer to psychology and to the criticism of Christianity that often results from a study of psychology. Let me make this clear. It does not matter what your background is, it does not matter what temperament you may happen to have been given in this world, all that does not make the slightest difference in the matter of salvation. We do not recognize such a thing as a 'religious complex'. We glory in the fact that the history of the Church proves abundantly that every conceivable type of temperament has been found, and is still to be found today, in the Church of the living God. But while I emphasize, with all my being, the fact that temperament does not make the slightest difference in the matter of our fundamental salvation, I am equally anxious to emphasize the fact that it does make a very great difference in actual experience in the Christian life, and that when you are trying to diagnose a condition such as that of spiritual depression, it is something with which you should start, it is something to put at the very beginning.

In other words, as I understand the Biblical teaching about this matter, there is nothing which is quite so important as that we should without delay, and as quickly as possible, get to know ourselves. For the fact of the matter is that though we are all Christians together, we are all different, and the problems and the difficulties, the perplexities and the trials that we are likely to meet are in a large measure determined by the difference of temperament and of type. We are all in the same fight, of course, as we share the same common salvation, and have the same common central need. But the manifestations of the trouble vary from case to case and from person to person. There is nothing more futile, when dealing with this condition, than to act on the assumption that all Christians are identical in every respect. They are not, and they are not even meant to be.

Here, again, I can best illustrate my point by choosing an example from another realm. We are all human beings, and as such we all have fundamentally the same constitution, and yet we know perfectly well that no two of us are alike, that in fact we are all different in so many respects. Now you will often come across people who advocate ways of living or methods of treating diseases which completely ignore that fundamental fact, and which are therefore obviously wrong. They would put the whole world on the same diet. They prescribe this universal diet which is going to cure everybody. That, I say, is impossible and quite wrong by definition. I have often said that the first fundamental law of dietetics is just that old word which tells us that: 'Jack Spratt could eat no fat, his wife could eat no lean'. Quite right! It is amusing in one sense but on the other hand it is a very vital, fundamental principle for dietetics. Constitutionally Jack Spratt and his wife are different, and to suggest that the same diet would be the best for both persons is to be guilty of a fundamental fallacy. They are both equally human beings, but as human beings they are different in their make-up. Or, to take another example, look at the tendency to insist upon all children in schools doing gymnastic exercises. There you have again the same obvious fallacy. We all differ in the length of our bodies and legs and it is unreasonable to lay down a hard and fast rule to cover all types. Some have an aptitude for these things and some have not, and to suggest that every child should go in for the same kind of physical activity is as monstrous as to put everybody on the same diet. We all need exercise, but not in the same way nor in the same amount.

All this is by way of illustration of the tendency in the direction of regimentation, and the point I am making is that you cannot lay down this kind of universal legislation as though men were machines. It is wrong in the physical realm as I have been showing, and it is infinitely more so in the spiritual realm.

It is quite clear that we can divide human beings into two main groups. There are the so-called introverts and the extroverts. There is the type of person who is generally looking inwards and the type of person who is always looking outwards, and it is of the greatest importance that we should realize not only that we belong to one or the other of these two groups, but further-more that this condition of spiritual depression tends to affect the one more than the other. We must start by knowing ourselves and by understanding ourselves.

There is a type of person who is particularly prone to spiritual depression. That does not mean that they are any worse than others. Indeed, I could make out a good case for saying that quite often the people who stand out most gloriously in the history of the Church are people of the very type we are now considering. Some of the greatest saints belong to the introverts; the extrovert is generally a more superficial person. In the natural realm there is the type of person who tends to be always analysing himself, analysing everything he does, and worrying about the possible effects of his actions, always harking back, always full of vain regrets. It may be something that has been done once and for ever but he cannot leave it alone. He cannot undo what has been done, but still he spends his time analysing and judging and blaming himself. You are familiar with that type of person. Now all that is transferred into the spiritual realm and into their spiritual life. In other words, it is obvious that the danger for such people is to become morbid. I have already said that I could mention names. Surely the great Henry Martyn belonged to this type. You cannot read the life of that man of God without seeing at once that he belonged to the introspective type. He was an introvert and he suffered from an obvious tendency to morbidity and introspection.

Those two terms remind us that the fundamental trouble with these people is that they are not always careful to draw the line of demarcation between self-examination and introspection. We all agree that we should examine ourselves, but we also agree that introspection and morbidity are bad. But what is the difference between examining oneself and becoming introspective? I suggest that we cross the line from self-examination to introspection when, in a sense, we do nothing but examine ourselves, and when such self-examination becomes the main and chief end in our life. We are meant to examine ourselves periodically, but if we are always doing it, always, as it were, putting our soul on a plate and dissecting it, that is introspection. And if we are always talking to people about ourselves and our problems and troubles, and if we are forever going to them with that kind of frown upon our face and saying: I am in great difficulty—it probably means that we are all the time centred upon ourselves. That is introspection, and that in turn leads to the condition known as morbidity.

Here, then, is the point at which we must always start. Do we know ourselves? Do we know our own particular danger? Do

2

we know the thing to which we are particularly subject? The Bible is full of teaching about that. The Bible warns us to be careful about our strength and about our weakness. Take a man like Moses. He was the meekest man, we are told, the world has ever known; and yet his great sin, his great failure was in connection with that very thing. He asserted his own will, he became angry. We have to watch our strength and we have to watch our weakness. The essence of wisdom is to realize this fundamental thing about ourselves. If I am naturally an introvert I must always be careful about it, and I must warn myself against it lest unconsciously I slip into a condition of morbidity. The extrovert must in the same way know himself and be on his guard against the temptations peculiar to his nature. Some of us by nature, and by the very type to which we belong, are more given to this spiritual disease called spiritual depression than others. We belong to the same company as Jeremiah, and John the Baptist and Paul and Luther and many others. A great company! Yes, but you cannot belong to it without being unusually subject to this particular type of trial.

But let us pass to the second big cause—physical conditions. Is anyone surprised again? Does someone hold the view that as long as you are a Christian it does not matter what the condition of your body is? Well, you will soon be disillusioned if you believe that. Physical conditions play their part in all this. It is very difficult to draw the line between this and the previous cause because temperament seems to some degree to be controlled by physical conditions and there are certain people who constitutionally, almost in a physical sense, are prone to this condition. In other words, there are certain physical ailments which tend to promote depression. Thomas Carlyle, I suppose, is an outstanding illustration of this. Or take that great preacher who preached in London for nearly forty years in the last century—Charles Haddon Spurgeon—one of the truly great preachers of all time. That great man was subject to spiritual depression, and the main explanation in his case was undoubtedly the fact that he suffered from a gouty condition which finally killed him. He had to face this problem of spiritual depression often in a most acute form. A tendency to acute depression is an unfailing accompaniment of the gout which he inherited from his forebears. And there are many, I find, who come to talk to me about these matters, in whose case it seems quite clear to me that the cause of the trouble is mainly physical. Into this group, speaking generally, you can put tiredness, overstrain, illness, any form of illness. You cannot isolate the spiritual from the physical for we are body, mind and spirit. The greatest and the best Christians when they are physically weak are more prone to an attack of spiritual depression than at any other time and there are great illustrations of this in the Scriptures.

Let us give a word of warning at this point. We must not forget the existence of the devil, nor allow him to trap us into regarding as spiritual that which is fundamentally physical. But we must be careful on all sides in drawing this distinction; because if you give way to your physical condition you become guilty in a spiritual sense. If you recognize, however, that the physical may be partly responsible for your spiritual condition and make allowances for that, you will be better able to deal with the spiritual.

Another frequent cause of spiritual depression is what we may describe as a reaction—a reaction after a great blessing, a reaction after some unusual and exceptional experience. I hope to call attention sometime to the case of Elijah under the juniper tree. There is no doubt in my mind that his main trouble was that he was suffering from a reaction, a reaction after what had happened on Mount Carmel (1 Kings 19). Abraham had the same experience (Genesis 15). For that reason when people come to me and describe some remarkable experience which they have had, while I rejoice with them and thank God, I always watch them carefully afterwards and am always on the look out and apprehensive on their behalf lest a reaction set in. That need not happen, but unless we are aware of the danger it may do so. If we but realized that when God is pleased to give us some unusual blessing we must be unusually watchful afterwards, we would avoid this reaction that so often tends to set in.

Then we come to the next cause. In a sense, and in the last analysis, that is the one and only cause of spiritual depression— it is the devil, the adversary of our souls. He can use our temperaments and our physical condition. He so deals with us that we allow our temperament to control and govern us, instead of keeping temperament where it should be kept. There is no end to the ways in which the devil produces spiritual depression. We must always bear him in mind. The devil's one object is so to depress God's people that he can go to the man of the world and say: There are God's people. Do you want to be like that? Obviously the whole strategy of the adversary of our souls, and God's adversary, is to depress us and to make us look as this man looked when he was passing through this period of unhappiness.

Indeed I can put it, finally, like this; the ultimate cause of all spiritual depression is unbelief. For if it were not for unbelief even the devil could do nothing. It is because we listen to the devil instead of listening to God that we go down before him and fall before his attacks. That is why this psalmist keeps on saying to himself: 'Hope thou in God for I shall yet praise Him. . . .' He reminds himself of God. Why? Because he was depressed and had forgotten God, so that his faith and his belief in God and in God's power, and in his relationship to God, were not what they ought to be. We can indeed sum it all up by saying that the final and ultimate cause is just sheer unbelief.

There then we have looked at the causes. What about the treatment in general? Very briefly at this point, the first thing we have to learn is what the Psalmist learned—we must learn to take ourselves in hand. This man was not content just to lie down and commiserate with himself. He does something about it, he takes himself in hand. But he does something which is more important still, that is he talks to himself. This man turns to himself and says: 'Why art thou cast down O my soul, why art thou disquieted within me?' He is talking to himself, he is addressing himself. But, says someone, is that not the one thing we should not do since our great trouble is that we spend too much time with ourselves? Surely it contradicts what you have already said. You warned us against morbidity and introspection, and now you tell us that we have to talk to ourselves!

How do we reconcile the two things? In this way. I say that we must talk to ourselves instead of allowing 'ourselves' to talk to us! Do you realize what that means? I suggest that the main trouble in this whole matter of spiritual depression in a sense is this, that we allow our self to talk to us instead of talking to our self. Am I just trying to be deliberately paradoxical? Far from it. This is the very essence of wisdom in this matter. Have you realized that most of your unhappiness in life is due to the fact that you are listening to yourself instead of talking to yourself? Take those thoughts that come to you the moment you wake up in the morning. You have not originated them, but they start talking to you, they bring back the problems of yesterday, etc. Somebody is talking. Who is talking to you? Your self is talking to you. Now this man's treatment was this; instead of allowing this self to talk to him, he starts talking to himself. 'Why art thou cast down, O my soul?' he asks. His soul had been depressing him, crushing him. So he stands up and says: 'Self, listen for a moment, I will speak to you'. Do you know what I mean? If you do not, you have had but little experience.

The main art in the matter of spiritual living is to know how to handle yourself. You have to take yourself in hand, you have to address yourself, preach to yourself, question yourself. You must say to your soul: 'Why art thou cast down'—what business have you to be disquieted? You must turn on yourself, upbraid yourself, condemn yourself, exhort yourself, and say to yourself: 'Hope thou in God'—instead of muttering in this depressed, unhappy way. And then you must go on to remind yourself of God, Who God is, and what God is and what God has done, and what God has pledged Himself to do. Then having done that, end on this great note: defy yourself, and defy other people, and defy the devil and the whole world, and say with this man: 'I shall yet praise Him for the help of His countenance, who is also the health of my countenance and my God'.

That is the essence of the treatment in a nutshell. As we proceed with our consideration of this subject we can but elaborate that. The essence of this matter is to understand that this self of ours, this other man within us, has got to be handled. Do not listen to him; turn on him; speak to him; condemn him; upbraid him; exhort him; encourage him; remind him of what you know, instead of listening placidly to him and allowing him to drag you down and depress you. For that is what he will always do if you allow him to be in control. The devil takes hold of self and uses it in order to depress us. We must stand up as this man did and say: 'Why art thou cast down? Why art thou disquieted within me?' Stop being so! 'Hope thou in God, for I shall yet praise Him for the help of His countenance,' He, 'who is the health of my countenance and my God.'

Therefore we conclude that a man is justified by faith without the deeds of the law.

Romans 3. 28

II

THE TRUE FOUNDATION

I WANT to consider this statement with you in the light of the fundamental text which we began to consider last time.

There can be no doubt but that the condition known as spiritual depression is a very common complaint, indeed the more one thinks about it and the more one speaks about it, the more one discovers how common it is. We are considering this condition because, as I have suggested, there are at least two great reasons for our doing so. The first is that it is very sad that anybody should remain in such a condition. But the second reason is still more serious and important, that is that such people are very poor representatives of the Christian faith. As we face the modern world with all its trouble and turmoil and with all its difficulties and sadness, nothing is more important than that we who call ourselves Christian, and who claim the Name of Christ, should be representing our faith in such a way before others, as to give them the impression that here is the solution, and here the answer. In a world where everything has gone so sadly astray, we should be standing out as men and women apart, people characterized by a fundamental joy and certainty in spite of conditions, in spite of adversity. Now that, I think you will agree, is the picture which is given of God's people everywhere in the Scriptures, whether it is the Old Testament or the New. Those men of God stood out in that way, and, whatever their circumstances and conditions, they seemed to possess a secret which enabled them to live triumphantly and to be more than conquerors. It therefore behoves us to examine this state of spiritual depression very closely.

We have already looked at the condition in general and considered some of its main causes. We have already seen that the essence of the treatment according to the Psalmist is that we must really face ourselves. In other words we must talk to ourselves instead of allowing ourselves to talk to us. We must take ourselves in hand, we must address ourselves as the Psalmist addressed himself and his soul, and ask the question: 'Why art thou cast down? why art thou disquieted within me?'—You have no right to be like this. Why are you depressed and cast down? He faces himself and talks to himself, he argues with himself and brings himself back to the position of faith. He exhorts himself to have faith in God, and then he is in a condition to pray to God.

I want to take up this method which is advocated by the Psalmist. The vital principle is that we must face ourselves and examine ourselves, and if we are among those that never seem to know the joy of salvation and the joy of the Lord, we must discover the cause. The causes are many, and it seems to me that the essence of wisdom in this matter is to deal with these causes one by one and to take them in detail. Nothing must be taken for granted. Indeed it could easily be established that the main cause of trouble in this matter is the fatal tendency to take things for granted. More and more do I find this to be the case as I talk to others about these matters. There are so many people who never seem to arrive at the true Christian position because they are not clear in their minds about certain primary matters, certain fundamental things that should be dealt with at the beginning.

At the risk of being misunderstood at this point, let us put it like this: The particular trouble with which we are dealing tends, I find, to be common among those who have been brought up in a religious manner rather than in those who have not been brought up in a religious manner. It is more likely to affect those who have been brought up in Christian homes and families and who have always been taken to a place of worship than those who have not. There are many such people who seem to go right through their lives in the way described by Shakespeare as 'bound in shallows and in miseries'. They never seem to get out of it. They are in the realm of the Church, and very interested in Christian things; and yet when you compare them with the New Testament description of the new man in Christ you see at once that there is a great difference. Indeed they themselves see that, and this is often the main cause of their depression and their unhappiness. They see other Christians rejoicing and they say: 'Well, I cannot say that I am like that. That person has got something that I have not got', and they would give the whole world if they could but get something which the other person has. They take up Christian biographies and read the lives of various saints who have adorned the life of the Christian Church, and they admit at once that they are not like them. They know that they have never been like them, and that there is something which those people obviously enjoyed which they themselves have never had.

There are large numbers of people in this unhappy situation. The Christian life seems to them to be a constant problem, and they are always asking the same question. 'Why cannot I get there? Why cannot I be like that?' They read books which are meant to give instruction about the Christian way of life, they attend meetings and conferences, always seeking this something which they do not find. And they are cast down, their souls are cast down and disquieted within them.

Now it is all-important, as we face such people, to be quite certain that they are clear in their minds about the primary and most fundamental principles of the Christian faith. Many and many a time I have found in talking to them that their real trouble lies just here. I would not say that they are not Christians but I am suggesting that they are what I would call miserable Christians, simply because they have not understood the way of salvation, and for that reason all their beliefs and efforts have been more or less useless. They often concentrate on the question of sanctification, but it does not help them because they have not understood justification. Having assumed that they were on the right road, they assume that all they have to do is to continue along it.

It is an interesting theological point as to whether such people are Christians or not. For myself I would say they are. The classic example is of course John Wesley. I would hesitate to say that John Wesley was not a Christian until 1738; but I am certain of this, that John Wesley had not understood the way of salvation as justification by faith only, until 1738. He had in a sense subscribed to the full teaching of the Bible, but he had not understood it, nor fully apprehended it. I have no doubt that if you had questioned him he would have given the correct answers even about the death of our Lord; and yet in experience he was not clear about justification by faith. You will recall that it was only as the result of his meeting with the Moravian brethren, and in particular the conversation he had with one called Peter Böhler, on a journey from London to Oxford, that he was truly made to understand this vital doctrine. There was a man who had been trying to find happiness in his Christian life by doing things, preaching to the prisoners in Oxford, giving up his fellowship of his college, and facing the hazards of crossing the Atlantic in order to preach to pagans in Georgia. He was trying to find happiness by living life in a given way. In fact the whole trouble with John Wesley really was that he had never understood or grasped the doctrine of justification by faith. He had not understood this verse that we are considering: 'Therefore we conclude that a man is justified by faith without the deeds of the law'. It seems almost impossible that such a man, who had been brought up in an unusually godly home and who had spent all his life and all his time in Christian work, should be wrong about a first and so fundamental a point and should have been wrong at the very beginning. But so it was.

I am suggesting that this is the case with large numbers of people still. They have assumed that they are right about the first things, but they never have been right about their justification, and it is just here that the devil causes confusion. It suits him well that such people should be concerned about sanctification and holiness and various other things, but they can never be right until they are right here, and that is why we must start with this. It is no use going on to deal with the superstructure if the foundation is not right. We therefore start with this great doctrine. This confusion is an old trouble. In a sense it is the masterpiece of Satan. He will even encourage us to be righteous as long as he has us confused at this point. That he is doing so at the present time is clear from the fact that the average person in the Church seems to regard men as Christian simply because they do good works, even though they may be entirely wrong about this preliminary truth. It is an old trouble, and it was the essential trouble with the Jews. It is what our Lord was continually saying to the Pharisees, and it certainly was the major argument which the Apostle Paul had with the Jews. They were entirely wrong with regard to the whole question of the Law, and the main problem was to show them the right view of it. The Jews believed that the Law was made by God in order that man might save himself by keeping it. They said that all one had to do was to keep the Law, and that if you kept the Law you would justify yourself, and that if you led your life according to the Law, God would accept you and you would be well pleasing in His sight. And they believed that they could do that, because they had never understood the Law. They put their own interpretation on it and made of it something that was well within their reach.

And so they thought that all was well. That is the picture of the Pharisees given in the Gospels and everywhere in the New Testament. It was the whole essential trouble with the Jews, and it is still the essence of the problem with many people. We have to realize that there are certain things about which we must be perfectly clear before we can really hope to have peace, and to enjoy the Christian life.

This preliminary point is one which we can well put by a general exposition of the teaching of this third chapter of the Epistle to the Romans. The first four chapters of this great and mighty Epistle are really devoted to this one theme. The one thing Paul was anxious to make clear was this message about the righteousness of God which is by faith in Jesus Christ. He had already said in chapter 1. 16, 17: 'I am not ashamed of the gospel of Christ for it is the power of God unto salvation to everyone that believeth, to the Jew first and also to the Greek. For therein is the righteousness of God revealed from faith to faith, as it is written the just shall live by faith'. Yes, but the question was, why did not everybody believe that? Why was this not accepted almost automatically by all who heard it, as the greatest good news that had ever come into the world? The answer is that they did not believe it because they did not see the need of it. They had the wrong view of righteousness. The righteousness of which Paul speaks means rightness with God. There is no happiness finally, there is no peace, there is no joy except we be right with God. Now that is agreed by all, that is assented to by the miserable Christian as well as the assured Christian. Yes, but the whole difference between the one and the other is that the former, the miserable Christian, is wrong in his ideas as to how this rightness with God is to be obtained. That was the trouble with the Jews also. They held, as I have reminded you, that this rightness is attained by conforming to the Law as they understood it, and keeping it. But their whole view of the Law was entirely wrong. They perverted it, with the result that the very thing which God had given them to further His way of salvation had become in their hands the main obstacle to it.

What then is the teaching? There are certain simple principles about which we must be quite clear before we can ever hope to enjoy this Christian salvation. The first is conviction of sin. We must be absolutely clear about our sinfulness. Here I follow the method of the Apostle Paul and raise an imaginary objection.

I imagine someone saying at once: 'Are you going to preach to us about sin, are you going to preach about conviction of sin? You say your object is to make us happy but if you are going to preach to us about conviction of sin, surely that is going to make us still more unhappy. Are you deliberately trying to make us miserable and wretched?' To which the simple reply is, Yes! That is the teaching of the great Apostle in these chapters. It may sound paradoxical—the term does not matter—but beyond any question that is the rule, and there are no exceptions. You must be made miserable before you can know true Christian joy. Indeed the real trouble with the miserable Christian is that he has never been truly made miserable because of conviction of sin. He has by-passed the essential preliminary to joy, he has been assuming something that he has no right to assume.

Let me put it again in a Scriptural statement. You remember the aged Simeon standing with the infant Lord Jesus Christ in his arms? He said a very profound thing when he said: 'This Child is set for the fall and for the rising again of many in Israel'. There is no rising again until there has been a preliminary fall. This is an absolute rule, and yet this is the thing that is being so sadly forgotten by so many today, and assumed by as many more. But the Scripture has its order, and its order must be observed if we are to derive the benefits of the Christian salvation. Ultimately, the only thing which is going to drive a man to Christ and make him rely upon Christ alone, is a true conviction of sin. We go astray because we are not truly convicted of our sin. That is why I say that this is in particular the problem of all those who have been brought up in a religious or Christian manner. Their chief trouble often is their wrong idea of sin. I remember such a person putting this very dramatically to me on one occasion. She was a woman who had been brought up in a very religious home, who had always attended a place of worship and been busily and actively engaged in the life of the Church. She was then a member in a church where a number of people had been converted suddenly from the world and from various kinds of evil living—drunkenness and such like things. I well remember her saying to me: 'You know, I almost wish that I had not been brought up in the way I have been brought up. I could wish that I had been living their kind of life in order that I might have their marvellous experience'. What did she mean? What she was really saying was that she had never seen herself as a sinner.

Why not? There are many reasons. That kind of person thinks of sin only in terms of action, in terms of sins. Not only that, but in terms of certain particular actions only. So their tendency is to think that because they have not been guilty of these particular things, that they are not really sinners at all. Indeed, sometimes they put it quite plainly and say: 'I have never really thought of myself as a sinner: but of course that is not surprising as my life has been sheltered from the beginning. I have never been tempted to do these things, and it is not surprising therefore that I have never felt myself to be a sinner'. Now there we see the very essence of this fallacy. Their thinking is in terms of actions, particular actions, and of comparisons with other people and their experiences, and so on. For this reason they have never had a real conviction of sin, and because of that they have never plainly seen their utter absolute need of the Lord Jesus Christ. They have heard it preached that Christ has died for our sins and they say that they believe that; but they have never really known its absolute necessity for themselves.

How then can such people be convicted of sin? That is Paul's subject in this third chapter of his Epistle to the Romans. He has really been dealing with it throughout the second chapter also. This is his way of doing it, this is his great thesis: 'There is none righteous, no not one, all have sinned and come short of the glory of God'. Who are these 'all'? He keeps on telling us, Jews as well as Gentiles. The Jews would of course agree that the Gentiles were certainly sinners, outside the pale, sinners against God. 'But wait a minute,' says Paul in effect, 'you are equally sinners'. The reason why the Jews hated Christ and crucified Him, the whole explanation of 'the offence of the Cross', the reason why Paul was treated as he was by his fellow countrymen who hated the Christian faith, was that the Christian faith said that the Jew was as much a sinner as the Gentile. It asserts that the Jew—the person who thought he had always lived a righteous and religious life—is as much a sinner as the most flagrant sinner amongst the Gentiles. 'All have sinned', Jews and Gentiles are equally condemned before God.

The same is true today, and if we are concerned about a conviction of sin, the first thing we have to do is stop thinking about particular sins. How difficult we all find this. We have all got these prejudices. We confine sin to certain things only, and because we are not guilty of these we think that we are not sinners. But that is not the way to know conviction of sin. It was not in that way that John Wesley came to see himself as a sinner. You remember what brought him to a conviction of sin? It began when he saw the way in which some Moravian Brethren behaved during a storm in mid-Atlantic. John Wesley was terrified by the storm and afraid to die; the Moravians were not. They seemed to be as happy in the hurricane and in the midst of the storm as they were when the sun was shining. John Wesley realized that he was afraid of death, he somehow did not seem to know God as these people knew Him. In other words he began to feel his need, and that is always the beginning of a conviction of sin.

The essential point is, that the way to know yourself a sinner is not to compare yourself with other people; it is to come face to face with the Law of God. Well, what is God's Law? Thou shalt not kill, thou shalt not steal? 'I have never done that, therefore I am not a sinner.' But, my friend, that is not the Law of God in its entirety. Would you like to know what the Law of God is? Here it is—'Thou shalt love the Lord thy God with all thy heart, and with all thy soul and with all thy mind and with all thy strength: this is the first commandment. And the second is like, namely this, Thou shalt love thy neighbour as thyself' (Mark 12. 30, 31). Forget all about drunkards and their like, forget all the people you read about in the press at the present time. Here is the test for you and me: Are you loving God with all your being? If you are not, you are a sinner. That is the test. 'All have sinned and come short of the glory of God.' God has made us and He has made us for Himself. He made man for His own glory and He intended man to live entirely for Him. Man was to be His representative, and was to dwell in communion with Him. He was to be the lord of the universe, he was to glorify God. As it is put in the Shorter Catechism: 'The chief end of man is to glorify God and to enjoy Him for ever', and if you are not doing so you are a sinner of the deepest dye, whether you know it and feel it or not.

Or let me put it like this. I find this is a very valuable way of approaching the subject. God knows I am preaching my own experience to you for I was brought up in a religious manner myself. I am also preaching my experience as one who has frequently to help people who have been brought up in the same way. Man is meant to know God. So the question is: Do you know God? I am not asking if you believe in God, or if you believe certain things about Him. To be a Christian is to have eternal life, and as our Lord says in John 17. 3: 'This is life eternal to know Thee the only true God, and Jesus Christ, whom Thou hast sent'. So the test we apply to ourselves is that. Not, 'Have I done this or that?' My test is a positive one: 'Do I know God? Is Jesus Christ real to me?' I am not asking whether you know things about Him but do you know God, are you enjoying God, is God the centre of your life, the soul of your being, the source of your greatest joy? He is meant to be. He made man in such a way that that was to be the position, that man might dwell in communion with God and enjoy God and walk with God. You and I are meant to be like that, and if we are not like that, it is sin. That is the essence of sin. We have no right not to be like that. That is sin of the deepest and worst type. The essence of sin, in other words, is that we do not live entirely to the glory of God. Of course by committing particular sins we aggravate our guilt before God, but you can be innocent of all gross sins and yet be guilty of this terrible thing, of being satisfied with your life, of having pride in your achievements and of looking down on others and feeling that you are better than others. There is nothing worse than that because you are saying to yourself that you are somehow nearer to God than they are, and yet the whole time you are not. If that is your attitude you are like the Pharisee in the temple who thanked God that he was not like the other man—'this publican'. The Pharisee had never seen the need of forgiveness and there is no more terrible sin than that. I know of nothing worse than the person who says: 'You know I have never really felt that I am a sinner'. That is the height of sin because it means that you have never realized the truth about God and the truth about yourself. Read the argument of the Apostle Paul and you will find that his logic is not only inevitable, but also unanswerable. 'There is none righteous, no not one.' 'We know that what things soever the law saith, it saith to them who are under the law; that every mouth may be stopped and all the world may become guilty before God.' If you have never realized your guilt or guiltiness before God you will never have joy in Christ. It is impossible. 'Not the righteous, sinners Jesus came to save.' 'They that are whole have no need of a physician, but they that are sick.'

There is the first thing—conviction of sin. If you have not a conviction of sin, and if you do not realize that you are unworthy before God, and that you are utterly condemned and a complete failure before God, pay attention to nothing else until you have it, until you come to this realization, because you will never find joy, you will never get rid of your depression until you are right about that. Conviction of sin is an essential preliminary to a true experience of salvation.

This brings me to the second principle. The second thing the true Christian realizes is God's way of salvation in Christ. This is the great good news. 'This is the thing I am preaching', says Paul, in effect, to the Romans, 'this righteousness that is of God, that is in Jesus Christ, His righteousness.' What is he talking about? It can be put in the form of a question if you like. What is your view of Christ? Why did He come into the world? What has God done in Christ? Is He merely a teacher, an example, and so on? I shall not waste your time by showing the utter futility of all that. No, this is something positive, this righteousness of God in Jesus Christ. Salvation is all in Christ, and unless you feel yourself shut up to Christ with everything else having failed, you are not a Christian, and it is not surprising that you are not happy. 'The righteousness of God in Jesus Christ' means that God sent Him into the world in order that He might honour the Law and so men might be forgiven. Here is One who gave perfect obedience to God. Here is One, God in the flesh, who has taken human nature unto Himself and, as man, has rendered perfect homage to God, perfect allegiance, perfect obedience. God's law He kept fully and absolutely without a failure. But not only that. Paul adds other things in this classic statement of the doctrine of the Atonement; 'Whom God hath set forth to be a propitiation through faith in His blood, to declare His righteousness for the remission of sins that are past, through the forbearance of God: to declare at this time His righteousness, that He might be just and the justifier of him which believeth in Jesus'. Which means this. Before man can be reconciled to God, before man can know God, this sin of his must be removed. God has said that He will punish sin, and that the punishment of sin is death and banishment from the face of God. This has to be dealt with. And what has happened? Well, says Paul, God has set Him forth as a propitiation. That is the means which God has employed. His being the propitiation for our sins means that God has made Him responsible for our sins. They have been placed upon Him and God has dealt with them and punished them there, and therefore because He has punished our sins in Christ, in His body upon the Cross, He can justly forgive us. You see this is high doctrine. It is a daring thing for the Apostle to say, but it has to be said and I repeat it. God, because He is righteous and holy and eternal, could not forgive the sin of man without punishing it. He said He would punish it, so He must punish it, and, blessed be His Name, He has punished it. He is just, therefore, and the justifier of them that believe in Jesus. The sin has been punished, so God, Who is just and righteous, can forgive sin.

How then does it work? It works like this. God accepts this righteousness of Christ, this perfect righteousness face to face with the Law which He honoured in every respect. He has kept it and given obedience to it, He has borne its penalty. The Law is fully satisfied. God's way of salvation, says Paul, is that. He gives to us the righteousness of Christ. If we have seen our need and go to God and confess it, God will give us His own Son's righteousness. He imputes Christ's righteousness to us who believe in Him, and regards us as righteous, and declares and pronounces us to be righteous in Him. That is the way of salvation, the Christian way of salvation, the way of salvation through justification by faith. So that it comes to this. That I see and I believe and I look to nothing and to no one except to the Lord Jesus Christ. I like Paul's way of putting it. He asks: 'Where is boasting then? It is excluded. By what law? of works? Nay, but by the law of faith'. You foolish Jews, says Paul, you are boasting about the fact that you have been circumcised, that you have the oracles of God and that you are God's people. You must cease to do that. You must not rest upon the fact that you have this tradition and that you are children of your forefathers. There is no boasting, you have to rest exclusively upon the Lord Jesus Christ and His perfect work. The Jew is not superior to the Gentile in this respect. 'All have sinned and come short of the glory of God.' We look to Christ and to Christ alone, and not to ourselves in any respect whatsoever.

To make it quite practical let me say that there is a very simple way of testing yourself to know whether you believe that. We betray ourselves by what we say. The Lord Himself said we should be justified by our words, and how true it is. I have often had to deal with this point with people, and I have explained the way of justification by faith and told them how it is all in Christ, and that God puts His righteousness upon us. I have explained it all to them, and then I have said: 'Well, now are you quite happy about it, do you believe that?' And they say, 'Yes'. Then I say: 'Well, then, you are now ready to say that you are a Christian'. And they hesitate. And I know they have not understood. Then I say: 'What is the matter, why are you hesitating?' And they say: 'I do not feel that I am good enough'. At once I know that in a sense I have been wasting my breath. They are still thinking in terms of themselves; their idea still is that they have to make themselves good enough to be a Christian, good enough to be accepted with Christ. They have to do it! 'I am not good enough.' It sounds very modest, but it is the lie of the devil, it is a denial of the faith. You think that you are being humble. But you will never be good enough; nobody has ever been good enough. The essence of the Christian salvation is to say that He is good enough and that I am in Him!

As long as you go on thinking about yourself and saying: 'Ah, yes, I would like to, but I am not good enough; I am a sinner, a great sinner,' you are denying God and you will never be happy. You will continue to be cast down and disquieted in your soul. You will think you are better at times and then again you will find that you are not as good as you thought you were. You read the lives of the saints and you realize that you are nowhere. So you keep on asking: 'What can I do? I still feel that I am not good enough'. Forget yourself, forget all about yourself. Of course you are not good enough, you never will be good enough. The Christian way of salvation tells you this, that it does not matter what you have been, it does not matter what you have done. How can I put this plainly? I try to say it from the pulpit every Sunday because I think it is the thing that is robbing most people of the joy of the Lord. It does not matter if you have almost entered into the depths of hell, if you are guilty of murder as well as every other vile sin, it does not matter from the standpoint of being justified with God. You are no more hopeless than the most respectable self-righteous person in the world. Do you believe that?

There is another good way of testing yourself. Do you believe that from the standpoint of salvation and justification with God that all our customary distinctions are abolished at a stroke and that what determines whether we are sinners or not is not what we have done, but our relationship to God? I say, therefore, that this is the test, that you acknowledge readily and say clearly that you look to Christ and to Christ alone and to nothing and no one else, that you stop looking at particular sins and particular people. Look at nothing and nobody but look entirely to Christ and say:

> 'My hope is built on nothing less
> Than Jesu's blood and righteousness,
> I dare not trust my sweetest frame,
> But wholly lean on Jesu's Name.
> On Christ the solid Rock I stand,
> All other ground is sinking sand.'

You must so believe that as to be able to go further and say with holy boldness:

> The terrors of law and of God
> With me can have nothing to do,
> My Saviour's obedience and blood
> Hide all my transgressions from view.'

Would you like to be rid of this spiritual depression? The first thing you have to do is to say farewell now once and for ever to your past. Realize that it has been covered and blotted out in Christ. Never look back at your sins again. Say: 'It is finished, it is covered by the Blood of Christ'. That is your first step. Take that and finish with yourself and all this talk about goodness, and look to the Lord Jesus Christ. It is only then that true happiness and joy are possible for you. What you need is not to make resolutions to live a better life, to start fasting and sweating and praying. No! you just begin to say:

> 'I rest my faith on Him alone
> Who died for my transgressions to atone.'

Take that first step and you will find that immediately you will begin to experience a joy and a release that you have never known in your life before. 'Therefore we conclude that a man is justified by faith without the deeds of the Law.' Blessed be the Name of God for such a wondrous salvation for desperate sinners.

And He cometh to Bethsaida; and they bring a blind man unto Him, and besought Him to touch him. And He took the blind man by the hand, and led him out of the town; and when He had spit on his eyes, and put His hands upon him, He asked him if he saw ought. And he looked up, and said, I see men as trees, walking. After that He put His hands again upon his eyes, and made him look up: and he was restored, and saw every man clearly. And He sent him away to his house, saying, Neither go into the town, nor tell it to any in the town.

Mark 8. 22, 26

III

MEN AS TREES, WALKING

I CALL your attention to this incident as part of our consideration of the theme that is engaging our attention at the
moment, the theme which I have described as 'spiritual depression'.

We are considering this subject not only because it is sad and
tragic that any Christian should ever be miserable, but because
of the whole state of the Church today. I have no hesitation in
asserting again that one of the reasons why the Christian Church
counts for so little in the modern world is that so many Christians
are in this condition. If all Christians simply began to function
as the New Testament would have us do, there would be no
problem of evangelism confronting the Church. The matter
would deal with itself immediately. It is because we are failing
as Christian people in our daily lives and deportment and witness
that the Church counts for so little and that so few are attracted
to God through our Lord Jesus Christ. So for that most urgent
reason alone it behoves us to deal with this question.

We have already taken a general view of the problem, and in
the previous chapter we considered one particular aspect of it.
We saw there that there are some Christians in this condition
because they have never really understood clearly the great
central doctrine of justification by faith. Indeed that was the
whole cause of the trouble before the Protestant Reformation.
The Protestant Reformation brought peace and happiness and
joy into the life of the Church in a way she had not known since
the early centuries, and it all happened because the central
doctrine of justification by faith was rediscovered. It made
Martin Luther rejoice and sing and he in turn was the means of
leading others to see this great truth. It produced this great
note of joy, and while we might hesitate to say that people who
have not clearly understood this matter are not Christians at all,
the moment they do understand it, they certainly cease to be
miserable Christians and become rejoicing Christians.

We now go on to another step and to a further consideration, and I want to consider it with you in terms of this extraordinary incident in the life and ministry of our Blessed Lord, recorded here in Mark 8. 22-26. You will observe at once that we are dealing with a different type, a different case; and we do so most conveniently in terms of this picture. It is in many ways one of the most remarkable of all the miracles ever performed by our Lord and Saviour. You recall the details of what He did to this blind man. He took him by the hand and led him out of the town, and He spat upon his eyes and put His hands upon him and then asked the man if he saw anything. The man said: 'Yes, I do see. I see men as trees, walking'. Then our Lord put His hands again upon the man's eyes and made him look up once more, and this time the man's sight was restored and 'he saw every man clearly'.

Now this is obviously something of very deep significance. What happened in this case was not accidental. We have other examples of our Lord healing blind people, and it is quite clear that He could have healed this man instantly by just saying to him: 'Receive thy sight'. Our Lord had that power; nothing was impossible to Him. He had done that in another case and He could have done it here. So what He did here He obviously did with great deliberation and of set purpose. Nothing our Lord did was done haphazardly or accidentally. All his actions were deliberate, and when He varied His technique He always had a very good reason for doing so. There was nothing peculiarly difficult about the case, and the variation in the treatment was not due to such a cause. It was due to our Lord's own determined plan to do the work in this given way in order that He might teach a lesson and give a certain message. In other words, all our Lord's miracles are more than events, they are in a sense parables as well. That does not mean that we do not believe in the actual incident as a fact in history. I am simply asserting that a miracle is also a parable, and if that is true of all the miracles, it is especially true of this one. For our Lord obviously varied the procedure here in order to bring out and to teach an important and vital lesson.

I am very ready to agree with those who suggest that perhaps the main lesson here was intended for the disciples. You remember what had gone before. The disciples when they went into the ship had forgotten to take a supply of bread. The result was that all they had with them in the ship was just one loaf. They began to be worried about this, and were most unhappy. Our Lord, speaking to them in the boat, said: 'Take heed, beware of the leaven of the Pharisees and of the leaven of Herod', and they reasoned among themselves saying: 'It is because we have no bread'. Because He mentioned the word 'leaven' they thought He must be talking about bread! They were literalists, they were lacking in spiritual understanding, and so the word 'leaven' made them think only of bread and of their failure to take a supply. They were unhappy and uneasy, therefore, and our Lord asks them a series of searching questions ending with this: 'Why is it that you do not understand?' 'Here am I', He says in effect, 'I have been preaching to you and teaching you and yet you still do not seem to understand. You are troubled because you have only one loaf, and yet you have witnessed two miracles which prove that with just a few loaves and fishes I could feed 5,000 or 4,000 people—how is it you do not understand?' I believe He dealt with the blind man as He did in order to give them a picture of themselves. He adopted this technique in the case before us, in order to enable the disciples to see themselves as they were.

It goes beyond that, however: it is a permanent lesson always for God's people. It is a terrible message. I am anxious to direct attention to it because there are many people like this man, there are many people who seem to be in the first stage through which this man passed in the process of healing. Our Lord, you remember, put the spittle on his eyes and asked: 'Do you see anything?' And he said: 'Yes, I do see, but I see men as trees, walking'. Do you understand the position? It is difficult to describe this man. You cannot say that he is blind any longer. You cannot say that he is still blind because he does see; and yet you hesitate to say that he can see because he sees men as trees, walking. What then —is he or is he not blind? You feel that you have to say at one and the same time that he is blind and that he is not blind. He is neither one thing nor the other.

Now that is precisely the condition with which I am anxious to deal at the moment. I am concerned about those Christians who are disquieted and unhappy and miserable because of this lack of clarity. It is almost impossible to define them. You sometimes talk to this type and you think: 'This man is a Christian'. And then you meet him again and you are thrown into doubt at once, and you say: 'Surely he cannot be a Christian if he can say a thing like that or do such a thing as that'. Whenever you meet this man you get a different impression; and you never quite know whether he is a Christian or not. You are not happy in saying either that he does see or that he does not see. Furthermore, the difficulty is that not only do others feel like this about these people, they feel it about themselves. Let me pay them that tribute, they are unhappy because they are not clear about themselves. Sometimes when they have been in a service they will say: 'Yes, I am a Christian, I believe this'. Then something happens and they say: 'I cannot be a Christian. If I were a Christian I could not have such thoughts. I would not want to do the things I do'. So they are as troubled about themselves as other Christians are about them; they feel they are, and they feel they are not Christians. They seem to know enough about Christianity to spoil their enjoyment of the world, and yet they do not know enough to feel happy about themselves. They are 'neither hot nor cold'. They see and yet they do not see. I think you will agree that I am describing the condition, alas, of large numbers of people. It is a distressing condition, and my whole message, as you may anticipate, is to say that nobody should be in it, and nobody should stay in it. I go still further—nobody need stay in that condition.

Let us follow our Lord's teaching. The best way to do that is to put the case of these people in a different form. I have been putting it in general. Let me now give a few particulars in order to help such persons to see themselves, and also to help us all to see the condition. What is that that these people can see? They do see something. This man said: 'Yes, I do see, I see men, but there is something wrong because I see them as trees, walking'.

What do these people see? Very often they are clear that there is something wrong with them as they are. They are unhappy about themselves. Something has happened to them which has given them a sense of dissatisfaction with themselves as they are. There was a time when they were perfectly satisfied with themselves. They went on living their kind of life and they thought that there was nothing wrong with it. But they are no longer like that. Something has happened to them which has given them an entirely new view of the kind of life they were living. I need not elaborate this, you have only to think of people who are living this kind of life at the moment, people who devour newspaper gossip, who regard as wonderful and enviable the life of the social round and the theatres, and always feel that 'all this is really life'. But these people are not now like that. They have come to see the emptiness, the vanity, the utter hollowness of it all, and they are profoundly dissatisfied with that kind of life. They see that, apart from anything else, it is not intelligent, that it is such an empty kind of life. They become unhappy about themselves and declare that they cannot go on as they are. Now there are many people in that position, and there are many who pass through that stage. It is a stage in which a man at any rate sees that everything else is wrong, though he has not yet seen that Christianity is right. That is what often drives him to cynicism, that is what often drives him to despair.

There have been some very dramatic instances of this. I remember very well the case of a man who was an outstanding surgeon in London and in great prominence. Suddenly to the amazement and astonishment of all who knew him it was announced that he had given it all up and had become a ship's doctor. What had happened to that man was this. He was a great man in his profession and he had legitimate ambitions with respect to certain honours in the profession. But disappointment in that respect suddenly opened his eyes to the whole situation. He arrived at the conclusion that there was no abiding satisfaction in the life he was living. He saw through it all, but he did not become a Christian. He just became cynical and left it all. There have been many other notable examples of men who have given up everything and have gone into some isolated position where they have found a measure of peace and happiness without becoming Christians. That is one possibility.

But they may even go further, they may see the excellencies of the Christian life as indicated in the Sermon on the Mount. They say: There is no question at all about it, the Christian life is the life, if only everyone lived like that! They may also have read the lives of the saints, and have recognized that these were men who had something wonderful about them. There was a time when they were not interested, but now they have come to see that the life depicted in the Sermon on the Mount is real life and living, and again, seeing life as portrayed in 1 Corinthians chapter 13, they say: 'If only we all lived like that, the world would be Paradise'. They have come to see that much very clearly.

They may even have come further than that, they may have

come to see that Jesus Christ is the only hope, that Jesus Christ is somehow the Saviour. You notice how I put it—that Jesus Christ is 'somehow the Saviour'. They have felt that He could help them, they have come to see that Christianity is the only hope for the world, and in some way they see and know that this Person Jesus can help them. There was a time when they were not interested, when they had dismissed Him without a serious thought; but that is no longer so. Having seen the emptiness of the world, having seen something of the life lived by certain Christians, and having realized that Jesus Christ is the One Who has made the difference, they see somehow that He is a Saviour. So they are interested in Him and concerned about Him. They see that much quite clearly.

Indeed we can go further and say this about them, that unlike the people we were dealing with in the previous chapter, these people have seen that they cannot save themselves. The trouble with the man who lacks a clear understanding of justification by faith is that he is still trying to put himself right; these people see that they cannot do that. They have tried so often, but they are dissatisfied; and as they see the true nature of the Christian quality of life, they see that man cannot lift himself up to that. They see that they cannot save themselves.

'Surely', says someone, 'you have gone too far, you grant them too much!' No! I am simply describing what these people can see, even as that man in the hands of our Lord when asked the question: 'Do you see?' replied: 'Yes'. He certainly could see, he could see men. And these people have come to see something, indeed they may see all of these things I have described to you.

Yet, alas, I have, in the second place, to say that they are still confused, that they still do not see clearly. They have simply seen men 'as trees walking'. In what respect is this true of them? The difficulty here is to know what to leave out; but I will try to select what I regard as the three main and important things.

First of all they have no clear understanding of certain principles. That is why I was careful to say that they have seen that Christ is 'somehow' the Saviour. But they do not see how He is the Saviour. They are not clear, for instance, about the death of Christ and its absolute necessity. Neither are they clear about the doctrine of the rebirth. You talk to them about these things and you will find that they are full of confusion. They say that they do not see, and they are quite right! They do not see, they do not understand why Christ had to die, they do not see the necessity of the rebirth. You are familiar with them, they are dissatisfied with their own lives, and they praise the Christian life. They are ready to talk about Christ as Saviour, but still they 'cannot see' certain truths. The result is that they are troubled and unhappy and miserable.

The second thing they do not see clearly is that their heart is not fully engaged. Though they are able to see many things, they do not really find their happiness in Christianity and in the Christian position. Somehow or another they are not moved by it, they do not find real joy in it. They always have to remind themselves of it and are ever trying to pull themselves up to it. They are not happy; they still seem to find their joy, as far as they have any, somewhere else; their heart is not fully engaged. I merely mention these things here because, God willing, I hope to deal with them in much greater detail later. I am now giving a synoptic view of the condition in general.

The third thing that is true about the people under discussion is that their will is divided. They are rebellious, they do not see why a man, because he calls himself a Christian, has got to do certain things and stop doing others. They think that is being narrow. Yet they denounce the old life and embrace the Christian life in general. They acknowledge Christ as Saviour and yet when it comes to the question of the application of His teaching through the will, there is confusion and they are not clear about it. They are always arguing about this, always asking if it is right for them to do this and that. There is a lack of ease in the realm of the will. I am not caricaturing these people. I am giving a very literal, accurate and detailed description of them. There are many of us who have been through this stage and know it from actual experience; and as our Lord adopted this particular procedure physically in the case of this blind man, He seems sometimes to do something similar in conversion. There are people who see things clearly at once; there are others who go through stages. We are dealing now with those who go through this particular stage and that is how I would describe their condition.

Let me come to the next matter. Why, when our Lord was out to teach, did He put His series of questions to the disciples, and then put it all in this dramatic form in this incident? Or, to put it in another way, what are the causes of this condition? Why should people be in this nondescript condition, Christian and not Christian, yes and no as it were, at the same time? There is no doubt but that sometimes the responsibility is entirely that of the evangelist concerned when they were first awakened. Evangelists are often the cause of the trouble. In their anxiety to report results they produce this very condition.

But it is not always the fault of the evangelist; it is quite frequently, perhaps as frequently, the fault of the people themselves, and here are some of the main reasons why they are in this state. First, these people generally object to clear-cut definitions; they dislike clarity and certainty. We need not at this point go into the specific reason for this. I think they object to clarity of thought and definition because of its demands. The most comfortable type of religion is always a vague religion, nebulous and uncertain, cluttered up with forms and ritual. I am not surprised that Roman Catholicism attracts certain people. The more vague and indefinite your religion, the more comfortable it is. There is nothing so uncomfortable as clear-cut Biblical truths that demand decisions. These people therefore say: 'You are being too precise, you are being too legalistic. No, no, I do not like this. I believe in Christianity, but you are being too rigid and too narrow in your conceptions'. You are familiar with that type. But if you start with the theory that Christianity is not clear-cut, do not be surprised if you find yourself, like this man, seeing 'men as trees, walking'. If you start your Christian life and experience by saying that you do not want an exact focus or a precise definition in your picture, you probably will not have it!

The second cause, and very often the real trouble with these people, is that they never fully accept the teaching and the authority of the Scriptures. I suppose that ultimately that is the whole cause of the trouble. They do not come to the Bible and submit themselves utterly and absolutely to it. If only we came to the Scriptures as little children and took them at their face value and allowed them to speak to us, this sort of trouble would never arise. These people will not do that. What they do is to mix their own ideas with spiritual truth. Of course they claim that basically they take it from the Scriptures, but, and that is the fatal word, they immediately proceed to modify it. They accept certain Biblical ideas, but there are other ideas and philosophies which they desire to bring with them from their old life. They mix natural ideas with spiritual ideas. They say that they like the Sermon on the Mount and I Corinthians, chapter 13. They claim that they believe in Christ as Saviour, but still they argue that we must not go too far in these matters, and that they believe in moderation. Then they begin to modify the Scriptures. They refuse to accept it authoritatively in every respect, in preaching and living, in doctrine and world outlook. 'Circumstances are changed', they say, 'and life is not what it used to be. We are now living in the twentieth century'. So they modify it here and there to suit their own ideas instead of taking Scriptural doctrine right through from beginning to end, and confessing the irrelevancy of talk about the twentieth century. This is God's Word which is timeless, and because it is God's Word we must submit to it and trust Him to employ His own methods in His own way.

Yet another cause of this condition is that almost invariably its victims are not interested in doctrine. Are you interested in doctrine? Sometimes these people are foolish enough to contrast what they regard as spiritual reading of the Scriptures with doctrine. They say that they are not interested in doctrine, that they like Bible expositions but do not like doctrine. They claim to believe the doctrines which are in the Bible and which come out of the Bible, but (it is almost incredible but it is true) they draw this fatal contrast between Biblical exposition and doctrine. But what is the purpose of the Bible except to present doctrine? What is the value of exposition unless it leads to truth? But it is not difficult to understand their position. It is the doctrine that hurts, it is the doctrine that focuses things. It is one thing to look at pictures and to be interested in words and shades of meaning. That does not disturb, that does not focus attention on sin, nor call for decision. We can sit back and enjoy that; but doctrine speaks to us and insists upon a decision. This is truth, and it examines us and tries us and forces us to examine ourselves. So, if we start by objecting to doctrine as such, it is not surprising that we do not see clearly. The whole purpose of all the creeds drawn up by the Christian Church, together with every confession of faith on doctrine and dogma was to enable people to see and to think clearly. This is how they came to be formulated. In the early centuries of the Christian Church, the gospel was preached from generation to generation. But some people began to say things that were wrong. Some, for example, said that

Christ did not really come in a human body, that it was but a phantom appearance. All sorts of things were said and many were made unhappy and bewildered. So the Church began to formulate her doctrines in the form of the Apostles' Creed, etc. Do you imagine that the early Fathers did that sort of thing simply because they enjoyed doing it? Not at all; it was done for a most practical reason. Truth must be defined and safeguarded, otherwise people will walk off into error. So, if we object to doctrine, it is not surprising if we do not see things clearly, it is not surprising if we are unhappy and miserable. There is nothing that so clears a man's spiritual sight as the apprehension and understanding of the doctrines of the Bible.

The last explanation of this condition I would say is that many people do not take the doctrines of the Scriptures in their right order. This is a most important point, and I hope to come back to it at some other time. But I do know this from personal experience. It is important that we should take the doctrines of Scripture in their right order. If you take the doctrine of regeneration before the doctrine of the atonement you will be in trouble. If you are interested in the rebirth and having new life, before you are clear about your standing with God, you will go wrong and you will eventually be miserable. The same applies to taking sanctification before justification. The doctrines must be taken in their right order. In other words, we can sum up all this by saying that the great cause of the condition which we are considering is a refusal to think things right through. It is the fatal danger of wanting to enjoy something before you really grasp it and possess it. It is men and women who refuse to think things right through, and who do not want to learn, and who become unteachable for various reasons—often self-protection—these are the people who generally become victims of this spiritual confusion, this lack of clarity, this seeing and not seeing at the same time.

That brings us to the last question. What is the cure for this condition? For the moment I shall give principles only. The first principle is evident: above everything else avoid making a premature claim that your blindness is cured. It must have been a great temptation to this man to do that. Here is a man who had been blind. Our Lord puts spittle upon his eyes and says to him: 'Do you see?' The man says: 'I see'. What a temptation it must have been to him to take to his heels and announce to the whole world: 'I can see'. The man, in a sense, could see, but so far his sight was incomplete and imperfect, and it was most vital that he should not testify before he had seen clearly. It is a great temptation and I can well understand it, but it is a fatal thing to do. How many are doing that at the present time (and are pressed and urged to do so), proclaiming that they see, when it is so patent to many that they do not see very clearly and are really still in a state of confusion. What harm such people do. They describe men to others as trees, walking. How misleading to the others!

The second thing is the exact opposite of the first. The temptation to the first is to run and to proclaim that they can see, before they see clearly; but the temptation to the second is to feel absolutely hopeless and to say: 'There is no point in going on. You have put spittle on my eyes and you have touched me. In a sense I see, but I am simply seeing men as if they were trees walking'. Such people often come to me and say that they cannot see the Truth clearly. In their confusion they become desperate and ask: 'Why cannot I see? The whole thing is hopeless'. They stop reading their Bible, they stop praying. The devil has discouraged many with lies. Do not listen to him.

What then is the cure? What is the right way? It is to be honest and to answer our Lord's question truthfully and honestly. That is the whole secret of this matter. He turned to this man and asked: 'Do you see ought?' And the man said, absolutely honestly: 'I do see, but I am seeing men as if they were trees walking'. What saved this man was his absolute honesty. Now the question is, where do we stand? The whole purpose of this sermon is just to ask that question—where do we stand? What exactly do we see? Have we got things clearly? Are we happy? Do we really see? We either do or we do not, and we must know exactly where we are. Do we know God? Do we know Jesus Christ? Not only as our Saviour but do we know Him? Are we 'rejoicing with joy unspeakable and full of glory'? That is the New Testament Christian. Do we see? Let us be honest; let us face the questions, let us face them with absolute honesty.

What then? Well, the last step is to submit yourself to Him, to submit yourself utterly to Him as this man did. He did not object to further treatment, he rejoiced in it, and I believe that if our Lord had not taken the further step he would have asked Him to do so. And you can do the same. Come to the Word of

God. Stop asking questions. Start with the promises in their right order. Say: 'I want the truth whatever it costs me'. Bind yourself to it, submit yourself to it, come in utter submission as a little child and plead with Him to give you clear sight, perfect vision, and to make you whole. And as you do so it is my privilege to remind you that He can do it. Yea, more, I promise you in His Blessed Name that He will do it. He never leaves anything incomplete. That is the teaching. Listen to it. This man was healed and restored and 'saw every man clearly'. The Christian position is a clear position. We are not meant to be left in a state of doubt and misgiving, of uncertainty and unhappiness. Do you believe that the Son of God came from heaven and lived and did all He did on earth, that He died on a Cross and was buried and rose again, that He ascended into heaven and sent the Holy Spirit, in order to leave us in a state of confusion? It is impossible. He came that we might see clearly, that we might know God. He came to give eternal life and 'This is eternal life, that they may know Thee the only true God and Jesus Christ Whom Thou hast sent'. If you are unhappy about yourself as a result of this examination come to Him, come to His Word, wait upon Him, plead with Him, hold on to Him, ask Him in the words of the hymn:

> 'Holy Spirit, Truth Divine,
> Dawn upon this soul of mine,
> Word of God, and inward Light,
> Wake my spirit, clear my sight.'

He is pledged to do it and He will do it, and you will no longer be an uncertain Christian seeing and not seeing. You will be able to say: 'I see, I see in Him all I need and more, and I know that I belong to Him'.

But God be thanked, that ye were the servants of sin, but ye have obeyed from the heart that form of doctrine which was delivered you.

Romans 6. 17

IV

MIND, HEART AND WILL

THAT is the statement as it is to be found in the Authorized Version. In the Revised Version you will find that instead of 'form of doctrine' you have 'standard of teaching'. But obviously, as we shall see, that means the same thing, and I call your attention to this verse because I want, by means of it, to continue our consideration of the cause and cure of 'spiritual depression'.

As we do so, we must be impressed by the fact that the forms which this particular condition may take seem to be almost endless. It comes in such different forms and guises that some people stumble at that very fact. They are amazed that there can be so many symptoms or manifestations of this one disease, this spiritual condition; and, of course, their ignorance of the problem in and of itself may lead to the very condition we are considering. The kind of person who thinks that once you believe on the Lord Jesus Christ all your problems are left behind and that the rest of the story will be 'they all lived happily ever after' is certain sooner or later to suffer from this spiritual depression. We are brought into this marvellous life, this spiritual condition by the grace of God. But we must never forget that over and against us is another power. We are citizens of the Kingdom of God, but the Bible tells us that we are opposed by another kingdom, which is also a spiritual kingdom, and that all along we are being attacked and besieged. We are in 'the fight of faith' and 'we wrestle not against flesh and blood but against principalities and powers, against the rulers of the darkness of this world, against spiritual wickedness in high places'. And while that is so, we must be prepared for the occurrence of this condition that we are considering, and we must be prepared for its manifestation in all types of people and in all kinds of ways.

There is nothing that so characterizes all the activities of Satan as his subtlety. He is not only able and powerful, he is subtle; indeed the Apostle Paul tells us that he can 'transform himself into an angel of light' if necessary. The one thing he desires to do is to ruin and destroy the work of God; and there is no work of

God which he is more anxious to destroy than the work of grace in and through our Lord and Saviour Jesus Christ. Therefore, from the moment we become Christian we become the special object of Satan's attention. That is why James says: 'My brethren, count it all joy when ye fall into divers temptations'. We are to rejoice because it is a proof of our faith. The moment we become Christian the devil is particularly concerned to get us down, and he has no more successful way of doing that than to make us miserable, or to make us suffer from what Charles Lamb has described as 'the mumps and measles of the soul'. Such Christians are like marasmic children, not growing, not manifesting health and vigour; and any Christian in that condition is more or less a denial of his own faith, and Satan is pleased. For that reason he is particularly concerned to produce this condition in us and there is no end to the ways in which it may affect us, and in which it may show itself in us—we must expect the manifestations of the condition to be protean.

I call your attention now to another general cause of this condition. It is the one which is described in the verse that we are looking at. Now this verse is a positive description of the Christian but we can use it in a negative way. The absence of conformity to the description which we have in the verse is one of the common causes of all spiritual depression. Here we have an absolute description of the Christian. Paul says: 'You were the servants of Satan, you were under the dominion of Satan. That is where you were, but you are no longer there'.   He thanks God that he can say this about them, that though they were once in that position, now, he says, they are no longer there. Why not? For this reason: 'You have obeyed from the heart that form of doctrine which was delivered to you', or, 'unto which you were delivered'. Now that is the Apostle's description of a Christian.

You notice that the point he is concerned to emphasize is the wholeness of the Christian life, the balance of the Christian life. It is a life in which one has 'obeyed'—there is the will—'from the heart'—there is the emotion, the sensibility—'the form of doctrine' which came to the mind and to the understanding. So that, in describing the Christian the thing he is emphasizing is that there is a wholeness about his life. The whole man is involved, the mind, the heart and the will, and a common cause of spiritual depression is the failure to realize that the Christian life is a whole life, a balanced life. Lack of balance is one of the most fruitful causes of trouble and discord and disquietude in the life of the Christian man.

Once more I have to indicate that the cause of this lack of balance can be laid, I fear too often, to the charge of the preacher or the evangelist. Lop-sided Christians are generally produced by preachers or evangelists whose doctrine lacks balance, or rotundity, or wholeness. More and more as we proceed with our studies we shall see how vitally important are the circumstances of the birth of the Christian. I sometimes think that someone should take this up as a matter of research and should investigate the relationship between the subsequent course of Christians and the particular means or methods employed in their conversion. It would, I am sure, be both significant and interesting. Children generally partake of the characteristics of their parents, and converts tend to take on certain characteristics of the ones who were used of God in their conversion. But not only that, the type and kind of meeting in which people come into the light, indeed all the circumstances of the new birth, tend to influence the subsequent history of these converts more than we often realize. We noticed it in a previous chapter and it is certainly very important with respect to the matter which we are considering now. It is this which explains the existence of different types of Christians showing certain characteristics. All the members of any one group are very much alike and have a certain stamp upon them; while others are different. Now the extent to which this is true, the extent to which we have these peculiar characteristics associated with a particular type of ministry, is the extent to which we are likely to be the victims of this lack of balance which ultimately will manifest itself in unhappiness and in misery.

The Apostle Paul takes this up because it always raises a practical problem. He was writing to the Christians at Rome. We cannot be sure whether he imagined this position in order to refute it, or whether it did actually obtain in Rome. It may be that there were people who were actually saying: 'Shall we then continue in sin that grace may abound?' or it may be the case that the Apostle, having established his doctrine of justification by faith only, suddenly says to himself: 'Now there is a danger in leaving it like that: some people may say: 'Very well, shall we continue in sin that grace may abound?'" for he has been saying that 'where sin abounded grace did much more abound'. There were people in the early Church that did argue like that, and

there are still many who tend to do the same thing. Their attitude
is: 'Very well, in the light of that doctrine it does not matter
what a man does, the more he sins the more God will be glorified
in forgiving him. Being a Christian, it doesn't matter what I do,
I shall be covered by grace.' What does the Apostle say to that?
His answer is, that you can only say a thing like that if you do
not understand the teaching. If you understood the teaching
you would never draw deductions like that; it would be impossible. He answers at once: 'God forbid. You that are dead to
sin (that is what I have been preaching) can no longer live
therein.' The Christian is now 'in Christ', therefore he has not
only died with Him, but has also risen with Him. It is only a man
who has never really grasped the teaching who can ask such
terrible questions as 'shall we then continue in sin that grace
may abound?' The Apostle's whole object in this chapter is to
show the importance of grasping the balance of truth, the importance of taking hold of the whole gospel, and of seeing that if
one but grasps it truly it leads inevitably to certain consequences.

Let me try to divide up the subject briefly. There are certain
principles enunciated here. The first is that spiritual depression
or unhappiness in the Christian life is very often due to our
failure to realize the greatness of the gospel. The apostle talks
about 'the form of doctrine delivered to you', he refers to the
'standard of teaching'. Now people are often unhappy in the Christian life because they have thought of Christianity, and the whole
message of the gospel, in inadequate terms. Some think that it is
merely a message of forgiveness. You ask them to tell you what
Christianity is and they will reply: 'If you believe in the Lord
Jesus Christ your sins are forgiven', and they stop at that. That
is all. They are unhappy about certain things in their past and
they hear that God in Christ will forgive them. They take their
forgiveness and there they stop—that is all their Christianity.
There are others who conceive of it as morality only. Their view
of themselves is that they do not need forgiveness, but they desire
an exalted way of life. They want to do good in this world, and
Christianity to them is an ethical, moral programme. Such
people are bound to be unhappy. Certain problems will inevitably
arise in their lives which are strictly outside morality—someone's
death, some personal relationship. Morality and ethics will not
help at that point, and what they regard as the gospel is useless
to them in that situation. They are unhappy when the blow

comes because they have never had an adequate view of the gospel. It has been but a partial view; they have simply seen one aspect. There are others who are interested in it simply as something good and beautiful. It makes a great aesthetic appeal to them. That is their way of describing the gospel and the entire message is to them just something very beautiful and wonderful which makes them feel better when they hear it.

I am putting all these incomplete and partial views over against what the Apostle here refers to as 'the form of doctrine', 'the standard of teaching', the great truth which he elaborates in this Epistle to the Romans with its mighty arguments and propositions and its flights of spiritual imagination. That is the gospel, all the (if I may borrow a phrase from Thomas Carlyle) 'infinities and immensities' of this Epistle, and of the Epistles to the Ephesians and to the Colossians—that is the gospel. We must have an accurate view of these things. But someone may say: 'When you talk about the Epistle to the Ephesians or the Epistle to the Colossians, surely you are not talking about "the gospel message". In the gospel message you just tell people about forgiveness of sins.' In a sense that is right, but in another sense it is wrong. I had a letter from a man who had been here on a Sunday night and he said that he made a discovery. The discovery he had made was that in a service which was obviously evangelistic there was something for believers. He said, 'I had never understood that that could happen. I never knew that it was possible that in one and the same service an evangelistic message could be preached to unbelievers and yet there could also be a message for believers which would disturb them. Now that man was making a great confession. He was telling me what his view had been hitherto of the evangel. It was this partial, incomplete view, just selecting one or two things. No, the way to evangelize is to give 'the whole counsel of God'. But people say that they are too busy, or, that they cannot follow all that. I would remind you that the Apostle Paul preached that sort of thing to slaves. 'Not many mighty, not many noble are called'. That is what he gave them—this tremendous presentation of truth. The gospel is not something partial or piecemeal: it takes in the whole life, the whole of history, the whole world. It tells us about the creation and the final judgment and everything in between. It is a complete, whole view of life, and many are unhappy in the Christian life because they have never realized that this way of life caters for the whole of man's life and covers every eventuality in his experience. There is no aspect of life but that the gospel has something to say about it. The whole of life must come under its influence because it is all-inclusive; the gospel is meant to control and govern everything in our lives. If we do not realize that, we are certain sooner or later to find ourselves in an unhappy condition. So many, because they indulge in these harmful and unscriptural dichotomies and only apply their Christianity to certain aspects of their lives, are bound to be in trouble. It is quite inevitable. That is the first thing we see here. We must realize the greatness of the gospel, its vast eternal span. We must dwell more on the riches, and in the riches, of these great doctrinal absolutes. We must not always stay in the gospels. We start there but we must go on; and then as we see it all worked out and put into its great context we shall realize what a mighty thing the gospel is, and how the whole of our life is meant to be governed by it.

That brings us to the second point, which is that in the same way as we often fail to realize the greatness and the wholeness of the message, we also fail to realize that the whole man must likewise be involved in it and by it—'Ye have obeyed from the heart the form of doctrine delivered unto you'. Man is a wonderful creature, he is mind, he is heart and he is will. Those are the three main constituents of man. God has given him a mind, He has given him a heart, He has given him a will whereby he can act. Now one of the greatest glories of the gospel is this, that it takes up the whole man. Indeed, I go so far as to assert that there is nothing else that does that; it is only this complete gospel, this complete view of life and death and eternity, that is big enough to include the whole man. It is because we fail to realize that, that many of our troubles arise. We are partial in our response to this great gospel.

Let me suggest some details in order to substantiate my point. There are some people in whose case the head only seems to be in use—the intellect, the understanding. They tell us that they are tremendously interested in the gospel as a point of view, as a Christian philosophy. These are the people who are always talking about the Christian outlook or, to use the present day jargon, the Christian insights. It is something purely philosophical, something entirely intellectual. I think you will agree that there are large numbers of people in that position at the present time.

Christianity is to them a matter of tremendous interest and they believe and proclaim that if only this Christian point of view could be applied in politics, in industry and in every other circle all our troubles would be solved. It is entirely the intellectual attitude and point of view.

There are others, not so many today, perhaps, as there used to be, whose sole interest in the gospel is their interest in theology and doctrine and metaphysics, and in great problems, arguments and discussions. I speak of past days; days that are gone. I do not want to defend them, but they were infinitely preferable to the present position. There were people then whose only interest in the gospel was their interest in theological problems; and they argued about them and discussed them. Their minds were very much engaged; this was their intellectual hobby and interest. But the tragedy was that it stopped at that interest, and their hearts had never been touched. Not only was there an absence of the grace of the Lord Jesus Christ in their lives but there was often an absence of the ordinary milk of human kindness. Those men would argue and almost fight about particular doctrines, but they were often hard men to approach. You would never go to them if you were in trouble; you felt that they would neither understand nor sympathize. Still worse, the truth they were so interested in was not at all applied in their lives; it was something confined to their studies. It did not touch their conduct or behaviour at all, but was confined entirely to the mind. Obviously they were bound, sooner or later, to get into difficulty and to become unhappy. Have you ever seen a man like that facing the end of his life? Have you seen him when he can no longer read, or when he is on his death-bed? I have seen one or two and I do not want to see another. It is a terrible thing when a man reaches that point when he knows that he must die, and the gospel which he has argued about and reasoned about and even 'defended' does not seem to help him because it has never gripped him. It was just an intellectual hobby.

But there are others in whose case the gospel seems to affect the heart only. This is commoner today. These are the people who feel that they have had an emotional release; they have passed through an emotional crisis. I do not want to disparage this, but there is a real danger in having a purely emotional experience only. These are people who may have some problem in their lives. They may have committed some particular sin.

They have tried to forget it but they cannot get away from it. At last they hear a message which seems tò give them deliverance from that one thing, and they accept it, and all is well. But they stop at that. They wanted this particular release and they have had it. That can be obtained from an incomplete presentation of the gospel, and it leads to a partial and incomplete experience. Such people, because they desire that primarily, have had an emotional experience and nothing else.

Or it may be that they were naturally interested in mysticism and the mystical phenomena. Some people are born natural mystics; there is something rather other-worldly about them, and they are interested in the mystical. There is great interest in this at the present time, in psychic phenomena, in this extra-sensory experience. There have always been people who have been interested in that kind of thing. They are natural mystics and they are drawn to something which seems to be offering a mystical experience. They come to the Scriptures because they feel that in them they are going to find satisfaction for this longing and desire for mystical experience. They seek for that and they get that. And they get nothing else.

Or it may be that certain people are in this position simply because they are moved aesthetically by the presentation of the gospel, by the atmosphere of the church, the painted windows, the monuments, the ritual, the hymns sung, the music, the sermon —any one or all of these things. Life has been hard and cruel to them and they have been embittered by circumstances. But they go to a particular service and somehow they find themselves comforted and soothed, and they feel happy and contented. That is all they wanted. They have it, and they want nothing more. They feel happy and away they go. But as certainly as they do so they will find themselves in a predicament and in a position where that will not help them. One day they will have to face some crisis and to see it through; but they have never learned to think things through. They have been content to live on their feelings.

Others again are in this one-sided position because they have responded to an appeal in a meeting. I remember a number of ministers telling me of how they worked in the enquiry room of a famous evangelist who once visited this country and who is now an old man and retired from the ministry. They would ask the people who came to the enquiry room why they had come.

Very often they got the reply that the person did not know. 'But', they said, 'you have come to the enquiry room. Why did you do so?' And the reply was: 'I have come because the preacher told us to come'. That preacher had a marvellous and exceptional gift for telling a story. He could dramatize, and he often ended his address with a moving story. Then he appealed to people to come forward and almost in a kind of trance they walked down the aisle and went to the enquiry room, they did not know why. They had been moved, they had been fascinated, but there seemed to be no conception of Truth, there was no relationship at all to 'the form of doctrine delivered'. Moved emotionally but by nothing else, they had arrived in the enquiry room. Now it is quite inevitable that such people should at some time or other find themselves in trouble. They will be unhappy and miserable; they will get depressed. These are people who have something in the heart but their head is not engaged at all, and oftentime, unfortunately, neither is the will. They are content to go on enjoying themselves emotionally and to experience feelings, and are not at all concerned about the application of Truth to the mind and to the will.

Then, finally, you have the same thing in those whose will is alone involved. It is possible, and it has happened unfortunately, for people to be persuaded to take up Christianity. They say that they believe that it is a good life and they solemnly decide to take it up. I think we should abolish this word decision. I do not like it. It seems to me that to talk about deciding for Christ is a denial of the text that we are considering, as I will show you. This 'making a decision', again, has often happened as the result of an appeal. If a great bombardment is made upon the wills of men there are certain wills that are sure to respond. They will decide because they have been called upon to decide, because they have been pressed to decide. Pressure has been put on the will. They have been told that they must decide, and they do decide: but they do not always know why they do so. And later on they will begin to ask questions, the devil will see to it that questions are raised in their minds. And they will find that they do not have an answer.

Let me sum up this point by putting it like this. These are the people who decide to take up Christianity instead of being taken up by Christianity. They have never known this feeling of constraint, this feeling of, 'I can do no other, so help me, God', that they must, that everything else has to be excluded, that the truth has so come to them that they must accept it. That is what Paul is saying in this chapter. 'God forbid', he says. 'What are you talking about? Do you not realize what the truth is? How can you say, "Shall we continue in sin that grace may abound?" It means that you do not know what grace is.' It is only people who have understood the truth who desire to do it. The tragedy of the others is that they have never seen it.

That, then, is the cause of the condition. But let me emphasize this. Sometimes, as I have been showing, you will find people who have one part of their personality engaged only—head only, heart only, will only. We will agree that they must be wrong. Yes, but let us be clear about this, it is equally wrong to have any two only. It is equally wrong to have the head and the heart only without the will, or the head and the will without the heart, or the heart and the will without the head. That is the thing I think the Apostle is impressing upon us. The Christian position is three-fold; it is the three together, and the three at the same time, and the three always. A great gospel like this takes up the whole man, and if the whole man is not taken up, think again as to where you stand. 'You have obeyed from the heart the form of doctrine delivered unto you.' What a gospel! What a glorious message! It can satisfy man's mind completely, it can move his heart entirely, and it can lead to wholehearted obedience in the realm of the will. That is the gospel. Christ has died that we might be complete men, not merely that parts of us may be saved; not that we might be lop-sided Christians, but that there may be a balanced finality about us.

But not only that, if we lack this proportion, we shall be in trouble later on, because man has been made by God in this balanced way. Have you ever thought of that? It is an interesting matter in psychology to notice how God has put these three powers within us—the mind, the heart and the will. And what tremendous powers they are. You would have thought that it would be impossible for the three to co-exist in one person; but God made man perfect. You see it all perfectly in the Lord Jesus Christ; and the object of salvation is to bring us to that perfection, to be so conformed to His image that the effects and traces of sin shall be removed and destroyed.

Let me say a final word about this balance. These things must always come in the right order. There is a definite order about this verse, and the order is obviously this. These people were servants held by sin: they are no longer that. Why not? The Apostle says the form of doctrine came to them—'you have obeyed from the heart the form of doctrine delivered unto you'. There they were in slavery. What has brought them out? The truth has been presented to them! They were not simply moved emotionally in the realm of the heart; it was not merely an appeal to the will. No, the Truth was presented. We must always put these things in the right order, and it is Truth first. It is doctrine first, it is the standard of teaching first, it is the message of the gospel first. We are not concerned simply to attract people emotionally or in the realm of the will, we are concerned to 'preach the Word'. The Apostles were not sent out simply to produce results and to change people. They were sent 'to preach the gospel', to 'preach the truth', to preach and declare 'Jesus and the resurrection'—this message, this form of doctrine, the deposit! Those are the terms used in the New Testament and the Church is certain to produce these spiritual monstrosities when she fails to put that first.

The Christian should know why he is a Christian. The Christian is not a man who simply says that something marvellous has happened to him. Not at all; he is able and ready 'to give a reason for the hope that is in him'. If he cannot, he had better make sure of his position. The Christian knows why he is what he is, and where he stands. He has had doctrine presented to him, he has received the truth. This 'form of sound teaching' has come to him. It came to his mind, and it must ever start with his mind. Truth comes to the mind and to the understanding enlightened by the Holy Spirit. Then having seen the truth the Christian loves it. It moves his heart. He sees what he was, he sees the life he was living, and he hates it. If you see the truth about yourself as a slave of sin you will hate yourself. Then as you see the glorious truth about the love of Christ you will want it, you will desire it. So the heart is engaged. Truly to see the truth means that you are moved by it and that you love it. You cannot help it. If you see truth clearly, you must feel it. Then that in turn leads to this, that your greatest desire will be to practise it and to live it.

That is Paul's whole argument. He says: Your talk about continuing in sin is unthinkable. If you only realized your unity with Christ, that you have been planted together in the likeness of

His death and have therefore risen with Him, you could never speak like that. You cannot be joined to Christ and be one with Him, and at the same time ask 'shall we continue in sin?' Does this great truth give me licence to go on doing those things which formerly appealed to me? Of course not. It is inconceivable. A man who knows and believes that he is 'risen with Christ' will inevitably desire to walk in newness of life with Him.

So Paul puts his mighty argument and demonstration and from this I draw my final conclusion, that in this realm we must always realize, when we talk to others, that the heart is never to be approached directly. I go further, the will is never to be approached directly either. This is a most important principle to bear in mind both in personal dealings and in preaching. The heart is always to be influenced through the understanding— the mind, then the heart, then the will. We have no right to make a direct attack upon the heart either in ourselves or anybody else. I have known evil-living men to find false comfort, to their own damnation, in the fact that they could still weep and be moved emotionally in a religious meeting. 'I cannot be all bad or else I would not respond like this', they have argued. But it is a false deduction—their emotional response was produced by themselves. Had it been a response to Truth their lives would have been changed. We must never approach the heart or the will directly. Truth is received through God's greatest gift to man, the mind, the understanding. God made man in His own image and there is no question but that the greatest part of this image is the mind with its capacity for apprehending truth. God has endowed us with that, and God sends truth to us in that way.

But God forbid that anyone should think that it ends with the intellect. It starts there, but it goes on. It then moves the heart and finally the man yields his will. He obeys, not grudgingly or unwillingly, but with the whole heart. The Christian life is a glorious perfect life that takes up and captivates the entire personality. O may God make us balanced Christians, men and women of whom it can be said that we are obviously, patently obeying from the heart the form of doctrine which has been delivered unto us.

Howbeit for this cause I obtained mercy, that in me first Jesus Christ might shew forth all longsuffering, for a·pattern to them which should hereafter believe on Him to life everlasting.

1 Timothy 1. 16

THAT ONE SIN

IN the last chapter we were considering those people who are unhappy and who never really enjoy their Christian life because of a failure to maintain a balance between mind and and heart and will. In this first Epistle to Timothy Paul speaks of this, and says that we must 'hold the faith and a good conscience; which some having put away concerning faith have made shipwreck; of whom is Hymenaeus and Alexander, whom I have delivered unto Satan that they may learn not to blaspheme' (1 Timothy 1. 19, 20). That lack of balance is one of the great causes not only of unhappiness, but of failure and of stumbling in the Christian life.

Now there are some who are amazed at all this. They have a glib, superficial view of Christianity which holds that so long as a person has signed a decision card he is a Christian and must, therefore, be perfectly happy. But, as experience and the history of the Church show very clearly, that is far from being the case, and if we have adopted that superficial view we shall soon be in some kind of trouble. The fact is that there are always Christian people who are in difficulties for various reasons, and you cannot read the New Testament Epistles without seeing the truth of what I am saying. If simply to believe and to accept salvation is everything, then these New Testament Epistles would never have been needed, indeed, in a sense, you would not need the Church at all. People would just be saved and go on happily for the rest of their lives as Christians. But there is abundant evidence that this is not the case. These New Testament people had believed and had become Christian, and yet it was necessary for the Apostles Paul and Peter and John and others to write letters to them because they were in trouble in one way or another. They were unhappy for various reasons, they were not enjoying their Christian life. Some were tempted to look back to the life out of which they had been saved; others were tempted severely, others persecuted cruelly. Thus the very existence of the New Testament Epistles shows us that unhappiness is a condition which does afflict Christian people. There is in this, therefore, a strange kind of comfort which is nevertheless very real. If anyone reading my words is in trouble, let me say this: The fact that you are unhappy or troubled is no indication that you are not a Christian; indeed, I would go further and say that if you have never had any trouble in your Christian life I should very much doubt whether you are a Christian at all. There is such a thing as false peace, there is such a thing as believing delusions. The whole of the New Testament and the history of the Church throughout the centuries bear eloquent testimony to the fact that this is a 'fight of faith', and not to have any troubles in your soul is, therefore, far from being a good sign. It is, indeed, a serious sign that there is something radically wrong, and there is a very good reason for saying that. For from the moment we become Christians we become the special objects of the attention of the devil. As he besieged and attacked our Lord, so does he besiege and attack all the Lord's people, 'Count it all joy', says James, 'when ye fall into divers temptations' or trials. That is the way your faith is proved, for not only is it a test of your faith, in a sense it is a proof that you have faith. It is because we belong to Him that the devil will do his utmost to disturb and upset us. He cannot rob us of our salvation, thank God, but while he cannot rob us of our salvation he can make us miserable. He can, if we are foolish enough to listen to him, seriously limit our enjoyment of our salvation. That is precisely what he tries to do constantly, and that in turn is why we have this teaching and instruction in the New Testament Epistles.

In this chapter, we are going to consider one very common way in which the devil attacks along this line. It is the one suggested not only by this particular verse before us but by the entire chapter in this biographical section—the section in which the Apostle refers to himself as a minister of the gospel of the Lord Jesus Christ. The problem here is the case of those who are miserable Christians or who are suffering from spiritual depression because of their past—either because of some particular sin in their past, or because of the particular form which sin happened to take in their case. I would say that in my experience in the ministry, extending now over many years, there is no more common difficulty. It is constantly recurring and I think that I have had to deal with more people over this particular thing than over anything else.

Now at first sight some of you may wonder and query whether such people are Christian at all. But you are quite wrong. They are Christians. Ask them to state the Christian faith and they do so perfectly. They seem to be quite clear about the doctrine of justification by faith. That is to say they see very clearly that they can never put themselves right. They are not relying upon their own lives or activities or anything they can ever do. They are fully aware of their complete helplessness and their entire dependence upon the grace of God in our Lord and Saviour Jesus Christ. They are quite clear about that, and can testify to it, and they have believed on the Lord Jesus Christ. Well, you ask, what is the matter with them? Their condition is that though they seem to be quite clear about this central doctrine, and though they speak as Christians, they are nevertheless unhappy, and they are unhappy because of something in their own past life. They come to you looking unhappy, indeed miserable, and they always talk about this thing, they invariably bring it up. As a rule it is some action, some deed—which may or may not have involved other people—some wrong committed by themselves. Generally it is some one thing, some big thing. That is the thing to which they constantly hark back. They harp upon it and they cannot leave it. They are always analyzing it and scrutinizing and condemning themselves because of it. And the result is that they are unhappy. Sometimes it is something they have said, some word which they once spoke.

Let me give you what is the most graphic illustration of this that I have ever come across in my own experience. I mention it simply to illustrate the point I am making. I remember an old man who was converted and became a Christian at the age of 77, one of the most striking conversions I have ever known. That man had lived a very evil life; there was scarcely anything he had not done at some time or another. But he came under the sound of the gospel and was converted in his old age. The great day came when he was received into the membership of the Church, and when he came to his first communion service on the Sunday evening it was to him the biggest thing that had ever happened. His joy was indescribable and we were all so happy about him. But there was a sequel, and this was the sequel. Next morning, even before I was up, that poor old man had arrived at my house, and there he stood looking the picture of misery and dejection, and weeping uncontrollably. I was amazed and astounded, especially in view of what had happened the previous night, the greatest night of his life, the climax of everything that had ever happened to him. I eventually succeeded in controlling him in a physical sense, and then asked him what was the matter. His trouble was this. After going home from that communion service he had suddenly remembered something that had happened thirty years ago. He was with a group of men drinking in a public house and arguing about religion. On that occasion he had said in contempt and derision that 'Jesus Christ was a bastard'. And it had all come back to him suddenly and there was, he felt sure, no forgiveness for that. This one thing! Ah, yes, he was quite happy to forget about the drinking and the gambling and the immorality. That was all right, that was forgiven. He understood that clearly. But this thing that he had said about the Son of God, the Saviour of the world—that! He could not be consoled, he could not be comforted. This one thing had cast him down to utter hopelessness. (I thank God that by the application of the Scriptures I was able to restore his joy to him.) But that is the kind of thing I am referring to, something a man has once said, or done, that haunts him and comes back to him, and makes him miserable and wretched, though he still subscribes to the full Christian faith. This condition, which appears to be contradictory, is a reality and we must recognize it as such. In other cases it may be the bondage of some promise or pledge, made but never kept, which causes the trouble. I have had many instances of this kind, of people who during an illness have made a certain pledge or promise to God that if only they might get well they would do so and so. But they had not kept their vows; indeed, they had meanwhile done something else which made the doing of that thing which they had promised impossible. And there they are, unhappy and held in the grip of this one thing.

That then is the kind of condition to which I am now calling attention. These are people who seem to be quite clear about the doctrine of salvation, except that they feel that in their case there is something—their sin, this particular sin or the form that sin has taken in their case—which somehow puts them in a different category. They say, 'Yes, I know—but . . .' They are held down, they are miserable Christians, they are suffering from this state of spiritual depression.

What is the real trouble here? Well, there are two main explanations of the condition. First and foremost, of course, it is the work of the devil; it is just Satan who, though he cannot rob us of our salvation, can definitely rob us of our joy. His great concern is to prevent anyone becoming a Christian, but when that fails, his one object then is to make them miserable Christians so that he can point men who are under a conviction of sin to them and say: 'That is Christianity; look at him or her. There is a picture of Christianity! Look at that miserable creature. Do you want to be like that?' No doubt the essential cause of most of these conditions is the devil himself.

But there is also a subsidiary cause, and this is the thing I want to emphasize here. I would again say that this condition is almost entirely due to an ignorance of doctrine—a failure to understand the New Testament doctrine of salvation clearly and this is of the very essence of the treatment of the condition. Let me put this plainly and bluntly in order that I may emphasize it even at the risk of being misunderstood. There is a sense in which the one thing that these people who are in this condition must not do is to pray to be delivered from it! That is what they always do, and that is what they have invariably been doing when they come seeking help—indeed, it is what they are generally told they must do. Now the Christian must always pray, the Christian must 'pray without ceasing', but this is one of those points at which the Christian must stop praying for a moment and begin to think! for there are particular problems in the Christian life concerning which I say that if you do nothing but pray about them you will never solve them. You must stop praying at times because your prayer may just be reminding you of the problem and keeping your mind fixed upon it. So you must stop praying and think, and work out your doctrine.

What are you to think of? The first thing I would suggest is that you think of this case of the Apostle Paul and of what he says here: 'I thank Jesus Christ our Lord who hath enabled me, for that He counted me faithful, putting me into the ministry; who was before a blasphemer and a persecutor and injurious, but I obtained mercy, because I did it ignorantly in unbelief. And the grace of our Lord was exceeding abundant with faith and love which is in Christ Jesus. This is a faithful saying and worthy of all acceptation, that Christ Jesus came into the world to save sinners, of whom I am chief. Howbeit for this cause I obtained mercy, that in me first Jesus Christ might shew forth all long-suffering, for a pattern to them which should hereafter believe on Him to life everlasting'. Now this is wonderful. You notice what the Apostle says; what he claims here is that in a sense the Lord Jesus Christ saved him in order to set him up as a model. A model in what respect? A model for those people who feel that their particular sin somehow or another passes the limit of grace and the mercy of God. The Apostle's argument is that his case alone is sufficient proof, once and for ever, that we must never reason along that line. In other words, here are people who believe that sins can be graded and they draw distinctions between particular sins. They classify them saying that some are forgivable and some apparently are not. To these the Apostle says that his own case is more than sufficient to deal with the argument. 'Whatever you may think,' he says, 'whatever you may have done, think of me, think of what I was, "a blasphemer, a persecutor and injurious".' Could anything be worse? He hated the very Name of Jesus Christ of Nazareth, he did his utmost to exterminate His followers, he went down to Damascus 'breathing out threatenings and slaughter' against them. He was in that condition, a blasphemer, a persecutor. 'Now', says the Apostle, 'I am a test case, and whatever you may think about yourself, put it up against my case and see where you stand.' That is the first argument. You think of his case and say to yourself: 'If he obtained mercy, if he could be forgiven, I must think again of this sin in my life'. That is where you start.

But the Apostle does not stop at that, because in a sense we must not differentiate between sin and sin. On the surface the Apostle seems to be doing that. He says: 'Christ Jesus came into the world to save sinners of whom I am chief', as if to say there are big sinners and lesser sinners and little sinners. He did not mean that, however: he cannot possibly mean that, for that would be to contradict his essential doctrine. What he does mean is that the nearer a man gets to God the greater he sees his sin. When a man sees the blackness of his own soul, he says: 'I am the chief of sinners'; and it is only a Christian who can say that. The man of the world will never make such a statement. He is always proving what a good man he is. But Paul seems to be saying more than that, as I have just been saying. He does seem to suggest in one way that these sins against the person of Christ are the sin of sins. But he makes his meaning plain when he puts it like this, in other words: 'I did it ignorantly, in unbelief.' In putting it like that he demolishes these grades of sin. Looking at it from one angle his sin was the worst sin conceivable, but from another angle it is the sum of all sins because finally there is only one sin and that is the sin of unbelief.

That is the great New Testament doctrine on this matter; it is the thing that these people have to grasp above everything else, that we must not think in terms of particular sins but always in terms of our relationship to God. We all tend to go astray at that point. That is why we tend to think that some conversions are more remarkable than others. But they are not. It takes the same grace of God to save the most respectable person in the world as the most lawless person in the world. Nothing but the grace of God can save anybody, and it takes the same grace to save all. But we do not think like that. We think some conversions are more remarkable than others. Because we are wrong in our doctrine, we differentiate between sin and sin, and think some sins are worse than others. It all comes back to our relationship to God; it is all a matter of belief or unbelief.

There are many striking examples of this in the Scriptures. The point at which a man like Joseph showed his spiritual insight and understanding supremely was this. When tempted by Potiphar's wife he said: 'How then can I do this great wickedness and sin against God?' What troubled Joseph was not the possibility of sinning against the woman but against God Himself. Now that is true spiritual thinking. We must not think so much about the sin itself. That is what we tend to do. What constituted sin for Joseph was the fact that it involved his relationship to God—'if I do that I will be sinning against God'. David saw the same thing. Murderer and adulterer that he was, this is what troubled him: 'Against Thee, Thee only have I sinned and done this evil in Thy sight'. He was not minimizing the wrong he had done to others; he knew all about that; but that was not the worst thing. It was God—his relationship to God. The moment you think of it like that you forget particular sins, and you forget that one is worse than another. 'My unbelief,' says Paul, 'that was the trouble'—not particular actions. It is indeed our relationship to God and His Law that matters.

The New Testament has some very striking teaching about this. I wonder whether you have observed the list of the works of the flesh that Paul gives in the 5th chapter of the Epistle to the Galatians? 'Now the works of the flesh are manifest which are these: adultery, fornication, uncleanness, lasciviousness'—we are

clear about them—horrible! 'Idolatry'—certainly—'witchcraft'—
obvious—ah, but suddenly—'hatred'—Hatred? But I thought
sin only applied to certain people who were adulterers and unclean? Not at all—hatred, variance, emulations, wrath, strife,
seditions, heresies. You notice how he mixes them up—envyings,
murders. Yes, not only actual, but in the heart. Drunkenness,
revellings and such like. What a list! And our Lord said the
same thing when He reminded us that it is 'out of the heart
proceed evil thoughts, murders, etc.'. He puts them together, not
only certain big sins but every sin, any sin, anything that suggests
a wrong relationship to God—lawlessness, breaking of the law.
James has put this point once and for ever in his Epistle in the
second chapter and the tenth verse: 'For whosoever shall keep
the whole law, and yet offend in one point, he is guilty of all'. So
you see we are all on the same level; and if the Evil One tries to
make you think that your sin is different, tell him in reply that it
does not matter what particular point a man breaks with respect
to the law, that if he breaks it in one point he is guilty of all. It
is not the one point in particular that really matters; it is the law
that matters. That is God's way of looking at sin. So do not
allow the devil to mislead you. It is the law, not any particular
sin, but our relationship to the Law of God, our relationship to
the Person of God Himself that matters.

That brings us to the third point. The trouble with this type
of unhappy Christian is that he does not really believe the Scriptures. Have you thought of that? You say: 'My trouble is that
terrible sin which I have committed'. Let me tell you in the Name
of God that that is not your trouble. Your trouble is unbelief.
You do not believe the Word of God. I am referring to the First
Epistle of John and the first chapter where we read this: 'If we
confess our sins, He is faithful and just to forgive us our sins and
to cleanse us from all unrighteousness'. That is a categorical statement made by God the Holy Spirit through His servant. There
is no limit to it; there is no differentiation between sin and sin.
I cannot see any qualification at all. Whatever your sin—it is as
wide as that—it does not matter what it is, it does not matter
what it was, 'if we confess our sins He is faithful and just to forgive
us our sins and to cleanse us from all unrighteousness'. So if you
do not believe that word, and if you go on dwelling on your sin,
I say that you are not accepting the Word of God, you are not
taking God at His word, you do not believe what He tells you

and that is your real sin. You remember what happened to Peter once (see Acts 10). Peter had gone to the housetop to rest and there he suddenly went into a trance and saw a great sheet coming down from heaven with all sorts of four-footed beasts in it and he heard a voice saying to him, 'Rise, Peter, slay and eat'. Peter continued saying: 'Not so, Lord; for I have never eaten anything that is common or unclean'. You remember what happened to him? The Voice of God from heaven came to him again and said: 'What God hath cleansed, that call thou not common (or unclean)'. 'Do you realize what you are doing?' said God in effect; 'you are persisting in calling common and unclean that which I have commanded you to slay and eat— "what God hath cleansed, that call thou not common".' That is precisely what I would say at this moment to anybody who may have been held in depression by the devil for a number of years over some particular sin, some unhappy past event in your life. I do not care what it is. What I say to you in the Name of God is this: 'What God hath cleansed—by the blood of His only Begotten Son—that call not thou common or unclean'. 'The blood of Jesus Christ His Son cleanseth us from all sin' and all unrighteousness. Believe the Word of God, my friend. Do not go on praying frantically to be forgiven that sin. Believe God's Word. Do not ask Him for a message of forgiveness. He has given it to you. Your prayer may well be an expression of unbelief at that point. Believe Him and His Word.

Another trouble with these people is that they do not seem to realize fully what our Lord did on the Cross on Calvary's Hill. They do believe in His sacrificial, atoning death, but they do not work out its implications. They have not fully grasped the doctrine. They know enough to be saved—I am speaking of Christians —but they are in a state of depression because they do not realize fully what this means. They forget that the angel announced to Joseph at the very beginning that He should 'save His people from their sins' (Matthew 1. 21). The angel did not say that He shall save from all sins except this one sin that you have committed. No! 'He shall save His people from their sins'. And listen to Peter saying the same thing: 'Who His own self bear our sins in His own body on the tree, that we, being dead to sins, should live unto righteousness: by whose stripes we are healed' (1 Peter 2. 24). There is no qualification there, no limit. Or listen to the words of the Apostle Paul when he says: 'He hath made Him to be sin for us who knew no sin' (2 Corinthians 5. 21). They were all put there, every one, there is no limit, there is nothing left. All the sins of His people are there, every one of them. Indeed, He said it Himself, did He not, on the Cross? He said: 'It is finished', absolutely finished. In what sense? It is finished in the sense that not only all the sins committed in the past were dealt with there, but all the sins that could ever be committed were also dealt with there. It is one sacrifice, once and forever. He would never come back to the Cross again. All the sins were dealt with there finally and completely, everything. Nothing was left undone—'It is finished'. What we remind one another of as we take the bread and the wine, and what we proclaim, is that completed finished work. There is nothing left undone, there is no qualification concerning particular sins. All the sins of those who believe on Him, every one, have been dealt with and God has blotted them out as a thick cloud. All the sins you may ever commit have been dealt with there, so when you go to Him it is 'the Blood of Jesus Christ His Son' that is going to cleanse you.

The next step, therefore, is that we must be clear about justification. I have dealt with this in a previous chapter, but let me remind you of it. Let us remember that our justification means not only that our sins are forgiven and that we have been declared to be righteous by God Himself, not merely that we were righteous at that moment when we believed, but permanently righteous. For justification means this also, that we are given by God the positive righteousness of His own Son, the Lord Jesus Christ. That is what justification means. It does not only mean that your sins are forgiven, but much more. It means that He clothes us also with the righteousness of Jesus Christ. He says in effect: 'You are righteous; I see, not a sinner, but a righteous child of My own; I see you in Christ covered by His holiness and right-eousness'. And when God does that to us, He does it once and for ever. You are hidden, you yourself and your whole personality and life stand in the righteousness of Christ before God. I say, therefore, with reverence and on the authority of the Word of God that God sees your sins no more; He sees the righteousness of Christ upon you. Lay hold of that.

Ultimately it all comes to this, that the real cause of the trouble is failure to realize our union with Christ. Many seem to think that Christianity just means that we are delivered in the sense that our sins are forgiven. But that is only the beginning, but one aspect of it. Essentially salvation means union with Christ, being one with Christ. As we were one with Adam we are now one with Christ. We have been crucified with Christ— 'I am crucified with Christ', says Paul. 'All that has happened to Him has happened to me. I am one with Him.' Read the fifth and sixth chapters of Paul's Epistle to the Romans. The teaching is that we have died with Christ, have been buried with Christ, have risen with Christ, are seated in the heavenly places in Christ and with Christ. That is the teaching of the Scriptures. 'Ye are dead and your life is hid with Christ in God' (Colossians 3. 3). The old man has been crucified and all that belonged to him. His sins have all been dealt with. You are buried with Christ, you are risen with Christ. 'Reckon ye yourselves then to be dead unto sin but alive unto God through Jesus Christ our Lord' (Romans 6. 11).

Let me sum it up in this way, therefore. You and I—and to me this is one of the great discoveries of the Christian life; I shall never forget the release which realizing this for the first time brought to me—you and I must never look at our past lives; we must never look at any sin in our past life in any way except that which leads us to praise God and to magnify His grace in Christ Jesus. I challenge you to do that. If you look at your past and are depressed by it, if as a result you are feeling miserable as a Christian, you must do what Paul did. 'I was a blasphemer,' he said, but he did not stop at that. Does he then say: 'I am unworthy to be a preacher of the gospel'? In fact he says the exact opposite: 'I thank Christ Jesus our Lord who hath enabled me, for that He counted me faithful putting me into the ministry, etc.'. When Paul looks at the past and sees his sin he does not stay in a corner and say: 'I am not fit to be a Christian, I have done such terrible things'. Not at all. What it does to him, its effect upon him, is to make him praise God. He glories in grace and says: 'And the grace of our Lord was exceeding abundant with faith and love which is in Christ Jesus'.

That is the way to look at your past. So, if you look at your past and are depressed, it means that you are listening to the devil. But if you look at the past and say: 'Unfortunately it is true I was blinded by the god of this world, but thank God His grace was more abundant, He was more than sufficient and His love and mercy came upon me in such a way that it is all forgiven, I am a new man', then all is well. That is the way to look at the past, and if we do not do that, I am almost tempted to say that we deserve to be miserable. Why believe the devil instead of believing God? Rise up and realize the truth about yourself, that all the past has gone, and you are one with Christ, and all your sins have been blotted out once and for ever. O let us remember that it is sin to doubt God's word, it is sin to allow the past, which God has dealt with, to rob us of our joy and our usefulness in the present and in the future. Hear again those words uttered from heaven to the doubtful, hesitant Apostle Peter: 'What God hath cleansed, that call not thou common'. Rejoice in this wondrous grace and mercy that has blotted out your sins and made you a child of God. 'Rejoice in the Lord always, and again I say rejoice.'

And last of all He was seen of me also, as of one born out of due time. For I am the least of the Apostles, that am not meet to be called an Apostle, because I persecuted the Church of God. But by the Grace of God I am what I am; and His Grace which was bestowed upon me was not in vain: but I laboured more abundantly than they all: yet not I, but the Grace of God which was with me.

1 Corinthians 15. 8-10

VI

VAIN REGRETS

IN these days men and women are ready to be interested in anything that is attractive. We are living in an age of advertisements and people are ready to believe anything that is said to them. They believe advertisements, they believe what they are told, and so it follows that were they to see something in Christian people that gave the impression that such people were living a life of joy and happiness and triumph, they would crowd in and would be anxious to discover the secret of such successful living. It is not an unfair deduction to make, therefore, that what accounts for the masses being outside is the condition of those who are inside. So often we give the impression that we are dejected and depressed; indeed, some would almost give the impression that to become a Christian means that you face many problems that never worried you before. So, looking at things superficially the man of the world comes to the conclusion that you find happier people outside the Church than inside the Church. He is quite wrong, of course, but we must recognize that some of us at any rate have to plead guilty to the charge, that far too often because we suffer from spiritual depression, and are more or less miserable Christians, we grossly and grievously misrepresent the gospel of Redeeming Grace.

Now all this, of course, is due to the fact that we are confronted by a very powerful adversary. The fact is that the moment we become Christian we become subjected to the most subtle and powerful assaults of one who is described in the Bible as 'the prince of the power of the air', 'the spirit who now ruleth in the children of disobedience', 'the god of this world', 'Satan', the 'Devil'. And as we go on with our study and consider the way in which the devil is able to come to us and to attack us, and the subtle way in which he deludes and leads us astray without our realizing it at all, we begin to understand why so many fail. And, of course, he is most subtle and most dangerous when he comes as 'an angel of light' and as a would-be friend of the Church and one who is interested in the gospel and in its propagation.

According to the Scriptures he does that (2 Corinthians 11), and it is at that point that he is most subtle of all. Not only is he powerful, he is subtle, and as we continue to consider these various forms and manifestations of depression that will become more and more clear.

In view of this we must prepare ourselves for him and for such attacks; and the way to do that is to study the Scriptures. There alone are we given an insight into his methods. 'We are not ignorant of his devices', says the Apostle Paul again to the Corinthians (2 Corinthians 2. 11), but the tragedy is that so many are ignorant of his devices that they do not believe in his existence, and even those who do, fail to remember that he is always there and that he can appear in many subtle forms. As we look objectively at what he does to us, we cannot but be amazed at our unutterable folly. As you look at some of these cases of spiritual depression you ask: 'How could a man have fallen into that?' It all seems so perfectly plain and obvious, yet we are all constantly falling into the same snare. That is due to the subtlety of the devil's method. He puts things to us in such an attractive manner that we find that we have fallen almost before we realize that anything has happened at all. There is only one way to deal with all this and that is to study his methods, and to study the various teachings of the Scripture itself with regard to this condition of spiritual depression. That is what we are endeavouring to do in our present studies.

We must now consider the case of other people who are crippled in the present as the result of looking back into the past, not this time to some particular sin, but rather to the fact that they spent so much time outside the Kingdom and are so late in coming into it. This again is an extremely common cause of spiritual depression. These people are depressed by the fact that they have wasted so much time, wasted so many long years, and that they have been so slow to become Christians at all. They are always bemoaning the fact that they have missed so many opportunities —opportunities of doing good and helping others and opportunities of service. They say, 'If only I had seen all this when I was young I would have volunteered for service, but I have only seen it now and it is too late'. Missed opportunities! Or they may put it in terms of what they might have attained to by now— if only. 'If only'—that is their cry. But they did not believe; and looking back at the years spent out in the world not understanding these things, they are full of vain regrets for what they might have been, for how they might have grown in grace and for the point at which they would have arrived by now. They look back in that way to the past and they regret it and bemoan it: they look back at the joys they might have had, the years of happy joyful experience they might have had. But it is too late, the opportunities have gone. Why were they so foolish; how could they have been so blind? Why were they so slow? They heard the gospel; they read good books; they even felt something at a certain point but nothing came of it and the opportunity was allowed to go. Now at long last they have understood, and are obsessed by the thought —'if only'.

Now this is a very common condition and it accounts for a state of spiritual depression in large numbers of people. How do we deal with this, what have we to say about it? Let me start by saying that while it is perfectly right for such people to regret the fact that they have been so slow to believe, it is quite wrong to be miserable about it. You cannot look back across your past life without seeing things to regret. That is as it should be; but it is just there that the subtlety of this condition comes in and we cross that fine line of distinction that lies between a legitimate regret and a wrong condition of misery and of dejection. The Christian life is a very finely balanced life. That is one of its most striking features. It has been compared to a man walking on a knife-edge with the possibility of falling easily on either side. All along we have to draw subtle distinctions and here is one of them, the distinction between a legitimate regret and a wrong condition of dejection and of misery.

How then do we avoid being miserable in this respect? We are going to consider that in terms of what the Apostle Paul says here about himself. This always seems to me to be a perfect illustration of what our Lord taught in the parable recorded in verses 1-16 of the twentieth chapter of Matthew, about the labourers in the vineyard who were hired at different hours of the day, some not until the eleventh hour. We shall be looking at it from the standpoint of the people who were engaged at the eleventh hour and who were the last to enter into the Kingdom.

But before we come to the specific treatment of the matter in terms of Scripture, let us consider it in a more general way. There are certain principles of common sense and general wisdom that need to be applied to this condition. There are some people who seem to think that it is wrong for a Christian ever to use common sense. They seem to think that they must always do everything in an exclusively spiritual manner. Now that seems to me to be very unscriptural. The Christian is in no respect inferior to the unbeliever; he is always superior. The Christian can not only do everything that the unbeliever does, he can do even more. That is the way to look at the Christian. He is a man who is to apply common sense to situations, and it is right and legitimate that he should do so. If you can conquer the devil at that level, conquer him at that level. It does not matter at what level you conquer the devil as long as you conquer him. If you can defeat him and get rid of him by using common sense and ordinary wisdom, do so. It is perfectly right and legitimate for the Christian to do that. I am saying all this because I often find that people are in difficulty about this matter and are spending their time in praying about a matter instead of doing something that is perfectly obvious from the standpoint of common sense.

Let me explain what I mean. I would suggest that the first thing for anyone to say to himself who is in this condition (and the same is true for one who has to help anybody who is in this condition) is that to be miserable in the present because of some failure in the past is a sheer waste of time and energy. That is obvious. That is common sense. The past cannot be recalled and you can do nothing about it. You can sit down and be miserable and you can go round and round in circles of regret for the rest of your life but it will make no difference to what you have done. Now that is common sense and it does not need special Christian revelation to demonstrate it. The world in its wisdom tells us it is 'no use crying over spilt milk'. Well, quote that to the devil! Why should a Christian be more foolish than anybody else? Why should you not apply natural common sense and human wisdom to a situation? But that is what many people fail to do. The result is that they are wasting their time and energy in vain regrets about things which they cannot change or undo, a purely foolish and irrational thing to do even from the mundane standard of common sense. Let us then lay this down as a principle. We must never for a second worry about anything that cannot be affected or changed by us. It is a waste of energy. If you can do nothing about a situation stop thinking about it; never again look back at it, never think of it. If you do, it is the devil defeating you. Vague useless regrets must be dismissed as irrational. My friend, stop dwelling on them! Quite apart from Christianity, it is a foolish thing to do, it is a sheer waste of energy and a waste of time.

But let us go further and realize that to dwell on the past simply causes failure in the present. While you are sitting down and bemoaning the past and regretting all the things you have not done, you are crippling yourself and preventing yourself from working in the present. Is that Christianity? Of course it is not. Christianity is common sense and much more—but it includes common sense. 'Ah', but you say, 'I can hear that in the world.' Well, if you can, hear it and act on it! Our Lord Himself has said that the children of this world are wiser in their generation than the children of light. He commended the unjust steward and I am simply doing the same thing. The world from its standpoint of common wisdom is perfectly right in this matter. It is always wrong to mortgage the present by the past, it is always wrong to allow the past to act as a brake upon the present. Let the dead past bury its dead. There is nothing that is more reprehensible, judged by common canons of thought, than to allow anything that belongs to the past to cause you to be a failure in the present. And this morbid concern about the past does so. The people I am describing are failing in the present. Instead of living in the present and getting on with the Christian life they are sitting down bemoaning the past. They are so sorry about the past that they do nothing in the present. How wrong it is.

My third argument from the standpoint of common sense and human wisdom is this: That if you really believe what you say about the past, if you really do bemoan the fact that you have wasted so much time in the past, the thing to do is to make up for it in the present. Is not that common sense? Here is a man who comes in utterly dejected and saying: 'If only—the time I have wasted!' What I say to him is this: 'Are you making up for that lost time? Why are you wasting this energy in telling me about the past which you cannot undo? Why don't you put your energy into the present?' I speak with vehemence because this condition has to be dealt with sternly and the last thing to do with such people is to sympathize with them. If you are suffering from this condition take yourself in hand and examine yourself from an ordinary common sense point of view. You are behaving like a fool, you are irrational, you are wasting your time and your energy. You do not really believe what you are saying. If you bemoan a wasted past, make up for it in the present, give yourself entirely to living at this present moment. That is what Paul did. He says: 'And last of all He was seen of me also as of one born out of due time'. He says in effect: I have wasted a lot of time, others have got ahead of me. But he is able to go on and to add: 'I laboured more abundantly than they all, yet not I, but the grace of God which was with me'.

Very well, there is the argument, there is the way of dealing with this thing from the standpoint of common sense and of ordinary common human wisdom. That is enough, it should be sufficient, but nevertheless let us go beyond that. The Christian, I say, is never less than the unbeliever, he is always more. He should have all the common sense and wisdom of the unbeliever, but he has something more in addition. And here we come to the statement of the great Apostle and to our Lord's teaching in the parable of the vineyard in Matthew 20.

Let us see what the Apostle has to say. We have seen what he said about the great sin in his life, we shall find the same thing with this problem also. The Apostle has been giving an account of the resurrection appearances. His immediate concern is about that great doctrine, but this is how he speaks: 'Last of all He was seen of me also'. Now the Apostle undoubtedly regretted the fact that he had come into the Christian life so late. Let us be clear about what he means when he says 'last of all'. He means that he was the last of the apostles to see the risen Lord. They had all seen Him in different ways together. Paul was not with them then; he was a blasphemer and a persecutor at that time. So 'last of all' means the last of the apostles. But not only was he the last of the apostles, he was literally the last person of all persons to see the risen Lord. No one has ever seen the risen Lord with his naked eyes since the Apostle Paul saw Him on the road to Damascus. He 'shewed Himself' to over 500 brethren at once. We do not even know their names, but He did show Himself to them and to these various witnesses that are recorded here. But the very last person of all to see Him was Saul of Tarsus. What happened on the road to Damascus was not that Paul had a vision—many have had visions since—but he literally saw the Lord of Glory. And that is what he says here: 'Last of all He was seen of me'. That is what made him an apostle, that he was a witness to the fact of the resurrection. But the thing he is emphasizing is this, that he was the very last of all. And not content with that, he says: 'Last of all He was seen of me also, as of one born out of due time'. There was something unnatural, untimely about his spiritual birth. He was not like the others. The others had listened to the Lord's teaching, they had been with Him all along, they had been at the Crucifixion, they had seen Him buried, they had been with Him for forty days after the resurrection, they had been with Him at the Ascension. They were with Him from the beginning and right through to the end. But Paul on the contrary had had a kind of unnatural, an untimely spiritual birth; he has come, in some odd, strange way and—last of all.

That is what he says about himself. And of course he could only think of that with regret. He should have been in at the beginning, he had had the facilities, he had had the opportunities; but he had hated the gospel. He 'verily thought within himself that he should do many things contrary to the Name of Jesus. . . .' He regarded Him as a blasphemer, he tried to exterminate His followers and the Church. There he was outside, but all the others were in. But—'last of all', and in this strange way, he came in. How easy it would have been for him to have spent the rest of his life in vain regrets about the past! He says here: 'Last of all he was seen of me, though I am the least of the apostles because I persecuted the Church'. It was all perfectly true, and he bitterly regretted it; but that did not paralyse Paul. He did not spend the rest of his life sitting in a corner and saying: 'I am the last to come in. Why did I do that? How could I have rejected Him?' That is what the people suffering from spiritual depression do. But Paul did not. What struck him was the amazing grace that brought him in at all. And so he entered into the new life with tremendous zeal, and though 'last of all' yet, in a sense, he became the first.

What then is the teaching? Let us take the Apostle's teaching and look at it in the light of this parable in the twentieth chapter of Matthew, for they both say the same thing. What matters first of all if you are a Christian is not what you once were, but what you are. Does that sound ridiculous? It is so perfectly obvious that what matters is not what you were but what you are. Yes, how obvious when I put it like this, but how difficult to see it sometimes when the devil attacks us. The Apostle said that he was 'not worthy to be called an apostle because he persecuted the Church of God', but he goes on to add: 'But by the grace of God

I am what I am'. What does it matter what I was? 'I am what I am.' Put your emphasis there. Do not be for ever thinking about what you were. The essence of the Christian position is that you should remind yourself of what you are. Certainly there is the past with all its sins. But say this to yourself:

> 'Ransomed, healed, restored, forgiven,
> Who like me His praise should sing.'

'I am what I am'—whatever the past may have been. It is what I am that matters. What am I? I am forgiven, I am reconciled to God by the Blood of His Son upon the Cross. I am a child of God. I am adopted into God's family, and I am an heir with Christ, a joint-heir with Him. I am going to glory. That is what matters, not what I was, not what I have been. Do what the Apostle did therefore if the enemy is attacking you along this line. Turn to him and say: 'What you are saying is perfectly true. I was all you say. But what I am interested in is not what I was but what I am, and "I am what I am by the grace of God".'

The second deduction is this—and they are all simple and obvious. It is not the time of your entry into the Kingdom that matters but the fact that you are in the Kingdom. That is the thing that matters. How foolish it is to mourn the fact that we were not in earlier, and to allow that to rob us of the things we might be enjoying now. It is like a man going to a great exhibition and discovering that there is a long queue. He has come rather late. He arrives at the exhibition but he has to wait a long time, he is about the last to get in. What would you think of such a man if, having got in through the door he simply stands at the door and says, 'What a shame I wasn't the first to get in, what a pity I wasn't in earlier'? You laugh at that, and rightly so, but I would point out that you are probably laughing at yourself, for that is precisely what you are doing spiritually. 'O that I have left it so late.' My friend, begin to enjoy the pictures, look at the sculpture, enjoy the treasures. What does the time of your entering matter? The fact is that you are in, and the exhibition is there, all spread out before you. It is not the time of your entry that matters. Go back to the twentieth of Matthew again. Those men were the last to enter the vineyard, it was the eleventh hour, but they were in. That was the thing that counted. They had been taken hold of, they had been employed, they had been brought in. It is the being in that matters, not when you come in, or how you come in. I could emphasize this at great length. One has so constantly to be saying it. It is not the mode or manner of conversion that matters, what matters is the fact that you are saved. But people will sit down and worry about how they came, the time, the mode, the manner, the method. It does not matter at all; what matters is that you are in. And if you are in, rejoice in it, and forget you were ever out.

But we must go even further. I suggest that this particular manifestation of spiritual depression is due to the fact that this person is still morbidly and sinfully preoccupied with self. I said just now that we have to be brutal with this condition. And it has to be said that the real trouble with these people is still 'self'. What are they doing? They are still judging themselves instead of leaving judgment to God. They lash themselves and scarify themselves metaphorically because they were so late and so long, and they go on condemning themselves. They appear to be very humble and full of contrition, but it is a mock modesty, it is a self-concern. Listen to Paul saying the self-same thing in the fourth chapter of this first epistle to the Corinthians. 'Let a man so account of us as of the ministers of Christ and stewards of the mysteries of God. Moreover, it is required in stewards that a man be found faithful. But with me it is a very small thing that I should be judged of you or of man's judgment; yea (and this is one of greatest things Paul ever said), yea, I judge not mine own self; for I know nothing by myself; yet am I not hereby justified; but He that judgeth me is the Lord' (verses 1-4). As Christians we must leave our judgment to Him. He is the Judge and you have no right to waste His time or your own time and energy in condemning yourself. Forget yourself, leave the judgment to Him; get on with the work. This whole trouble is due to this morbid preoccupation with self in the matter of judgment. Not only that, it is indicative of a proneness still to think in terms of what we can do. This kind of person comes to us in apparent modesty and says, 'If only I had come sooner what a lot of work I could have done'. In a sense that is quite right, but in another sense it is quite wrong, and utterly false. The parable of our Lord about the labourers in the vineyard was designed to demolish that argument.

Let me put it positively as I close. I have said that part of the trouble with these people is that they are still morbidly preoccupied with themselves, that they have not learned as Christians that they are to deny self and take up the Cross and follow Him and to leave themselves, past, present and future in His hands. Ah, yes, but why are they morbidly preoccupied with themselves? The answer is that they are not sufficiently occupied with Him. It is our failure to know Him and His ways as we should know them—that is the real trouble. If we only spent more of our time in looking at Him we should soon forget ourselves. I said just now that once you are in that exhibition you must not stand at the door bemoaning the fact of your late entry, but rather look at the treasures. Let me take that into the spiritual realm. You have come into the spiritual life. Well, stop looking at yourself and begin to enjoy Him. What is the difference between a Christian and a non-Christian? Paul in the second Epistle to the Corinthians, chapter 3, says it is this, that the non-Christian is a man who looks at Christ and God with a veil over his eyes and therefore cannot see. What is the Christian? This is his description (verse 18). 'But we all'—every one of us as Christians—'we all with open face (the veil has gone), beholding as in a glass the glory of the Lord, are changed into the same image from glory to glory.' That is the Christian. He spends his time in looking at Christ, in gazing upon Him. He is so enraptured by the sight of Him that he has forgotten himself. If you were to feel more interest in Christ you would be less interested in yourself. Begin to look at Him, gaze upon Him with this open, unveiled face. And then go on to learn that in His Kingdom what matters is not the length of service but your attitude towards Him, your desire to please Him. Go back again to the parable. He does not count service as other people do. He is interested in the heart. We are interested in time, we all clock in and count the time we have spent, the work we have done. Like the first men in the parable we claim to have done all, and boast of the time we have spent in the work. And if we are not among those who went in at the beginning we are concerned because we have not done this and that, and because we have missed all this time. Our Lord is not interested in our work in this way. It is the widow's mite He is interested in. It is not the amount of money, it is the woman's heart. And it is the same in that parable in the twentieth chapter of Matthew. For the same reason He gave the people who had been in the vineyard for only one hour the same as He gave to those who had been in all day. That is also the case that Paul puts here. 'Last of all He revealed Himself unto me also.' But thank God that does not make any difference. His grace goes before, 'by the grace of God I am what I am'. He is not interested in time, He is interested in relationship.

That brings me to the last principle. Nothing matters in the Kingdom but the grace of God. That is the whole point of the parable. God has a different way of looking at things. He does not see as men do; He does not compute as they do; it is all grace from beginning to end. The last people got a penny exactly as did the first; they were given the same wages as the first. Indeed, He impresses the truth upon us by saying: 'That many that are last shall be first and the first last'. We have to cease thinking in this carnal, human, fleshly manner. In the Kingdom of God and of Christ the standpoint is that of grace, and of grace alone; and it cuts across all other regulations. It is His grace that matters—'by the grace of God I am what I am'. So stop looking at what you have not done and the years you have missed and realize that in His Kingdom it is His grace alone that matters. You who have come in last may find yourselves first one day to your own amazement, and like the people in the parable at the end of Matthew 25, you will ask: 'When did I do this, when did I do that?' He knows, He sees, His grace is sufficient.

Very well, I end with an exhortation from the Old Testament. 'In the morning', therefore, 'sow thy seed: but in the evening withhold not thy hand, for thou knowest not whether shall prosper either this or that, or whether they both shall be alike good.' I wonder whether I am addressing someone who has spent a lifetime outside Christ, in sin and the world, someone who has come into the Kingdom in old age, and who has been tempted in the way I have been describing. If so my word to you is this: 'In the evening, the evening of your life, withhold not your hand in this marvellous Kingdom of grace. It is supernatural. You may find on the Judgment Day that you have a much bigger reward than those who were saved in their youth'. What a glorious gospel. Youth is the great word today—Youth. The question of age is irrelevant in God's kingdom and it is unscriptural to emphasize it as we do. 'In the morning sow thy seed'; yes, but with equal force I would say, 'In the evening withhold not thy hand'.

And then, remember what is perhaps one of the most comforting and wonderful things that is found anywhere in Scripture. It was spoken to the prophet Joel as he was given that great vision and understanding of the coming of Christ, the Christ that was to come. This was the word he was given to utter: 'I will restore to you the years that the locust hath eaten' (Joel 2. 25). He has promised to do it; He can do it. The wasted years, the barren years, the years that the locusts and the canker-worms and the caterpillars and all these other things have devoured, until there was nothing apparently left, of them He says: 'I will restore to you the years that the locust hath eaten'. If you think of it in terms of what you can do with your strength and power, then time is of the essence of the contract. But we are in a realm in which that does not matter. He comes in and He can give us a crop in one year that will make up for ten—'I will restore to you the years that the locust hath eaten'. That is the character of our Master, that is our Saviour, that is our God. I say, therefore, in the light of this: Never look back again; never waste your time in the present; never waste your energy; forget the past and rejoice in the fact that you are what you are by the grace of God, and that in the Divine alchemy of His marvellous grace you may yet have the greatest surprise of your life and existence and find that even in your case it will come to pass that the last shall be first. Praise God for the fact that you are what you are, and that you are in the Kingdom.

For God hath not given us the spirit of fear; but of power, and of love, and of a sound mind.

2 Timothy 1. 7

VII

FEAR OF THE FUTURE

IN these words we are directed to yet another cause of the condition which we have described in general as spiritual depression. There is almost no end to the ways in which this condition, this disease of the soul, may take us or may attack us. We have demonstrated how our adversary, the devil, is subtle, and can even transform himself into an angel of light, and that is very true. But it is equally true to say of him that he is relentless. I mean by that, that he does not cease or give up. He does not care what methods he employs so long as he can bring us down and discredit the work of God; and he is not concerned about consistency. He does not hesitate to vary his procedure, his approach, he does not hesitate to contradict what he had said to us previously; he has but one object and one concern and that is to bring into disrepute the Name and the work of God, and expecially, of course, the great work of God in our redemption through our Lord and Saviour Jesus Christ.

When God originally made and created this world, we are told that 'God saw everything that He had made, and, behold, it was very good'. He was well pleased with it; it was perfect. And it was because of that that the devil in his jealousy and his malice was determined to mar and ruin that work and to concentrate his efforts especially upon the supreme work of God which was the creation of man. If only he could bring man down, then the very acme of creation would be marred. So he concentrated, as we remember, upon the woman and beguiled her and she in turn misled her husband; and so man fell. But the story of humanity does not end at that point. God purposed and planned a great way of redemption. This is beyond any question the outstanding glory of God. Redemption is a greater work even than creation, and especially when we consider the way in which God has achieved it, even through the sending of His only Begotten Son into this world in all the marvel and the wonder and the miracle of the Incarnation, but above all in delivering Him up to the Death upon the Cross. This is the supreme thing—that sinful fallen man can be redeemed and restored, and ultimately the whole of creation also. Obviously, therefore, the supreme concern of the adversary, the devil, the opponent, is to endeavour somehow or other, to bring this work of God to discredit and to dishonour. To this end he makes a special object of attacking the heirs of salvation, Christian people, and there is nothing which so suits his purpose as to depress us and to bring us down, to give the impression that this boasted salvation is but a figment of the imagination, and that we who believe it have believed 'cunningly devised fables'. And what better way of doing that than to bring us into such a condition that we give the impression of being depressed, burdened and miserable?

We have seen how the devil seeks to depress us by getting us to concentrate our gaze upon the past, so that by dwelling on the past we become cast down. But if that fails, we may anticipate that he will change his procedure entirely and begin to make us look to the future. This is exactly what he does, and that is what we have in this particular verse that we are looking at now. We are going to consider the case of those who are suffering from spiritual depression because they are afraid of the future—fear of the future.

Now this again is a very common condition and it really is most extraordinary to notice the way in which the enemy often produces the self-same fundamental condition in the same people by these apparently diametrically opposed methods. When you have put them right about the past, they immediately begin to talk about the future, with the result that they are always depressed in the present. You have satisfied them about forgiveness of sin, yes, even that particular sin which was so exceptional. You have shown them that, though they have wasted years, He will 'restore the years that the locust hath eaten'. And then they say, 'Ah, yes, but . . .', and they begin to talk about fears concerning the future and what lies ahead.

There is a great deal of teaching with respect to this in the Scriptures, but I am sure I am right when I say that the supreme example of this particular condition is undoubtedly this man Timothy to whom the Apostle wrote this Epistle together with the previous one. It was, without doubt, his peculiar problem and it is certain that the Apostle wrote both these letters to him because of that. He was very dependent upon Paul because of his fears of difficulties and dangers to come, and the whole

object of both the Epistles is to put Timothy right with respect
to this problem of facing the future. Now we must not spend our
time with Timothy as such, I merely quote him as an example of
one who was spiritually depressed because of his fear of the future.

What are the causes of this condition? Why is it that people
suffer from fear of the future? What are the reasons which they
give for it? What are the particular aspects of the difficulty and
what are the problems which it tends to produce and about
which its victims are always speaking? Well, there can be no
doubt at all that first and foremost among causes we must put
temperament—the particular make-up. We are all born different.
No two of us are exactly the same; we have our own particular
characteristics, our virtues, our failures, our weaknesses and our
blemishes. The human person is very delicately and finely
balanced. Fundamentally we all have the same general characteristics, but the relative proportions vary tremendously from
case to case, and so our temperaments vary and differ. It is very
important that we should bear that in mind. 'But, ah,' says
someone, 'we are Christians now, and when a person becomes
a Christian all such differences are demolished.' Now that is the
essential fallacy with respect to this whole matter. There is no
profounder change in the universe than the change which is
described as regeneration; but regeneration—the work of God
in the soul by which He implants a principle of divine and
spiritual life within us—does not change a man's temperament.
Your temperament still remains the same. The fact that you
have become a Christian does not mean that you cease to have to
live with yourself. You will have to live with yourself as long as
you are alive, and yourself is your self and not somebody else's
self. Paul was essentially the same man after his salvation and
conversion as he was before. He did not become somebody else.
Peter is still Peter, John is still John, temperamentally and in
essential characteristics. That is where the glory of the Christian
life is seen. It is like the variety in nature and creation. Look at
the flowers. No two are identical. It is in the variety within the
fundamental unity that God displays the wonders of His ways.
And it is exactly the same in the Christian Church. We are all
different, our temperaments are different, we are all ourselves.
That is one of the great glories of the Church. God distributes his
gifts through the Holy Spirit in divers manners, though our
essential personality remains exactly the same as it was before

our conversion. I mean by personality our temperament, the peculiar way in which we do things. We do the same things but we do them differently. As Christians we must all do the same essential things, but the way in which we do them is different. Think of the difference in preachers preaching the same gospel and living the same Christian life; yet their manner of presentation is different, and is meant to be different. And God uses these differences in order to spread the gospel. He can use one man to make the message appeal to a certain type, while another person could not be used in that respect. Different presentations appeal to different people, and rightly so, and God makes use of all.

So first of all we put temperament; and there are some people who by temperament are nervous, apprehensive, frightened. Paul himself was, I believe, an instance of this. He was a nervous man, lacking in self-confidence in the natural sense. He went to Corinth 'in weakness and fear and much trembling'. He was a naturally timorous man—'without were fightings, within were fears'. That was the man by nature. It was especially true of Timothy also, and there are people who are born like that. There are other people who are self-confident and assured; they are afraid of nothing; they will tackle anything; they will stand up anywhere. They do not know the meaning of nerves. These two types of people are Christians and yet in that respect they are different, vitally and fundamentally different. There are some Christians who can only with the greatest difficulty, be persuaded to speak in public, and there are others who are the exact opposite. This question of temperament is, therefore, an important one in our consideration of the causes of this particular form of anxiety and depression.

Then there are other things which emerge as you consider the case of the people who fear the future. You will find that they are always concerned about the nature of the task confronting the Christian. They have a very high conception of the Christian cause (if we may judge by the things they say), they have an exalted idea of the Christian life. These people realize that it is not an easy thing to be a Christian, that it is not just a matter of being converted and then lying on a bed of roses for the rest of your life. No, they see it as a high calling, a fight of faith; they see the exalted character of the life; they see it means following Christ. They read their New Testament and—invariably they are intelligent people—they are aware of the greatness of the task and of the calling. But that in turn tends to depress them because they are equally aware of their own smallness. In other words they have a fear of failure. They are afraid of letting down the cause. They say: 'I like the gospel. I believe my sins are forgiven. I want to be a Christian, but I am so afraid I will fail. All is well while I am in meetings or in the company of Christian people, but I have to live and I know myself and my weakness, I know the greatness of the task and I know the difficulties.' They are afraid of failure; they do not want to let down God and the Lord Jesus Christ and His Church on earth. Who are they to live the Christian life? The greatness of the task and their acute awareness of their own deficiences and needs oppresses them. Or it may be that they just suffer from a kind of general fear of the future, while they cannot put their finger on anything in particular. You ask them if they are afraid of any one special thing and they do not know, but they have this general fear, this apprehensiveness with regard to the future, of things that may happen, of things they may be called upon to suffer. I have often had to deal with such people. I remember a lady telling me: 'Well, yes, I do believe, but I do not know that I can call myself a Christian.' When I said: 'Why can't you?' Her reply was something like this: 'I have been reading about people in the past and people in the present who are being persecuted for Christ's sake, and I have tried to imagine myself having to face that position'. She had a little boy of three at the time and she said: 'You know, if it really became a question of denying my faith or giving up this boy I do not know what I would say; I do not think I would be strong enough; I doubt if I would have the courage to put Christ first at all costs or perhaps to suffer death if necessary'. And she therefore thought she had no right to call herself a Christian. Now she had never been, and indeed might never be, put to such a test, but she was conscious of the possibility and it was depressing her. Such spiritual depression is due to fear of the future—often imaginary fears.

We must not stay with these descriptions though we could multiply the cases. The remarkable thing is that it is possible for such things so to grip us as to paralyse us completely in the present; such people are very often in danger of being so absorbed and gripped by these fears that they really become ineffective in the present. There is no doubt at all that that was the essence of the trouble with Timothy. Paul was in prison and Timothy began to wonder what was going to happen to him. What if Paul were to be put to death? How could he, Timothy, face alone the difficulties that were arising in the Church and the persecution that was beginning to show itself and in which he Timothy himself, might be involved? So Paul had to be quite firm with him: and he tells him that he must not be ashamed of him and his suffering—'Be not thou therefore ashamed of the testimony of our Lord, nor of me His prisoner, but be thou partaker of the afflictions of the gospel according to the power of God'. Fear of the future was undoubtedly the essence of Timothy's trouble.

The question for us is, how are we to deal with the condition; how is it to be treated? Once more I cannot think of any better way than to adopt the procedure we adopted with our previous problem. There are certain preliminary general considerations before we come to the precise teaching of Scripture. So I would lay down certain propositions. The first thing here again is to discover, and to know exactly where to draw the line between legitimate forethought and paralyzing forethought. Now it is right that we should think about the future, and it is a very foolish person who does not think about it at all. But what we are always warned against in Scripture is about being worried about the future. Take no thought for the morrow,' means 'Do not be guilty of anxious care about the morrow'. It does not mean that you do not take any thought at all, otherwise the farmer would not plough and harrow and sow. He is looking to the future, but he does not spend the whole of his time wondering and worrying about the end results of his work. No, he takes reasonable thought and then he leaves it. Here again the whole question is where to draw the line. Thinking is right up to a point, but if you go beyond that point it becomes worry and anxiety and it paralyses and cripples. In other words, although it is very right to think about the future, it is very wrong to be controlled by it. The difficulty with people who are a prey to these fears is that they are controlled by the future, they are dominated by thoughts of it, and there they are wringing their hands, doing nothing, depressed by fears about it. In fact, they are completely governed and mastered by the unknown future, and that is always wrong. To take thought is right, but to be controlled by the future is all wrong. Now that is a fundamental proposition and the world has discovered it. It has told us not to cross our bridges until we get to them. Put that into your Christian teaching, for the world is right there, and the Christian must accept that wisdom. Don't cross your bridges until you come to them. Indeed, many Scriptural statements to the same effect have become proverbial—'take no thought for the morrow', 'Sufficient unto the day is the evil thereof'. Certainly the New Testament raises that concept and puts it in its spiritual form. But it is true on the lowest level—'Sufficient unto the day is the evil thereof'. That is sound common sense. As we saw before, it is a waste of time to be concerned about the past which you cannot affect; but it is equally wrong to be worried about the future which at the moment is obscure. 'One step enough for me.' Live in the present to the maximum and do not let your future mortgage your present any more than you should let the past mortgage your present.

Now let us go on to what the Apostle says. He raises the reasoning to a higher level and gives us specific teaching of a two-fold character. First of all, it is a reprimand, and secondly it is a reminder. Now both these are absolutely vital and essential. The first thing he does is to reprimand Timothy. He turns on him and says: 'For God hath not given us the spirit of fear'. Now that is a reprimand. Timothy at the moment was guilty of the spirit of fear, he was gripped by it; so Paul reprimands him—'God hath not given us the spirit of fear but of power and of love and of a sound mind'. The principle, the doctrine here, is that our essential trouble, if we suffer from this particular manifestation of spiritual depression, is our failure to realize what God has given us, and is giving us, in giving us the gift of the Holy Ghost. That was really the trouble with Timothy as it is the trouble with all such Christians. It is a failure to realize what God has done for us, and what God is still doing in us. In fact, we can employ words which our Lord once used in a slightly different connection. In answering James and John who wanted to call fire from heaven to consume certain of the Samaritans, He said: 'Ye know not what spirit ye are of'. Now that is what Paul is saying to Timothy. There it was negative, here it is positive. The Apostle has to tell Timothy to stir up the gift of God.

Our fears are due to our failure to stir up—failure to think, failure to take ourselves in hand. You find yourself looking to the future and then you begin to imagine things and you say: 'I wonder what is going to happen?' And then, your imagination runs away with you. You are gripped by the thing; you do not stop to remind yourself of who you are and what you are, this thing overwhelms you and down you go. Now the first thing you have to do is to take a firm grip of yourself, to pull yourself up, to stir up yourself, to take yourself in hand and to speak to yourself. As the Apostle puts it, we have to remind ourselves of certain things. And as I understand it, the big thing that Paul is saying in effect to Timothy is: 'Timothy, you seem to be thinking about yourself and about life and all you have to do as if you were still an ordinary person. But, Timothy, you are not an ordinary person! You are a Christian, you are born again, the Spirit of God is in you. But you are facing all these things as if you are still what you once were, an ordinary person'. And is not that the trouble with us all in this connection? Though we are truly Christian, though we believe the truth, though we have been born again, though we are certainly children of God, we lapse into this condition in which we again begin to think as if none of these things had happened to us at all. Like the man of the world, the man who has never been regenerated, we allow the future to come to us and to dominate us, and we compare our own weakness and lack of strength with the greatness of the calling and the tremendous task before us. And down we go as if we were but our natural selves. Now the thing to do, says Paul to Timothy, is to remind yourself that we have been given the gift of God's Holy Spirit, and to realize that because of this our whole outlook upon life and the future must therefore be essentially different. We must think of suffering in a new way, we must face everything in a new way. And the way in which we face it all is by reminding ourselves that the Holy Spirit is in us. There is the future, there is the high calling, there is the persecution, there is the opposition, there is the enemy. I see it all. I must admit also that I am weak, that I lack the necessary powers and propensities. But instead of stopping there I must go on to say: 'Yes, I know it all, but——' And the moment I use that word 'but I am doing what the Apostle wants me to do. I say: 'But—but the Spirit of God is in me; God has given me His Holy Spirit'. The moment I say that the whole outlook changes. In other words, we have to learn to say, that what matters in any of these positions is not what is true of us but what is true of Him. Timothy by nature was weak and the enemy was powerful, and the task was great. Yes, but he must not think of himself alone or of the situation in terms of himself—'God hath not given us the spirit

of fear. He hath given us the Spirit of power'. So do not think of
your own weakness; think of the power of the Spirit of God. It is
when we begin to do that that we balance our doctrine and see
the whole position clearly.

I have already been at pains to emphasize that all our temperaments are different, and I want to emphasize it again. But at
this point I would say that, although our temperaments are
different, our temperaments should not make any difference at
all face to face with the task. Now here is the miracle of redemption. We are given our temperaments by God. Again all our
temperaments are different and that also is of God. Yes, but it
must never be true of us as Christians that we are controlled by
our temperaments. We must be controlled by the Holy Ghost.
You must put them in that order. Here are powers and capacities
and here is your particular temperament that uses them, but the
vital point is that as a Christian you should be controlled by the
Holy Spirit. What is so tragically wrong in a Christian is that he
should allow himself to be controlled by his temperament. The
natural man is always controlled by his temperament, he cannot
help himself; but the difference that regeneration makes is that
there is now a higher control even over temperament. The
moment the Holy Spirit enters in, He controls everything including temperament, and so He enables you to function in your own
particular way through your temperament. That is the miracle of
redemption. Temperament remains, but temperament no longer
controls. The Holy Spirit is in control.

Let us now work it out in detail. 'God hath not given us the
spirit of fear'. What, then, is the spirit He has given us? Notice.
'God hath not given us the spirit of fear but of power——.' That
is what He puts first and rightly so. We have a task, we know our
own weakness. Yes, but here is a power even for weaklings, and
it means power in the most comprehensive sense conceivable.
Are you afraid that you will not be able to live the Christian life?
The answer is: 'Work out your own salvation with fear and trembling, for it is God that worketh in you both to will and to do'. The
fear and the trembling remain. That is partly your temperament,
but you are enabled to work by the power 'that worketh in you
both to will and to do'. So you do not become a person who is not
afraid and one who is no longer subject to fear. You still have
to work out your own salvation in fear and trembling, but there is
power in spite of that. It is the power of God working in you

'both to will and to do of His good pleasure'. But this has reference not only to the question of living the Christian life, and battling with temptation and sin, it means also power to endure, power to go on whatever the conditions, whatever the circumstances, power to hold on and to hold out. Let me go further, it means that the most timorous person can be given power in all things, even to die. You see it in the apostles, you see it in a man like Peter who was afraid of death, afraid to die. He even denied his Lord because of that fear. He said: I do not know Him, I have had nothing to do with Him. He denied with oaths and cursings his own blessed Lord, his greatest benefactor, in order to save his life. But look at him afterwards in the book of the Acts of the Apostles. The Spirit of power had entered into him and now he is ready to die. He will face the authorities, he will face anybody. That is one of the most glorious things in the long annals of the history of the Church, and it is still happening. I never tire of telling Christians to read the stories of the martyrs and the Confessors and the Protestant Fathers, of the Puritans and the Covenanters. Read their stories and you will find not only strong, courageous men, you will find weak women and girls and even little children dying gloriously for Christ's sake. They could not in and of themselves, but they were given the spirit of power. Now that is what Paul means here. He says to Timothy: 'Do not talk like that. You are talking as a natural man. You are talking as if you yourself with your own power have to face it all. But God has given you the spirit of power. Go forward. He will be with you. You won't know yourself; you will be amazed at yourself. And even though it may mean facing death, you will rejoice that you have been accounted worthy to suffer shame and even death for His glorious Name's sake'. Power! It is given. And what you and I have to do, as we are tempted to be depressed by the things which are against us, is to say: 'I have the Holy Spirit, and He is the Spirit of power'.

Then the next thing he mentions is 'love'. Now I find this most interesting and fascinating, I wonder how many of you would have put love at this point in our list? Why, do you think, does he put it here? What does he mean by it? 'God hath not given us the spirit of fear but of power———.' Yes, I understand that I need power. But love—why love? It is surely not love that this timorous person needs? Why does he put this second, the spirit of love? Here is a superb bit of psychology, for what after

all, is the main cause of this spirit of fear? The answer is 'self'—
self-love, self-concern, self-protection. Had you realized that the
essence of this trouble is that these fearful people are really too
absorbed in self—how can I do this, what if I fail? 'I'—they are
constantly turning in upon themselves, looking at themselves and
concerned about themselves. And it is just here that the spirit of
love comes in, for there is only one way to get rid of yourself.
There is only one cure for self. You will never deal with self
yourself. That was the fatal fallacy of those poor men who became
monks and anchorites. They could get away from the world
and from other people, but they could not get away from themselves. Your self is inside you and you cannot get rid of him,
the more you mortify yourself the more your self will torment
you.

There is only one way to get rid of self, and that is that you
should become so absorbed in someone or something else that
you have no time to think about yourself. Thank God, the Spirit
of God makes that possible. He is not only 'the spirit of power',
but He is also 'the spirit of love'. What does it mean? It means
love to God, love to the great God who made us, love to the great
God who has made the way of redemption for us miserable
creatures—for us who deserve nothing but hell. He has 'loved us
with an everlasting love'. Think of that, says Paul to Timothy,
and as you become absorbed in the love of God you will forget
all about yourself. 'The spirit of love!' It will deliver you from
self-interest, self-concern, and from depression about self, because
depression results from self and self-concern. It gets rid of self at
all points. So talk to yourself about this eternal, amazing love of
God—the God Who ever looked upon us in spite of sin and
planned the way of redemption and spared not His own Son but
delivered Him up for us all.

What then? Go on to think of the love of the Son in its breadth,
its length, its depth, its height; go on to know the love of Christ
which passeth knowledge. Think of Him who came from the
Courts of Heaven and laid aside the insignia of His eternal glory
and was born as a babe, worked as a carpenter and endured the
contradiction of sinners against Himself. Think of Him into
whose holy face men spat and on whose brow they pressed a
crown of thorns and into whose hands and feet the nails were
hammered. There He is on the Cross. What is He doing there?
There He died for us, that you and I might be forgiven and

reconciled to God. Think of His love, and as you come to know something about it, you will forget yourself.

And then, love of the brethren. Think of other people, their needs, their concerns. Shall I go on? Timothy seems to have been saying to himself, 'I might be put to death'. Paul says: 'Think of other people, look at those people perishing in their sins. Forget yourself'. Cultivate love for the lost and love for the brethren in the same way, and love for the greatest and noblest cause in the world, this blessed, glorious gospel. Work it out for yourselves. This is what the Apostle means by the spirit of power and the spirit of love. If you are consumed by this spirit of love you will forget yourself. You will say that nothing matters save the Christ who gave Himself for you, that nothing is too much for you to give. You will, like Count Zinzendorf, have but one passion and it will be 'He and He alone'. 'The spirit of love!'

And, lastly, 'a sound mind'—'not the spirit of fear but the spirit of power and of love and of a sound mind'. What does this mean? It is the right antidote for the spirit of fear—self-control, discipline, a balanced mind. Though you and I may be timorous and nervous, the Spirit that God has given us is the Spirit of control, the Spirit of discipline, the Spirit of judgment. Our Lord had already said all this before Paul thought of it. Paul is but repeating and giving an exposition of our Lord's own teaching. You remember what He said to His disciples when He sent them out to teach. He warned them that they might be hated and persecuted and that a day might come when they would have to give up their lives, or certainly be put on trial for their lives. But He went on to say: 'When they deliver you up, take no thought how or what ye shall speak; for it shall be given you in that same hour what ye shall speak'. You will be on trial in court and they will be doing everything to catch you in your words, but do not worry, says our Lord, for it shall be given you in that same hour what ye shall speak. You need not be afraid, you will not lose your nerve; you will not be so excited and alarmed that you will not know what to speak; it will be given you in that self-same hour what to speak. The spirit of wisdom and of a sound mind!

I can put this point very briefly in one illustration. It is the story of a comparatively young girl in the days of the Covenanters in Scotland. She was going to attend a Communion Service held by the Covenanters on a Sunday afternoon, and, of course, such Communion Services were absolutely prohibited. The soldiers of the King of England were looking everywhere for people who were going to meet together to partake in this Communion Service, and as this girl turned a corner on her way she came face to face with a band of soldiers, and she knew that she was trapped. For a moment she wondered what she was going to say, but immediately on being questioned she found herself answering: 'My Elder Brother has died and they are going to read His will this afternoon, and He has done something for me and has left something for me, and I want to hear them read the will'. And they allowed her to go on. 'God hath not given us the spirit of fear but of power and of love and of a sound mind'—wisdom, discretion, understanding. He will make you as wise as serpents; you will be able to make absolutely true statements to your enemies but the enemy will not understand, and you can escape. Ah, yes, her Elder Brother had died. Christ had died for her and in the Communion Service the will was going to be read out again and she was going to be reminded of what He had left for her and done for her. You see, the most ignorant and the most nervous in the Kingdom of Christ is given a sound mind and the spirit of wisdom. Don't worry, says Christ, it shall be given you in that self-same hour what ye ought to speak. He will tell you what to do, He will tell you what to say, He will, if necessary, restrain you. We are not living on ourselves. We must not think of ourselves as ordinary people. We are not natural men; we are born again. God has given His Holy Spirit, and He is the spirit 'of power and of love and of a sound mind'. Therefore to those who are particularly prone to spiritual depression through timorous fear of the future, I say in the Name of God and in the words of the Apostle: 'Stir up the gift', talk to yourself, remind yourself of what is true of you. Instead of allowing the future and thoughts of it to grip you, talk to yourself, remind yourself of who you are and what you are, and of what Spirit is within you; and, having reminded yourself of the character of the Spirit, you will be able to go steadily forward, fearing nothing, living in the present, ready for the future, with one desire only, to glorify Him who gave His all for you.

Wherefore I put thee in remembrance that thou stir up the gift of God, which is in thee by the putting on of my hands.

2 Timothy 1. 6

VIII

FEELINGS

THIS is a great statement, but our primary interest in it is this exhortation which the Apostle here addresses to Timothy, to the effect that he should 'stir up' the gift that is in him. And I call your attention to it as part of our general consideration of the subject which we have described as 'spiritual depression'. We are trying to diagnose and treat the case of the so-called miserable Christian. We have been at pains to indicate that the very term, in and of itself, directs our attention to that which is so essentially wrong about the condition. These words are really incompatible and yet we must put them together because they are an accurate description of certain people—miserable Christians. It should be impossible, but actually it is a fact. There should not be such a thing, but there is such a thing, and it is our business, as we understand the teaching of the Scriptures, both the Old Testament and the New, to deal with this condition.

There are those, I know, who will not recognize the condition at all but will brush it aside impatiently, and say that a Christian is one who sings all the day long, and that that, ever since they were converted, has been their story—never a ripple on the surface of the soul, and all has been well. Since they will not recognize the condition at all, they have grave doubts about those who are given to depression and even doubt whether such people are Christians at all. We have shown repeatedly that the Scriptures are much kinder to such friends, and do grant clearly by their teaching that it is possible for a Christian to be depressed. Not that they justify this, but they do recognize the fact, and it is the business of anyone who is concerned about the nurture and care of the soul to understand such cases and to apply to them the remedy that God has provided so freely in the words of Scripture.

We have considered already many causes of this condition and still we go on. They are almost endless, for we are confronted, as I have reminded you, by a very subtle and powerful adversary who knows us so well, so much better than we know ourselves, and his one great object and endeavour is to detract from the glory of God and from the glory of the Lord Jesus Christ. Now there is no more effective way in which he can do that than to make Christian people miserable and depressed, because, whether we like it or not, the fact is that the world still judges God and the Lord Jesus Christ by what it sees in us, and we cannot blame them for that. We make certain claims; the very designation of Christian which we apply to ourselves is a claim and a challenge, and the world is entitled to look at us. 'You are making a great claim,' says the world, and then looking at us, it says, 'Is that Christianity? Is that the thing to which you are inviting us?' There can be no question at all, and let us be clear about this, that the thing above everything else that accounts for the fact that the masses of the people are outside the Christian Church today, is the condition of those of us who are inside the Church. Read the story of any revival that has ever taken place and you will find that the beginning of it is always the same. One man, or sometimes a number of people, suddenly become alive to the true Christian life, and others begin to pay attention to them. The world outside is stirred and begins to pay attention. Revival always begins in the Church, and the world outside seeing it, begins to pay attention. That is why our condition as believers is so important.

We have considered the way in which the devil gets us to concentrate on the past—some sin we have committed, the time we have wasted—how we bemoan it all and are miserable in the present because we are worrying about the past. And we have seen how if that does not work, he changes his tactics completely, and tries to depress us in the present by filling us with fears and forebodings about the future.

Now we move on to another theme, very closely connected of course, and very closely associated with these fears and apprehensions with respect to the future. This theme is indicated in this sixth verse and it concerns the whole problem of feelings—feelings in the Christian life. Perhaps there is nothing so frequently encountered as a cause of spiritual depression and unhappiness in the Christian life as this very problem of feelings. Where do they come in, and what should they be? People are constantly troubled about the matter, and I am sure that all who have ever been engaged in pastoral work will agree that there is no particular subject that brings people so often to the pastor as this very problem of feelings. Now that is very natural because, after all, we all desire to be happy. That is something that is innate in human nature; nobody wants to be miserable, though I am aware of the fact that there are people who seem to enjoy being miserable and some who seem to find their happiness in being unhappy!

I regard it as a great part of my calling in the ministry to emphasize the priority of the mind and the intellect in connection with the faith; but though I maintain that, I am equally ready to assert that the feelings, the emotions, the sensibilities obviously are of very vital importance. We have been made in such a way that they play a dominant part in our make-up. Indeed, I suppose that one of the greatest problems in our life in this world, not only for Christians, but for all people, is the right handling of our feelings and emotions. Oh, the havoc that is wrought and the tragedy, the misery and the wretchedness that are to be found in the world simply because people do not know how to handle their own feelings! Man is so constituted that the feelings are in this very prominent position, and indeed, there is a very good case for saying that perhaps the final thing which regeneration and the new birth do for us is just to put the mind and the emotions and the will in their right positions. We shall proceed to consider that as we analyse this subject. It is obviously a very great subject, which no one can deal with briefly, but it is important that we should take a comprehensive view of the subject.

There is a preliminary point here which to me, at any rate, is of interest. It is, as I suggested at the beginning, that there is a curious relationship between this particular problem and that other problem of being nervous and frightened of the future. These things tend to go together, so it is not surprising that the two things are found in this one chapter. Timothy, obviously, was a naturally nervous person, but equally he was a person given to depression; and the two things are often to be found in the same kind of person. Once more, therefore, we must indicate that there are certain people who are more prone to depression in a natural sense than others. Let me also underline again and re-emphasize this vital statement in connection with this whole consideration, that though we are converted and regenerated, our fundamental personality is not changed. The result is that the person who is more given to depression than another person before conversion, will still have to fight that after conversion.

We all have certain common problems in the Christian life, but we all have special problems also. We vary in our gifts—we have not all the same talents: and it is exactly the same in the matter of our difficulties, 'The heart knoweth its own sorrow' and every man has his own burden to carry. We all have something which is peculiarly difficult for us, and it is generally something that belongs to the realm of our temperament or natural make-up. So the person who is naturally given to introspection and morbidity and depression, will still have to bear that in mind in the Christian life. The danger for such a person will be to become depressed, and particularly in connection with this question of the feelings.

It seems to me, therefore, that the most profitable thing to do is to look at this subject in a general way, and perhaps return to the particular later. Therefore, let us make a number of general statements about feelings and about their place in the Christian life. One of the first questions facing us is this: Where do feelings come in, what is their place, what should be their position in the Christian experience? I would put to you a number of general statements in this connection. First and foremost, obviously, in a truly Christian experience, the feelings must be engaged. They are meant to be involved. We saw that when we considered that great statement which Paul made to the Romans in the sixth chapter and the seventeenth verse. The whole emphasis there is that the gospel of Jesus Christ is so great and glorious that it takes up the whole man and not merely a part of man. All I want to indicate now, therefore, is that our feelings as well as our minds and our will should be actively engaged. If you and I have never been moved by our feelings, well, we had better examine the foundations again. If a poet like Wordsworth, thinking of nature, could say: 'For I have felt a Presence that disturbs me with the joy of elevated thoughts'—if a mystical poet could say a thing like that—how much more should you and I be able to say it with such a gospel, such a message, such a Saviour, such a God, with such a power and influence as the Holy Spirit of God. You cannot read through your New Testament without seeing at a glance that joy is meant to be an essential part of the Christian experience. One of the most striking things that conversion does is to take us out of some horrible pit, some miry clay and establish our feet upon a rock, and establish our goings and to put a new song in our mouth. Feelings are meant to be engaged, and when the gospel comes to us it does involve the whole man. It moves his mind as he sees its glorious truths, it moves his heart in the same way, and it moves his will.

The second statement which I want to make is this—and these are very simple and elementary points, but we are often in trouble because we forget them. The second is, that we cannot create feelings, we cannot command them at will. Let me put this quite plainly. You cannot generate feelings within yourself. You can, perhaps, make yourself weep and bring tears to your own eyes, but that does not of necessity mean real feelings. There is a false sentimentality very different from true emotion. That is something beyond our control; we cannot create it. However much you try you will not succeed. Indeed, in a sense, the more you try to produce feelings within yourself, the more you are increasing your own misery. Looked at psychologically it is one of the most remarkable things about man that in this respect he is not master of himself. He cannot generate or produce feelings, he cannot bring them into being, and to attempt to do so directly is always to exacerbate the trouble.

That leads us to my next statement, which is that, clearly, there is nothing that is quite so variable about us as our feelings. We are very variable creatures, and our feelings are, of everything that belongs to us, the most variable of all. That is because they are dependent upon so many factors; there are so many things that influence the feelings, not only temperament, but physical conditions also. The ancient people, as you know, used to believe that feelings were located in the different organs of the body. In a sense they were right, the phlegm of which they spoke, the atrabiliar mood—'all seems yellow to the jaundiced eye, etc.' There is an element of truth here. Physical conditions affect us profoundly. And again let us be careful to observe that the fact that you have become a Christian does not mean that you immediately lose all these constitutional tendencies. They are still there, and, therefore, with all these factors our moods tend to vary. We must have been amazed at ourselves many times that, on waking up in the morning, we find ourselves in a mood or condition quite different from the day before. Nothing you know of accounts for it. Yesterday you may have been perfectly happy and you went to sleep anticipating another great and glorious day, but you find yourself in the morning waking up depressed and in a wrong mood. Suddenly, without any explanation, you just find yourself like that. Now that is the essence of the problem. In other words, our feelings are variable, and I would emphasize the danger of being controlled by them. We have already seen that the same is true of our temperament, whatever it may be. We are all given our temperament by God. He has made no two of us the same, and we must remain different. Yes, we have our temperament, but there is nothing that is so wrong and un-Christian as to allow our temperament to rule us. Of course, there are people who glory in doing that. We all know the person who says: 'I always speak my mind. I always say what I think'. Think of the damage done by such people as they trample self-right-eously over the susceptibilities of other people! What if everybody did it? They say: 'I am that sort of person'. The answer to them is that they should not be! That does not mean that they can change their temperament, but it does mean that they should control it. In other words, temperament is a gift from God, but as the result of the Fall, and of sin, temperament is to be kept in its place. It is a wonderful gift, but to be controlled. Now it is exactly the same with feelings. Our feelings are always seeking to control us, and unless we realize this, they will undoubtedly do so. That is what we mean when we talk about moods and moodiness. The mood seems to descend upon us. We do not want it, but there it is. Now the danger is to allow it to control and grip us. We wake up in a bad mood in the morning, and the tendency is to go on like that throughout the day and to remain like that until something happens to put us right. There is a great instance of that in the Old Testament in the case of Saul, King of Israel. Our danger is to submit ourselves to our feelings and to allow them to dictate to us, to govern and to master us and to control the whole of our lives.

Finally under this heading I would draw attention to the danger of thinking that we are not Christians at all because we have not had some particular type of feeling or experience. This from a spiritual standpoint is one of the commonest manifestations of this condition. I am thinking of people who hear others, while talking or giving their testimony, testifying to some wonderful feeling, and they say to themselves: 'I have never had that'. And they begin to wonder whether they are Christians at all. Let me repeat what I have already said; feelings must be engaged in true Christianity, but the mere fact that we have not had certain particular feelings does not of necessity mean that we are not Christian. Feelings are essential, but if we postulate certain particular feelings as being essential we may very well become victims of the devil and spend the whole of our life in unhappiness and 'bound in shallows and in miseries', though the whole time we are truly Christian.

This to me is a fascinating theme, but I must avoid the temptation of allowing myself to be drawn into a digression. There is no doubt, however, but that this particular point raises not only the question of temperament, but also of nationality. There is no doubt but that there are certain national types that are more given to particular views of life. There are certainly people in the Christian faith, and they generally belong to the Celtic races, some of whom would go so far as to say that it is wrong for a Christian to be too happy. They are so afraid of feelings that they are almost ready to say that feelings of happiness and joy are almost certainly due to that which is false. That kind of thing is not confined to races only, it is characteristic of certain denominations also. There was a sermon preached by J. C. Philpot, one of the founders of the Strict Baptists, bearing this title: 'The child of Light walking in darkness and the child of darkness walking in the Light', based upon the last two verses of the fiftieth chapter of the Prophet Isaiah. In the sermon, he held that you can kindle false feelings, that you can work up a wonderful kind of fire and experience but that it will not last. 'The true child of God,' he says, 'because he realizes the plague of his own heart and his own sinfulness, walks through this world heavily and laboriously, conscious of his sin and of the greatness and the majesty of God'. Now I have great sympathy with his main emphasis but I suggest that in that sermon that great and godly preacher went too far, because the final impression he leaves with us is that if you are happy there is probably something wrong with you and you are not a Christian at all. Now that is going too far. There are undoubtedly people who think that they are Christians, whose experience is certainly psychological rather than spiritual. Frothy and lighthearted happiness is not Christian joy, but that must not lead us to say that joy is never Christian.

Well, what do the Scriptures tell us about all this? How are we to deal with this problem of feelings? I shall put forward a number of suggestions. The first is a very practical one—it is just this. If you are at all depressed at this moment you should make certain that there is no obvious cause for the absence of joyous

8

feelings. For instance, if you are guilty of sin, you are going to be miserable. 'The way of the transgressor is hard.' If you break God's laws and violate His rules you will not be happy. If you think that you can be a Christian and exert your own will and follow your own likes and dislikes, your Christian life is going to be a miserable one. There is no need to argue about it, it follows as the night the day, that if you are harbouring some favourite sin, if you are holding on to something that the Holy Spirit is condemning through your conscience, you will not be happy. And there is only one thing to do, confess it, acknowledge it, repent, go to God at once and confess your sin, open your heart, bare your soul, tell Him all about it, hold nothing back and then believe that because you have done so, He forgives you. 'If we confess our sins, He is faithful and just to forgive us our sins and to cleanse us from all unrighteousness'. If unconfessed sin is the cause of your unhappiness I should be wasting my time and yours by going on with my list of other causes. How many are trapped at this point. Let us be perfectly clear about it; let your conscience speak to you; listen to the voice of God as He speaks through the Spirit that is within you, and if He is placing His finger upon something, get rid of it. You cannot hope to solve this problem while you are harbouring some sin.

But taking that for granted, and assuming that that is not the cause, the next thing I would say is this. Avoid the mistake of concentrating overmuch upon your feelings. Above all, avoid the terrible error of making them central. Now I am never tired of repeating this because I find so frequently that this is a cause of stumbling. Feelings are never meant to take the first place, they are never meant to be central. If you put them there you are of necessity doomed to be unhappy, because you are not following the order that God himself has ordained. Feelings are always the result of something else, and how anyone who has ever read the Bible can fall into that particular error passes my comprehension. The Psalmist has put it in the 34th Psalm. He says: 'Taste and see that the Lord is good'. You will never see until you have tasted; you will not know it, you will not feel it until you have tried it. 'Taste and see', it follows as the night the day. Seeing before tasting is impossible. That is something that is constantly emphasized everywhere in the Scriptures. After all, what we have in the Bible is Truth; it is not an emotional stimulus, it is not something primarily concerned to give us a joyful experience.

It is primarily Truth, and Truth is addressed to the mind, God's supreme gift to man; and it is as we apprehend and submit ourselves to the truth that the feelings follow. I must never ask myself in the first instance: What do I feel about this? The first question is, Do I believe it? Do I accept it, has it gripped me? Very well, that is what I regard as perhaps the most important rule of all, that we must not concentrate overmuch upon our feelings. Do not spend too much time feeling your own pulse taking your own spiritual temperature, do not spend too much time analysing your feelings. That is the high road to morbidity.

This whole matter is very subtle and the subtlety often comes in in this way. You read the lives of the great saints of all the centuries and you will find that every one has emphasized the importance of self-examination. Irrespective of what particular view of theology they may have held, they are all one at this point. They urge that we must examine ourselves, that we must search our own hearts. Now the very fact that they have done so has meant that naturally and inevitably we, too, have to look at our feelings. They want us to make sure that we are not mere intellectualists who are interested in arguing about theology. They want to make sure that we are not moralists who are just interested in a code of morals. But the tendency always is that in following them we make too much of the feelings. The saintly Henry Martyn was surely an instance of this. But perhaps the classic instance was a man who lived in America in the seventeenth century, whose name was Thomas Sheppard. He is a perfect example of a man making himself wretched. He went from the heart of England to America and was one of the greatest saints who ever trod the face of this earth and the author of such great books as 'The Parable of the Ten Virgins'. That poor man was constantly depressed because of his great concern about his feelings and the danger of false feelings. He made himself wretched.

So the next point I would make is this, that we must recognize that there is all the difference in the world between rejoicing and feeling happy. The Scripture tells us that we should always rejoice. Take the lyrical Epistle of Paul to the Philippians where he says: 'Rejoice in the Lord always and again I say rejoice'. He goes on saying it. To rejoice is a command, yes, but there is all the difference in the world between rejoicing and being happy. You cannot make yourself happy, but you can make yourself rejoice, in the sense that you will always rejoice in the Lord. Happiness is something within ourselves, rejoicing is 'in the Lord'. How important it is then, to draw the distinction between rejoicing in the Lord and feeling happy. Take the fourth chapter of the Second Epistle to the Corinthians. There you will find that the great Apostle puts it all very plainly and clearly in that series of extraordinary contrasts which he makes: 'We are troubled on every side (I don't think he felt very happy at the moment) yet not distressed', 'we are perplexed (he wasn't feeling happy at all at that point) but not in despair', 'persecuted but not forsaken', 'cast down, but not destroyed'—and so on. In other words the Apostle does not suggest a kind of happy person in a carnal sense, but he was still rejoicing. That is the difference between the two conditions.

That brings me to the practical point which is that the great thing in this respect is to know how to stir ourselves up. That is the whole essence of this matter. As I have been reminding you, the whole danger is that when the mood comes upon us, we allow it to dominate us and we are defeated and depressed. We say that we would like to be delivered, and yet we do nothing about it. The Apostle says to Timothy: 'Stir up the gift'—we must away with 'dull sloth and melancholy'.

You have to speak to yourself. I have said this many times before and I shall go on saying it, for there is a sense in which what the Scriptures do is to teach us how to speak to ourselves. I have reminded you that you must speak to yourself, this horrible self. Speak to it and then 'stir up the gift'. Remind yourself of certain things. Remind yourself of who you are and what you are. You must talk to yourself and say: 'I am not going to be dominated by you, these moods shall not control me. I am going out, I am breaking through'. So get up and walk, and do something. 'Stir up the gift'. This is the constant exhortation of the Scriptures. If you allow these moods to control you, you will remain miserable, but you must not allow it. Shake them off. Do not recognize them. Say again, 'Away dull sloth'.

But how do you do that? In this way—your business and mine is not to stir up our feelings, it is to believe. We are never told anywhere in Scripture that we are saved by our feelings; we are told that we are saved by believing. 'Believe on the Lord Jesus Christ and thou shalt be saved.' Never once are feelings put into the primary position. Now this is something we can do. I cannot make myself happy, but I can remind myself of my belief. I can exhort myself to believe, I can address my soul as the Psalmist did in Psalm 42: 'Why art thou cast down O my soul, and why art thou disquieted within me? Hope thou' . . . believe thou, trust thou. That is the way. And then our feelings will look after themselves. Do not worry about them. Talk to yourself, and though the devil will suggest that because you do not feel, you are not a Christian, say: 'No, I do not feel anything, but whether I feel or not, I believe the Scriptures. I believe God's Word is true and I will stay my soul on it, I will believe in it come what may'. Put belief in the first place, hold on to it. Yes, J. C. Philpot was right at that point, the child of the light is sometimes found walking in darkness but he goes on walking. He does not sit down and commiserate with himself—that is the thing—the child of light walking in darkness. He does not see the face of the Lord at this point, but he knows that He is there; so he goes on.

Better still, let me put it like this. If you want to be truly happy and blessed, if you would like to know true joy as a Christian, here is the prescription—'Blessed (truly happy) are they who do hunger and thirst after righteousness'—not after happiness. Do not go on seeking thrills; seek righteousness. Turn to yourself, turn to your feelings and say: 'I have no time to worry about feelings, I am interested in something else. I want to be happy but still more I want to be righteous, I want to be holy. I want to be like my Lord, I want to live in this world as He lived, I want to walk through it as He walked through it'. You are in this world, says John in his First Epistle, even as He was. Set your whole aim upon righteousness and holiness and as certainly as you do so you will be blessed, you will be filled, you will get the happiness you long for. Seek for happiness and you will never find it, seek righteousness and you will discover you are happy—it will be there without your knowing it, without your seeking it.

Finally, let me put it in this way: 'Do you want to know supreme joy, do you want to experience a happiness that eludes description? There is only one thing to do, really seek Him, seek Him Himself, turn to the Lord Jesus Christ Himself. If you find that your feelings are depressed do not sit down and commiserate with yourself, do not try to work something up but—this is the simple essence of it—go directly to Him and seek His face, as the little child who is miserable and unhappy because somebody else has taken or broken his toy, runs to its father or its mother.

So if you and I find ourselves afflicted by this condition, there is only one thing to do, it is to go to Him. If you seek the Lord Jesus Christ and find Him there is no need to worry about your happiness and your joy. He is our joy and our happiness, even as He is our peace. He is life, He is everything. So avoid the incitements and the temptations of Satan to give feelings this great prominence at the centre. Put at the centre the only One who has a right to be there, the Lord of Glory, Who so loved you that He went to the Cross and bore the punishment and the shame of your sins and died for you. Seek Him, seek His face, and all other things shall be added unto you.

For the kingdom of Heaven is like unto a man that is an householder, which went out early in the morning to hire labourers into his vineyard. And when he had agreed with the labourers for a penny a day, he sent them into his vineyard. And he went out about the third hour, and saw others standing idle in the marketplace, And said unto them; Go ye also into the vineyard, and whatsoever is right I will give you. And they went their way. Again he went out about the sixth and ninth hour, and did likewise. And about the eleventh hour he went out, and found others standing idle, and saith unto them, Why stand ye here all the day idle? They say unto him, Because no man hath hired us. He saith unto them, Go ye also into the vineyard; and whatsoever is right, that shall ye receive. So when even was come, the lord of the vineyard saith unto his steward, Call the labourers, and give them their hire, beginning from the last unto the first. And when they came that were hired about the eleventh hour, they received every man a penny. But when the first came, they supposed that they should have received more; and they likewise received every man a penny. And when they had received it, they murmured against the goodman of the house, Saying, These last have wrought but one hour, and thou hast made them equal unto us, which have borne the burden and heat of the day. But he answered one of them, and said, Friend, I do thee no wrong: didst not thou agree with me for a penny? Take that thine is, and go thy way: I will give unto this last, even as unto thee. Is it not lawful for me to do what I will with mine own? Is thine eye evil, because I am good? So the last shall be first, and the first last: for many be called, but few chosen.

Matthew 20. 1-16

IX

LABOURERS IN THE VINEYARD

I CALL your attention to the particular teaching that is
enshrined in this parable as part of our general consideration
of the subject of spiritual depression, or, if you prefer it, the
subject of unhappiness in the life of the Christian—the miserable
Christian. I feel that we have arrived at a turning point. So far,
we have been considering difficulties which I would put into the
category of preliminary difficulties, those initial stumbling blocks
—difficulties arising from a lack of clarity with regard to the
entry into the faith and the Christian life.

Now we must take a step forward. We have not by any means
dealt with all the preliminary difficulties, our treatment has not
been exhaustive in that sense; but we have tried to pick out the
more important causes of stumbling and of difficulty and of
unhappiness. The kind or group of difficulties we now want to
consider are those which tend to arise after that stage of the pre-
liminaries. These difficulties, of course, may come at any point,
but they do constitute a kind of group on their own.

As we come to consider them, we must again remind ourselves
that the Scripture makes it very plain and clear that there is no
part of this Christian life which is without its dangers. Nothing
is so false to the teaching of the New Testament as to give the
impression that the moment you believe and are converted, all
your troubles are at an end and you will never have another
problem. Alas, that is not true, and it is not true because we have
an enemy, the Adversary of our souls. But not only do we have to
contend with the enemy, there is still the old nature within, and
these two together make it certain that we shall have troubles and
difficulties; and it is our business to understand the teaching of
the Scripture with respect to these, lest we be caught by the guile
and the subtlety of the enemy. He follows us as he followed our
Lord, all the way. When he had tempted and tried our Lord in
the wilderness for forty days, we are told that at the end of it he
only left Him 'for a season'. He did not leave Him permanently,
he came back again and again and followed Him all the way.

Look at his activities in Gethsemane at the very end, indeed he was still attacking when our Blessed Lord was dying on the Cross. Now to say that is not to be depressing, it is to be realistic, and to be realistic is always encouraging. There is nothing worse or more reprehensible than to drug people with some kind of soporific and then to allow them to wake up suddenly to find difficulties they are not prepared for. It is our business to anticipate these things in the light of Scripture. 'To be forewarned is to be forearmed', and we have before us always that mighty Scripture which teaches: 'Take unto you, therefore, the whole armour of God'. We are simply trying in these studies to put on the separate pieces of this strong armour that God has provided for us.

The point I would emphasize now, therefore, is that while it is of vital and supreme importance to start correctly, it is not enough. We must continue in the same way, for, if we do not, we shall soon find ourselves unhappy. In other words, I am laying down the proposition, that though we may be clear about the things that we have been considering hitherto—though the gospel has been presented to us and we have been converted, though we have started correctly and are in the Christian life, though we have heeded the warnings about the initial difficulties —yet if we do not continue, if we do not maintain our course in the same way, we shall soon get into trouble. There is a great illustration of this in the Gospel according to St. John, the eighth chapter, verses 30 ff. Our Lord was preaching one afternoon about the relationship between Himself and the Father, and we are told that: 'As He spake those words many believed on Him'. Then our Lord looked at them and said: 'If ye continue in My words then are ye My disciples indeed and ye shall know the Truth and the Truth shall make you free'. They seemed to be starting well but they must continue if they were to be truly free. It is exactly the same with some of the people depicted in the parable of the sower. There were those who received the Truth with great joy but they did not last. In other words the importance of continuing is a very vital principle and that is what I want to consider with you in the light of this parable.

As we come to look at it, it is very important that we should approach it correctly and understand it truly. It can be said with reverence that this is a very dangerous parable if we do not interpret it correctly. There are many who take hold of one thing only in it, namely 'the eleventh hour'. They think to themselves:

'I need not worry about my salvation now; I will do so at the eleventh hour, like the people who went in at the eleventh hour and got paid the same as those who had started early in the morning'. There is no more fatal mistake than this. As Bishop Ryle says of the dying thief: 'Few are ever saved on their death-beds. One thief on the cross was saved that none should despair; but only one, that none should presume'. Another dangerous thing is to turn the parable into an allegory, to take hold of each detail in the teaching and impose upon it some spiritual truth. That has often been done, but that is all due to the fact that we fail to remember that this is a parable, and the point to remember about a parable is that it is generally meant to illustrate one truth only. That is why, for instance, in the thirteenth chapter of this Gospel according to St. Matthew you find that our Lord spoke a whole series of parables about the Kingdom of Heaven. You cannot see it all in one. One shows one aspect and another another; they are all complementary, and each one is meant to convey one aspect of truth only. We must be very careful, therefore, that we do not turn the details into some kind of allegorical representation of the truth.

This parable, therefore, like all the other parables, is meant to teach one great truth. What is that? The answer, surely, is to be found in the word 'FOR' —'For the Kingdom of Heaven'. It is a pity that when they came to divide the Scriptures up into chapters they introduced a division at this point. Obviously the theme is a continuation of what we have at the end of the nineteenth chapter, and what we have there is the incident of the rich young ruler, so called, and our Lord's comments to the disciples about that young man who had gone away sorrowful. You remember what Peter said to Him: 'We have forsaken all and followed Thee, what shall we have therefore?' Now it was because of this that our Lord spoke this parable. Peter put his question. He said in effect: 'Look, Lord, we have left everything, we have come after you, we have given up everything, what are you going to give us?' Our Lord answered his question and said: 'Verily I say unto you, that ye which have followed Me, in the regeneration when the Son of Man shall sit in the throne of His glory, ye also shall sit upon twelve thrones, judging the twelve tribes of Israel; And every one that hath forsaken houses, or brethren, or sisters, or father, or mother, or wife, or children, or lands for My Name's sake shall receive an hundredfold, and shall inherit everlasting life. But many that are first shall be last: and the last shall be first. "FOR" the Kingdom of Heaven is like unto a man that is an householder, etc.' In other words, the whole point of this parable is addressed to Peter because of that claim which he made. Our Lord heard Peter's question and He answered Peter's question, but He obviously detected a very wrong and false note in that question; so it was in order to rebuke him, to reprimand him and to warn him most seriously, that our Lord spoke the parable. That, it seems to me, is proved conclusively by the way in which He repeats this statement about 'many that are first shall be last and the last shall be first'. You get it at the beginning and you get it at the end.

Here, then, is the principle on which we must concentrate. What is it? What is the doctrine? It is that in the Christian life all is of grace from the very beginning to the very end. That is the message, that is the doctrine, that is the principle. Now we glanced at the teaching of this parable in a previous study but we were concerned then to take up the one point, that, because of this great principle of grace, those who do come in at the end are equally in with those who went in at the beginning. We were dealing then with the discouragement that often comes to men who may be converted in their old age. We saw that it is never too late, that salvation is not only for young people, but for all. Sometimes a man who is converted rather late in life is tempted of the devil in this way because salvation has come to him so late, and because of the years he has wasted. To such a man it is a great comfort that our Lord called these men and sent them in at the eleventh hour. We then looked at it from that point of view, but now in this study the emphasis is rather upon those who went in at the beginning. There can be no doubt at all but that the primary object of the parable is to address them and to issue to them this most serious and solemn warning.

The point about these people is that they started in the right way and then got into trouble later on. How often does that happen! That is why it is dealt with so frequently in the New Testament in such phrases as: 'Ye did run well, who did hinder you?' There is a sense in which all the New Testament Epistles were written to help just this kind of person. These early Christians had believed and come into the early Church, but they had become depressed, and the Epistles were written in order to help them. It is something that is constantly threatening us, and it is a danger that tends to dog our footsteps throughout the Christian life. It is not enough to start correctly, we must continue in the right way. I am going to deal with many illustrations of this. The danger to many has been to go back into bondage and it is a very real danger at the present time because of the cults that thrive round and about us. People who have known the glorious liberty of the children of God sometimes go back into bondage and become miserable and unhappy. Very well, let us try to look at this as it is presented in this parable.

First of all let us try to analyse the cause of the trouble. Why did these men, who were sent into the vineyard early in the morning, cut such a sorry figure at the end? Here they are discontented and murmuring and grumbling—what was the cause of the trouble? I would lay down as the first principle that their attitude towards themselves and their work was clearly wrong. I tend to agree with those who say that there is significance in this word 'agreed' in the second verse 'And when he had agreed with the labourers', etc. Now it is the truth that we are only told about this agreement in the case of these first people. We are told later on, you remember: 'About the third hour he saw others standing idle in the market-place and said unto them: Go ye also into the vineyard and whatsoever is right I will give you'. And so he said to all the subsequent labourers. There is no talk about an agreement. He simply says: 'You go and work and what is right I will give you'.And they went quite happily. But with the first people, who murmured at the end about the wages paid, there seems to be a suggestion that they demanded an agreement. Thus one feels at the very beginning that there was something wrong in their attitude. They have this tendency to strike a bargain, to make certain demands and to stipulate certain things. Whether we are right or wrong in sensing this about them, surely we are right in saying that they are very conscious of their work, they are very conscious of what they are doing; as they are working, they are in a sense keeping an eye upon themselves doing it. What a terrible thing that is! But are we not all guilty of it? God knows the greatest problem that any man who preaches the gospel ever has to face is that while he is preaching he is in danger of looking at himself and watching himself and always being conscious of himself. It comes into all our service, it comes into everything we do. It is very true of the natural man of course. He is play-acting all the time and watching himself, and this thing tends to follow us into the Christian life. These men, clearly, were very conscious of everything they did. It is obvious from what they say that they had been watching themselves all the time.

Let us go on to the next point, which is that they were assessing their work. They were keeping an account of the others also, and keeping a careful record of all they did and how long they had been working, as well as how many hours they themselves had spent and how much they themselves had done—'the heat and burden of the day'. They knew it all in detail and kept a careful record and account of it. That is our Lord's first statement about these people. Let us pause with that for a moment and let it sink deeply into us. Our Lord is concerned to denounce that attitude. It is fatal in the Kingdom of God. He detected it in Peter's statement. 'We have left all and followed Thee, what do we get?' The suggestion of bargain and demand is implicit there. The fundamental attitude is so wrong and so entirely antithetical to the realm of the Spirit and of the Kingdom, as we shall see. But there it is and this wrong attitude is bound to lead to trouble eventually, as it did in the case of these men. What is so pathetic and tragic about this is that it brings a man into trouble at the very point where our Lord is most gracious in His dealings. What makes this parable so terrible is that these men are exposed for what they really were, and the terrible spirit which possessed them is revealed just when the householder in his graciousness gave a penny to the last exactly as to the first. It is then that it comes out and leads to trouble. Look at these men. Because of their initial wrong attitude, because of their forgetfulness of the principle of grace, they expected to receive more than the others, and they felt that they deserved more. Of course they were perfectly logical, they were quite consistent with themselves. Starting on their principle and from their attitude it is the logical conclusion. That is why I say that to start in that way inevitably leads to this position. They had a feeling that they were entitled to more and that they should be given more; they expected more and because they did not get it they were upset.

The next thing we are told is that they began to murmur. Now their happiness and their joy have gone altogether, and here they are murmuring because they were not given something extra. Is not that a terrible thing? But how true it is that Christian people can be guilty of this very thing that our Lord here depicts—

this tendency to murmur as the children of Israel did of old, and as these people did at this point, commiserating with yourself, feeling you are not having your rights, feeling you are being dealt with harshly. There is a great deal of emphasis upon this in the New Testament. You remember how the Apostle Paul addresses a word about it to the Philippians. He reminds them that they are to be as luminaries in the heavens, they are to 'do all things without murmurings and disputings: that ye may be blameless and harmless, the sons of God, without rebuke, in the midst of a crooked and perverse nation, among whom ye shine as lights in the world; holding forth the word of life' (Philippians 2. 14-16). What a tragic thing it is that Christian people can be miserable and murmuring instead of rejoicing in Christ Jesus. It is an outcome of the fact that they have forgotten that everything is of grace. They have forgotten this great principle that goes right through the Christian life from the very beginning to the very end.

But that is not all. It leads to another thing, namely, a contempt for others and at the same time a certain amount of jealousy of others. The men in the parable say, 'Here these last have wrought but one hour and thou hast made them equal unto us, which have borne the burden and heat of the day'. It is the principle of the elder brother in the parable of the Prodigal Son and again is illustrated in many places in the New Testament. This tendency comes in and attacks Christian people who have been faithful in their witness and who have done most excellent work. It comes in most subtle ways and makes them miserable because they feel that others have been rewarded in a greater way than they have. Those who have read Mr. Hugh Redwood's account of himself in the years of his backsliding will know that this was precisely the cause of his trouble. A change of officers in the Salvation Army made him feel he was no longer the favourite. Somebody else was brought forward and made the favourite and he began to feel sorry for himself, and back he went into sin. Read his book 'God in the Shadows' and there you will find the account in detail. That is the kind of thing illustrated here. These men felt a contempt for the others, they were jealous of those men who were given so much when they had done so little. Their whole attitude was selfish and self-centred.

But above all, and this is the most serious and the most terrible thing of all, they had a feeling in their heart that the householder was unjust. In this condition they had persuaded themselves that this man was not righteous in his dealing with them. They were absolutely wrong, there was not a vestige of foundation for that attitude, but they felt it. And so the Christian is tempted of the devil to feel that God is not being fair. The devil comes to him and says: 'Look at how much you have done, and what are you getting for it? Look at that other fellow, he has done nothing yet look at what he is getting'. That is what the devil says, and these people listen to him: 'We who have borne the heat and burden of the day are only getting a penny—the same as these others who have only been working for an hour'. That is the spirit, and the thing that makes it so serious is that in that condition the Christian, unless he is very careful, will soon be ascribing unrighteousness to God. He will be feeling that God is not fair to him, that God is not giving him his rights, that God is not giving him his due.

What a miserable thing self is, what an ugly thing, what a foul thing. We are all guilty, of this, every one of us, in some shape or form. The devil comes to us and we listen, and we begin to doubt whether God is just and righteous in His dealings with us. Self needs to be exposed for what it is. Sin in its ugliness and foulness needs to be unmasked. It is not surprising that our Lord dealt with this wrong spirit in the way He did in this parable. It is the greatest enemy of the soul, and it leads to misery and unhappiness. It is bound to do so for every reason. It is utterly wrong, and there is nothing to be said in its defence.

That brings me to the cure. What is the treatment? It is to understand the controlling principle of the Kingdom of God. That principle which seems so obvious but which we are so prone to forget in detail. Our Lord puts it here once and for ever. I am simply putting what He said in other words. The principle is that in the Kingdom of God everything is essentially different from everything in every other kingdom. For, He says in effect, the Kingdom of God is not like that which you have always known, it is something quite new and different. The first thing we have to realize is that 'if any man be in Christ he is a new creature (he is a new creation), old things are passed away, behold all things are become new.' If only we realized as we should, that here we are in a realm in which everything is different! The whole foundation is different, it has nothing to do with the principle of the old life. We have to work this out in detail, but first let me underline again that new principle. We must say to ourselves every day of our lives: 'Now I am a Christian, and because I am a Christian I am in the Kingdom of God and all my thinking has got to be different. Everything here is different. I must not bring with me those old ideas, those old moods and concepts of thought'. We tend to confine salvation to one thing, namely to forgiveness, but we have to apply the principle throughout the Christian life.

Very well, bearing that in mind, here are some of the details. The first thing is this. Do not think in terms of bargains and rights in the Kingdom of God. That is absolutely fatal. There is nothing so wrong as the spirit which argues that because I do this, or because I have done that, I have a right to expect something else in return. This is met with frequently. I know very good evangelical Christian people, who seem to be thinking like that. 'Now,' they say, 'if we pray for certain things, we are bound to have them, for instance if we pray all night for revival we must have revival.' I have sometimes described this as the 'penny in the slot' idea of Christianity. You put in your coin and you draw out a bar of chocolate or whatever else you want. Now this is that same attitude. Because men in the past have prayed all night that revival might come and revival has come, therefore let us have an all-night prayer meeting and revival will come. But that surely is to deny the whole principle which our Lord is teaching. I do not care what it is, whether prayer or anything else, in no respect must I ever argue that because I do something I am entitled to get something—never. And of course the principle can be seen to be true in practice. Think of the many such prayer meetings that have been held. And yet the revival has not come, and I am going to venture to say that I thank God that it has not. What would the position be if we could command these things at will? But we cannot. Let us get rid of this bargaining spirit, that if I do this then that will happen. You cannot have revival whenever you want it and as a result of doing certain things. The Holy Spirit is Lord, and He is a Sovereign Lord. He sends these things in His own time and in His own way. In other words we must realize that we have no right to anything at all. 'But', says someone, 'does not Paul teach about judgment and rewards in the Second Epistle to the Corinthians, in the fifth chapter?' Certainly he does, and he does so likewise in the third chapter of the First Epistle to the Corinthians, and our Lord Himself in the twelfth chapter of Luke talks about those who are beaten with many stripes and those who receive few stripes and so on. Well, what of that? The reply is that even the rewards are of grace. He need not give them, and if you think you can determine and predict how they are to come you will be quite wrong. Everything is of grace in the Christian life from the very beginning to the very end. To think in terms of bargains and to murmur at results, implies a distrust of Him, and we need to watch our own spirits lest we harbour the thought that He is not dealing with us justly and fairly.

If you start in that way you end by robbing yourself. I like the way in which our Lord teaches that. If you strike a bargain with God, well then it is almost certain that you will just get your bargain and no more. These men at the very beginning had this agreement for one penny per day. 'Very well,' said the householder, 'I will give you a penny.' But when the others came he said to them: 'You go and work and I will give you that which is right'. And they received much more than they expected. These last people got a penny; but they never expected it, and they had much more than they imagined. But the first got nothing but the penny. O Christian friends, do not make bargains with God. If you do, you will get only your bargain; but if you leave it to His grace, you will probably get more than you ever thought of. Of the Pharisees our Lord says: 'Verily they have their reward'. They do these things in order to be seen of men; they are seen of men, that is what they wanted and that is all they will get, they will get no more.

Very well, let us go on to the next principle. Do not keep a record or an account of your work. Give up being book-keepers. In the Christian life we must desire nothing but His glory, nothing but to please Him. So do not keep your eye on the clock, but keep it on Him and His work. Do not keep on recording your work and labour, keep your eye on Him and His glory, on His love and His honour and the extension of His Kingdom. Keep your attention on that and on nothing else. Have no concern as to how many hours you have given to the work, nor how much you have done. In effect leave the book-keeping to Him and to His grace. Let Him keep the accounts. Listen to Him saying it Himself: 'Let not thy left hand know what thy right hand doeth'. That is the way you are to work in His Kingdom, you are to work in such a way that your left hand does not know what your right hand is doing. For this reason: 'Thy Father which seeth in secret shall reward thee openly'. There is no need to waste time keeping the accounts, He is keeping them. And what wonderful accounts they are. May I say it with reverence, there is nothing I know of that is so romantic as God's method of accountancy. Be prepared for surprises in this Kingdom. You never know what is going to happen. The last shall be first. What a complete reversal of our materialistic outlook, the last first, the first last, everything upside down. The whole world is turned upside down by grace. It is not of man, it is of God, it is the Kingdom of God. How excellent this is.

Let me make a personal confession. This kind of thing has often happened to me in my ministry. Sometimes God has been gracious on a Sunday and I have been conscious of exceptional liberty, and I have been foolish enough to listen to the devil when he says: 'Now, then, you wait until next Sunday, it is going to be marvellous, there will be even larger congregations'. And I go into the pulpit the next Sunday and I see a smaller congregation. But then on another occasion I stand in this pulpit labouring, as it were left to myself, preaching badly and utterly weak, and the devil has come and said: 'There will be nobody there at all next Sunday'. But, thank God, I have found on the following Sunday a larger congregation. That is God's method of accountancy. You never know. I enter the pulpit in weakness and I end with power. I enter with self-confidence and I am made to feel a fool. It is God's accountancy. He knows us so much better than we know ourselves. He is always giving us surprises. You never know what He is going to do. His book-keeping is the most romantic thing I know of in the whole world.

Our Lord spoke of it again in the third parable in the twenty-fifth chapter of the Gospel according to St. Matthew. You remember His description of the people who will come at the end of the world expecting a reward but to whom He will give nothing, and then the others to whom He will say: 'Come ye blessed of My Father, inherit the Kingdom prepared for you'. And they will say: 'We have done nothing. When have we seen you naked, when have we seen you hungry or thirsty and given you drink?' And He will say, 'Because you have done it unto the least of My brethren you have done it unto Me'. What a surprise that will be. This life is full of romance. Our ledgers are out of date; they are of no value. We are in the Kingdom of God and it is God's accountancy. It is all of grace.

Very well, that brings us to the last principle, which is that we should not only recognize that it is all of grace, but rejoice in the fact that it is so. That was the tragedy of these men. They see a penny given to those who only work for one hour, and instead of rejoicing at the sight of it, they begin to murmur and complain, to feel that it is unjust and that they are not being dealt with fairly. The secret of a happy Christian life is to realize that it is all of grace and to rejoice in that fact. 'So likewise ye,' says our Lord in another place, 'when ye shall have done all those things which are commanded you say, "We are unprofitable servants: we have done that which was our duty to do".' That is His view, that is His teaching, and that is the secret of it all. Was not that His own way? It was, according to St. Paul, who says: 'Look not every man on his own things, but every man also on the things of others. Let this mind be in you which was also in Christ Jesus'. You see what that means. He did not look at Himself, He did not consider Himself and His own interests only; He made Himself of no reputation, He laid aside the insignia of His eternal glory. He did not regard His equality with God as something to hold on to and say: 'Come what may I will not let it go'. Not at all, He laid it aside, He humbled Himself, He forgot Himself, and He went through and endured and did all He did, looking only to the glory of God. Nothing else mattered to Him but that the Father should be glorified and that men and women should come to the Father. That is the secret. Not watching the clock, not assessing the amount of work, not keeping a record in a book, but forgetting everything except the glory of God, the privilege of being called to work for Him at all, the privilege of being a Christian, remembering only the grace that has ever looked upon us and removed us from darkness to light.

It is grace at the beginning, grace at the end. So that when you and I come to lie upon our deathbeds, the one thing that should comfort and help and strengthen us there is the thing that helped us at the beginning. Not what we have been, not what we have done, but the grace of God in Jesus Christ our Lord. The Christian life starts with grace, it must continue with grace, it ends with grace. Grace, wondrous grace. 'By the grace of God I am what I am.' 'Yet not I, but the grace of God which was with me.'

Now it came to pass on a certain day, that He went into a ship with His disciples: and He said unto them, Let us go over unto the other side of the lake. And they launched forth. But as they sailed He fell asleep: And there came down a storm of wind on the lake; and they were filled with water, and were in jeopardy. And they came to Him, and awoke Him, saying, Master, Master, we perish. Then He arose, and rebuked the wind and the raging of the water: and they ceased, and there was a calm. And He said unto them, Where is your faith? And they being afraid wondered, saying one to another, What manner of Man is this! for He commandeth even the winds and water, and they obey Him.

Luke 8. 22-25

X

WHERE IS YOUR FAITH?

I WANT to call attention particularly to this question which was addressed by our Lord and Saviour Jesus Christ to the disciples. He said to them: 'Where is your faith?' Indeed I would call your attention to this entire incident as a part of our consideration of the subject of spiritual depression. We have already considered a number of causes of the condition and this particular incident in the life and ministry of our Lord brings us face to face with yet another cause.

The one that is dealt with here is the whole problem and question of the nature of faith. In other words, there are many Christians who get into difficulty and are unhappy from time to time because they clearly have not understood the nature of faith. 'Well', you may say, 'if they have not understood the nature of faith, how can they be Christians?' The answer is that what makes one a Christian is that one is given the gift of faith. We are given the gift of faith by God through the Holy Spirit and we believe on the Lord Jesus Christ and that saves us; but that does not mean that we have fully understood the nature of faith. So it comes to pass that, while we may be truly Christian and genuinely saved through receiving this gift of faith, we may subsequently get into trouble with our spiritual experience because we have not understood what faith really is. It is given as a gift, but from there on we have to do certain things about it.

Now this very striking incident brings out the vital importance of distinguishing between the original gift of faith and the walk of faith, or the life of faith which comes subsequently. God starts us off in this Christian life and then we have to walk in it. 'We walk by faith, not by sight', is the theme that we are now considering.

Before I come actually to that particular theme, I must say a few words about this great incident in and of itself. Looked at from any standpoint it is a very interesting and important incident. It has a great deal to tell us, for instance, about the Person of our Lord Himself. It brings us face to face with what is described as a paradox, the seeming contradiction in the Person of our Lord Jesus Christ. There He was, weary and tired, so tired, in fact, that He fell asleep. Now this incident is recorded by the three so-called synoptic Gospels, Matthew, Mark and Luke, and it is really important from the standpoint of understanding the Person of the Lord Jesus Christ. Look at Him. There is no doubt about His humanity, He is fatigued, He is tired and weary, so much so that He just falls asleep, and, though the storm has arisen, He still goes on sleeping. He is subject to infirmity, He is a man in the body and flesh like all the rest of us. Ah, yes, but wait a minute. They came to Him and awoke Him saying: 'Master, carest Thou not that we perish?' Then He arose and rebuked the wind and the raging of the sea, and they ceased and there was a calm—one of the others describes it as 'a great calm'. Now it is not surprising that the disciples, seeing all this, wondered and said one to another: 'What manner of Man is this! for He commandeth even the winds and water and they obey Him'. Man, and yet obviously God. He could command the elements, He could silence the wind and stop the raging of the sea. He is the Lord of nature and of creation, He is the Lord of the universe. This is the mystery and the marvel of Jesus Christ—God and Man, two natures in One Person, two natures unmixed yet resident in the same Person.

We must start here, because if we are not clear about that there is no purpose in our going on. If you do not believe in the unique deity of the Lord Jesus Christ, you are not a Christian, whatever else you may be. We are not looking at a good Man only, we are not interested merely in the greatest Teacher the world has ever seen; we are face to face with the fact that God, the Eternal Son, has been in this world and that He took upon Him human nature and dwelt amongst us, a Man amongst men—God-Man. We are face to face with the mystery and the marvel of the Incarnation and of the Virgin Birth. It is all here, and it shines out in all the fullness of its amazing glory. 'What manner of Man is this?' He is more than Man. That is the answer—He is also God.

However, that is not, it seems to me, the special purpose of this particular incident. You get that revelation in other places also, it shines out right through all the Gospels; but the separate particular incidents in which it is seen, generally also have some special and peculiar message of their own to teach us. In this case there can be no doubt that that message is the lesson with regard to the disciples and their condition at this point—it is the great lesson concerning faith and the nature or the character of faith. I do not know what you feel, but I never cease to be grateful to these disciples. I am grateful for the record of every mistake they ever made, and for every blunder they ever committed, because I see myself in them. How grateful we should be to God that we have these Scriptures, how grateful to Him that He has not merely given us the gospel and left it at that. How wonderful it is that we can read accounts like this and see ourselves depicted in them, and how grateful we should be to God that it is a divinely inspired Word which speaks the truth, and shows and pictures every human frailty.

So we find our Lord rebuking these men. He rebukes them because of their alarm, because of their terror, because of their lack of faith. Here they were in the boat with Him, and the storm arose, and soon they were in difficulties. They baled out the water, but the boat was filling up and they could see that in a few moments it was going to sink. They had done everything they could but it did not seem to be of any avail, and what amazed them was that the Master was still sleeping soundly in the stern of the vessel. So they awoke Him and said: 'Master, Master, carest Thou not that we perish?'—are You unconcerned about it all? And He arose, and having rebuked the wind and the sea, He rebuked them.

Now we must be careful to observe this rebuke and to understand what He was saying. In the first place, He was rebuking them for being in such a state at all. 'Where is your faith?' He says. Matthew puts it: 'O ye of little faith!' Here as elsewhere 'He marvelled at their unbelief'. He rebuked them for being in that state of agitation and terror and alarm while He was with them in the boat. That is the first great lesson we have to apply to ourselves and to one another. It is very wrong for a Christian ever to be in such a condition. I do not care what the circumstances may be, the Christian should never be agitated, the Christian should never be beside himself like this, the Christian should never be at his wit's end, the Christian should never be in a condition in which he has lost control of himself. That is the first lesson, a lesson we have emphasized before because it is an essential part of the New Testament teaching. A Christian should never, like the worldly person, be depressed, agitated, alarmed, frantic, not knowing what to do. It is the typical reaction to trouble of those who are not Christian, that is why it is so wrong to be like that. The Christian is different from other people, the Christian has something which the non-Christian does not possess, and the ideal for the Christian is that which is stated so perfectly by the Apostle Paul in the fourth chapter of the Epistle to the Philippians: 'I have learned, in whatsoever state I am, therewith to be content . . . I can do all things through Christ which strengtheneth me'. That is the Christian position, that is what the Christian is meant to be like. The Christian is never meant to be carried away by his feelings, whatever they are— never. That is always wrong in a Christian. He is always to be controlled, as I hope to show you. The trouble with these men was that they were lacking in self-control. That is why they were miserable, that is why they were unhappy, that is why they were alarmed and agitated, though the Son of God was with them in the boat. I cannot emphasize this point too strongly. I lay it down as a simple proposition that a Christian should never lose self-control, should never be in a state of agitation or terror or alarm, whatever the circumstances. That is obviously our first lesson. The position of these people was alarming. They were in jeopardy and it looked as if they were going to be drowned the next moment, but our Lord says in effect: 'You should not be in that condition. As My followers you have no right to be in such a state even though you are in jeopardy'.

That is the first great lesson, and the second is, that what is so wrong about being in this condition is that it implies a lack of trust and of confidence in Him. That is the trouble and that is why it is so reprehensible. That is why He reprimanded these men at that point. He said in effect: 'Do you feel like this in spite of the fact that I am with you? Do you not trust Me?' Mark reports them as saying: 'Master, carest Thou not that we perish?' Now I do not think that they were referring only to themselves or to their own safety. I do not think that they were so self-centred. I do not think that they simply meant: Don't You care that *we* are going to drown? without considering Him at all. I believe they were including Him as well, that they thought they were all going to be drowned. 'Master, carest Thou not that we perish?' But still, this agitation and alarm always carries with it a lack of implicit trust and confidence in Him. It is a lack of faith in His concern for us and in His care for us. It means that we take charge and are going to look after the situation ourselves, feeling either that He does not care, or perhaps that He cannot do anything. That is what makes this so terrible, but I wonder whether we always realize it. It seems obvious as we look at it objectively in the case of these disciples; but when you and I are agitated or disturbed and do not know what to do, and are giving the impression of great nervous tension, anybody looking at us is entitled to say: 'That person has not much faith in his or her Lord. There does not seem to be much point in being a Christian after all, there is not much value in Christianity as I see it in that person'. Now during the war we were all subject to these trials in an exceptional way, but even now in days of peace anything that comes across our path and puts us in difficulty, at once shows whether we believe in Him and trust in Him, by our response and reaction to it. There seems to me, therefore, on the very surface to be these two great lessons. We must never allow ourselves to be agitated and disturbed whatever the circumstances because to do so implies a lack of faith, a lack of trust, a lack of confidence in our blessed Lord and God.

However, let us look at the passage in detail, let us now draw some general principles out of the incident and its great teaching. First of all, in looking at this whole question of faith, let me say a word about what I might call 'the trial of faith'. Scripture is full of this idea of the trial of one's faith. Take the eleventh chapter of the Epistle to the Hebrews. That is, in a sense, nothing but a great exposition of this theme of the trial of faith. Every one of those men was tried. They had been given great promises and they had accepted them, and then everything seemed to go wrong. It is true of all of them. Think of the trial of a man like Noah, the trial of a man like Abraham, the trials that men like Jacob and especially Moses had to endure. God gives the gift of faith and then the faith is tried. Peter, in his First Epistle in the first chapter, says exactly the same thing. He says: 'Though ye are in heaviness for a season' because of certain circumstances, the object of that is 'that the trial of your faith which is more precious than of gold that perisheth, though it be tried with fire, might be found unto praise and honour and glory at the appearing of Jesus Christ'. That is the theme of all the Scriptures. You find it in the history of the Patriarchs and of all the Old Testament saints, you find it running through the New Testament. Indeed, it is peculiarly the theme of the last book of the Bible, the Book of Revelation.

Let us then be clear about this. We must start by understanding that we may well find ourselves in a position in which our faith is going to be tried. Storms and trials are allowed by God. If we are living the Christian life, or trying to live the Christian life, at the moment, on the assumption that it means just come to Christ and you will never have any more worry in the whole of your life, we are harbouring a terrible fallacy. In fact it is a delusion and it is not true. Our faith will be tried, and James goes so far as to say: 'Count it all joy when ye fall into divers temptations (trials)' (James 1. 2). God permits storms, He permits difficulties, He permits the wind to blow and the billows to roll, and everything may seem to be going wrong and we ourselves to be in jeopardy. We must learn and realize that God does not take His people and lead them into some kind of Elysium in which they are protected from all 'the slings and arrows of outrageous fortune'. Not at all, we are living in the same world as everybody else. Indeed, the Apostle Paul seems to go further than that. He tells the Philippians: 'Unto you it is given in the behalf of Christ, not only to believe on Him, but also to suffer for His sake' (Philippians 1. 29). 'In the world', says our Lord, 'ye shall have tribulation but be of good cheer; I have overcome the world' (John 16. 33). 'Be of good cheer'—yes, but remember that you will have the tribulation. Paul and Barnabas going on their missionary journey visited the churches and warned them, 'that we must through much tribulation enter into the Kingdom of God' (Acts 14. 22).

We must start by realizing that 'to be forewarned is to be forearmed' in this matter. If we have a magical conception of the Christian life, we are certain to find ourselves in trouble, because, when difficulties come, we shall be tempted to ask: 'Why is this allowed?' And we should never ask such a question. If we but realized this fundamental truth, we never would ask it. Our Lord goes to sleep and allows the storm to come. The position may indeed become quite desperate and we may appear to be in danger of our lives. Everything may seem to be against us, yet— well here it is, a Christian poet has said it for us:

> 'When all things seem against us
> To drive us to despair' . . .

But it does not drive him to despair because he goes on to say:

> 'We know one gate is open
> One ear will hear our prayer'.

But things may be desperate: 'All things seem against us, to drive us to despair'. Let us then be prepared for that. Yes, but we must go further. While all this is happening to us, our Lord appears to be utterly unconcerned about us. That is where the real trial of faith comes in. The wind and the billows were bad enough and the water coming into the ship. That was terrible, but the thing that to them was most terrible of all was His apparent unconcern. Still sleeping and not apparently caring. 'Master, carest Thou not that we perish?' He appears to be unconcerned, unconcerned about us, unconcerned about Himself, unconcerned about His cause, unconcerned about His Kingdom. Just imagine the feelings of these men. They had followed Him and listened to His teaching about the coming of the Kingdom, they had seen His miracles and were expecting marvellous things to happen; and now it looked as if everything was going to come to an end in shipwreck and drowning. What an anti-climax and all because of His unconcern! We must be very young indeed in the Christian life if we do not know something about this. Do we not all know something of this position of trial and difficulty, yes, and of a feeling that God somehow does not seem to care? He does not do anything about it. 'Why does He allow me, a Christian, to suffer at the hands of a non-Christian?' says many a person. 'Why does He allow things to go wrong with me and not with the other person?' 'Why is that man successful while I am unsuccessful? Why does not God do something about it?' How often do Christian people ask such questions. They have asked it about the whole state of the Church today. 'Why does He not send revival? Why does He allow these rationalists and atheists to take the ascendancy? Why does He not break in and do something, and revive His work?' How often we are tempted to say such things, exactly as these disciples in the boat were!

The fact that God permits these things and that He often appears to be quite unconcerned about it all really constitutes what I am describing as the trial of faith. Those are the conditions in which our faith is tried and tested, and God allows it all, God permits it all. James even tells us to 'count it all joy' when these things happen to us. This is a great subject—the trial of faith. We do not talk much about it these days, do we? But if we went back to the seventeenth or eighteenth century we would find that it was then a very familiar theme. I suppose that in many ways it was the central theme of the Puritans. It was certainly prominent later on in the evangelical awakening of the eighteenth century. The trial of man's faith and how to overcome these things, the walk of faith, and the life of faith, was their constant theme.

Let us now go on to the second question—What is the nature of faith, the character of faith? This is above everything the particular message of this incident and I feel that it is brought out especially clearly in this record of it in the Gospel according to St. Luke. That is why I am taking the incident from that particular Gospel and emphasizing the way in which our Lord puts the question: 'Where is your faith?' There is the key to the whole problem. You observe our Lord's question. It seems to imply that He knows perfectly well that they have faith. The question He asks them is: 'Where is it? You have got faith, but where is it at this moment? It ought to be here, where is it?' Now that gives us the key to the understanding of the nature of faith.

Let me first of all put it negatively. Faith, obviously, is not a mere matter of feeling. It cannot be, because one's feelings in this kind of condition can be very changeable. A Christian is not meant to be dejected when everything goes wrong. He is told to 'rejoice'. Feelings belong to happiness alone, rejoicing takes in something much bigger than feelings; and if faith were a matter of feelings only, then when things go wrong and feelings change, faith will go. But faith is not a matter of feelings only, faith takes up the whole man including his mind, his intellect and his understanding. It is a response to truth, as we shall see.

The second thing is still more important. Faith is not something that acts automatically, faith is not something that acts magically. This, I think, is the blunder of which we have all, at some time or another, been guilty. We seem to think that faith is something that acts automatically. Many people, it seems to me, conceive of faith as if it were something similar to those thermostats which you have in connection with a heating apparatus, you set your thermostat at a given level, you want to maintain the temperature at a certain point and it acts automatically. If the temperature is tending to rise above that, the thermostat comes into operation and brings it down; if you use your hot water and the temperature is lowered, the thermostat comes into operation and sends it up, etc. You do not have to do anything about it, the thermostat acts automatically and it brings the temperature back to the desired level automatically. Now there are many people who seem to think that faith acts like that. They assume that it does not matter what happens to them, that faith will operate and all will be well. Faith, however, is not something that acts magically or automatically. If it did, these men would never have been in trouble, faith would have come into operation and they would have been calm and quiet and all would have been well. But faith is not like that and those are utter fallacies with respect to it.

What is faith? Let us look at it positively. The principle taught here is that faith is an activity, it is something that has to be exercised. It does not come into operation itself, you and I have to put it into operation. It is a form of activity.

Now let me divide that up a little. Faith is something you and I have to bring into operation. That is exactly what our Lord said to these men. He said: 'Where is your faith?' which means, 'Why are you not taking your faith and applying it to this position?' You see, it was because they did not do so, because they did not put their faith into operation, that the disciples had become unhappy and were in this state of consternation. How then does one put faith into operation? What do I mean by saying that faith is something we have to apply? I can divide my answer in this way. The first thing I must do when I find myself in a difficult position is to refuse to allow myself to be controlled by the situation. A negative, you see. These men were in the boat, the Master was asleep and the billows were rolling, the water was coming in, and they could not bale it out fast enough. It looked as if they were going to sink, and their trouble was that they were controlled by that situation. They should have applied their faith and taken charge of it, and said: 'No, we are not going to panic'. They should have started in that way, but they did not do so. They allowed the position to control them.

Faith is a refusal to panic. Do you like that sort of definition of faith? Does that seem to be too earthly and not sufficiently spiritual? It is of the very essence of faith. Faith is a refusal to panic, come what may. Browning, I think had that idea when he defined faith like this: 'With me, faith means perpetual unbelief kept quiet, like the snake 'neath Michael's foot'. Here is Michael and there is the snake beneath his foot, and he just keeps it quiet under the pressure of his foot. Faith is unbelief kept quiet, kept down. That is what these men did not do, they allowed this situation to grip them, they became panicky. Faith, however, is a refusal to allow that. It says: 'I am not going to be controlled by these circumstances—I am in control'. So you take charge of yourself, and pull yourself up, you control yourself. You do not let yourself go, you assert yourself.

That is the first thing, but it does not stop at that. That is not enough, because that may be nothing but resignation. That is not the whole of faith. Having taken that first step, having pulled yourself up, you then remind yourself of what you believe and what you know. That again is something these foolish disciples did not do. If only they had stopped a moment and said: 'Now then what about it? Is it possible that we are going to drown with Him in the boat? Is there anything He cannot do? We have seen His miracles, He turned the water into wine, He can heal the blind and the lame, He can even raise the dead, is it likely that He is going to allow us and Himself to be drowned in this way? Impossible! In any case He loves us, He cares for us, He has told us that the very hairs of our head are all numbered!' That is the way in which faith reasons. It says: 'All right, I see the waves and the billows but'—it always puts up this 'but'. That is faith, it holds on to truth and reasons from what it knows to be fact. That is the way to apply faith. These men did not do that and that is why they became agitated and panic stricken. And you and I will become panic stricken and agitated if we fail to do the same. Whatever the circumstances, therefore, stand, wait for a moment. Say: 'I admit it all, but——' But what? But God! but the Lord Jesus Christ! But what? The whole of my salvation! That is what faith does. All things may seem to be against me 'to drive me to despair', I do not understand what is happening; but I know this, I know that God has so loved me that He sent His only begotten Son into this world for me, I know that while I was an enemy, God sent His only Son to die on the Cross on Calvary's Hill for me. He has done that for me while I was an enemy, a rebellious alien. I know that the Son of God 'loved me and gave Himself for me'. I know that at the cost of His life's blood I have salvation and that I am a child of God and an heir to everlasting bliss. I know that. Very well, then, I know this, that 'if when we were enemies, we were reconciled to God by the death of His Son, much more, being reconciled, we shall be saved by His life' (Romans 5. 10). It is inevitable logic, and faith argues like that. Faith reminds itself of what the Scripture calls 'the exceeding great and precious promises'. Faith says: 'I cannot believe that He who has brought me so

far is going to let me down at this point. It is impossible, it would
be inconsistent with the character of God'. So faith, having
refused to be controlled by circumstances, reminds itself of what
it believes and what it knows.

And then the next step is that faith applies all that to the
particular situation. Again, that was something these men did
not do, and that is why our Lord puts it to them in this way:
'Where is your faith?'—'You have got it, why don't you apply it,
why don't you bring all you know to bear on this situation, why
don't you focus it on this particular problem?' That is the next
step in the application of faith. Whatever your circumstances at
this moment, bring all you know to be true of your relationship
to God to bear upon it. Then you will know full well that He will
never allow anything to happen to you that is harmful. 'All
things work together for good to them that love God.' Not a hair
of your head shall be harmed, He loves you with an everlasting
love. I do not suggest that you will be able to understand everything that is happening. You may not have a full explanation
of it; but you will know for certain that God is not unconcerned.
That is impossible. The One who has done the greatest thing of
all for you, must be concerned about you in everything, and
though the clouds are thick and you cannot see His face, you
know He is there. 'Behind a frowning providence He hides a
smiling face.' Now hold on to that. You say that you do not see
His smile. I agree that these earthborn clouds prevent my
seeing Him, but He is there and He will never allow anything
finally harmful to take place. Nothing can happen to you but
what He allows, I do not care what it may be, some great disappointment, perhaps, or it may be an illness, it may be a
tragedy of some sort, I do not know what it is, but you can be
certain of this, that God permits that thing to happen to you
because it is ultimately for your good. 'Now no chastening for
the present seemeth to be joyous, but grievous; nevertheless
afterward it yieldeth the peaceable fruit of righteousness . . .'
(Hebrews 12. 11).

That is the way faith works. But you and I have to exercise it.
It does not come into operation automatically. You have to
focus your faith on to events and say: 'All right, but I know this
about God, and because that is true I am going to apply it to
this situation. This, therefore, cannot be what I think it is, it
must have some other explanation'. And you end by seeing that

it is God's gracious purpose for you, and having applied your faith, you then hold on. You just refuse to be moved. The enemy will come and attack you, the water will seem to be pouring into the boat, but you say: 'It is all right, let the worst come to the worst'. You stand on your faith. You say to yourself: 'I believe this, I am resting on this, I am certain of this and though I do not understand what is happening to me I am holding on to this!'

That brings me to my final word, which is my third principle —the value of even the weakest or smallest faith. We have looked at the trial of faith, we have looked at the nature of faith, let me say a closing word on the value of even the weakest and smallest faith. However poor and small and however incomplete the faith of these disciples was on this occasion, they at any rate had a sufficient amount of faith to make them do the right thing in the end. They went to Him. Having been agitated and distressed and alarmed and exhausted, they went to Him. They still had some kind of feeling that He could do something about it, and so they woke Him and said: 'Master, are you not going to do something about it?' That is very poor faith you may say, very weak faith, but it is faith, thank God. And even faith 'like a grain of mustard seed' is valuable because it takes us to Him. And when you do go to Him this is what you will find. He will be disappointed with you and He will not conceal that. He will rebuke you, He will say: 'Why did you not reason it out, why did you not apply your faith, why do you appear agitated before that worldly person, why do you behave as if you were not a Christian at all, why didn't you apply your faith as you should have done? I would have been so pleased if I could have watched you standing like a man in the midst of the hurricane or storm— O why didn't you?' He will let us know that He is disappointed in us and He will rebuke us; but, blessed be His Name, He will nevertheless still receive us. He does not drive us away. He did not drive these disciples away, He received them and He will receive us. Yes, and He will not only receive us, He will bless us and He will give us peace. 'He rebuked the wind and the sea and there was a great calm.' He produced the condition they were so anxious to enjoy, in spite of their lack of faith. Such is the gracious Lord that you and I believe in and follow. Though He is disappointed in us often and though He rebukes us, He will never neglect us; He will receive us, He will bless us, He will give us peace, indeed He will do for us what He did for these men. With this peace He gave them a still greater conception of Himself than they had had before. They marvelled, and were full of amazement at His wonderful power. He, as it were, threw that into the bargain on top of all the blessings.

If you find yourself in this position of trial and trouble and testing, take it as a wonderful opportunity of proving your faith, of showing your faith, of manifesting your faith and bringing glory to His great and Holy Name. But if you should fail to do that, if you should apparently be too weak to apply your faith, if you are being so besieged and attacked by the devil and by hell and by the world, well, then, I say, just fly to Him at once and He will receive you and will bless you, He will give you deliverance, He will give you peace. But remember always that faith is an activity, it is something that has to be applied. 'Where is your faith?' Let us make certain that it is always at the place and at the point of need and of testing.

And straightway Jesus constrained His disciples to get into a ship, and to go before Him unto the other side, while He sent the multitudes away. And when He had sent the multitudes away, He went up into a mountain apart to pray: and when the evening was come, He was there alone. But the ship was now in the midst of the sea, tossed with waves: for the wind was contrary. And in the fourth watch of the night Jesus went unto them, walking on the sea. And when the disciples saw him walking on the sea, they were troubled saying, It is a spirit; and they cried out for fear. But straightway Jesus spake unto them, saying, Be of good cheer; it is I; be not afraid. And Peter answered Him and said, Lord, if it be Thou, bid me come unto Thee on the water. And He said, Come. And when Peter was come down out of the ship, he walked on the water, to go to Jesus. But when he saw the wind boisterous, he was afraid; and beginning to sink, he cried, saying, Lord, save me. And immediately Jesus stretched forth His hand, and caught him, and said unto him, O thou of little faith, wherefore didst thou doubt? And when they were come into the ship, the wind ceased. Then they that were in the ship came and worshipped Him, saying, Of a truth thou art the Son of God.

Matthew 14. 22-33

XI

LOOKING AT THE WAVES

THIS incident which we are going to consider next has many features in common with that in our last study in the eighth chapter of the Gospel according to St. Luke, the main point being that this incident, exactly like the other, concentrates attention on the nature and the character of faith and the importance of our having a right view of it. But, of course, it does so in a slightly different manner. There, the major trouble we saw to be the failure to realize that faith is an activity, something that must be applied. 'Where is your faith?' The disciples had it, but they were not focusing it upon their particular problem. Here, as we shall see, while in general we are still considering the question of the true character of faith, it is from a somewhat different aspect.

However, we cannot come to our main consideration, important as it is, without noticing one preliminary matter which is absolutely vital and essential. Again as in the incident of the storm at sea, the first thing we notice here is the Person, the personality if you like, of our Blessed Lord. Here, once more, He stands out in all the fulness of His Godhead and of His unique deity. We see Him, Himself, walking upon the waves, though they were stormy and turbulent, and we see Him likewise enabling His servant, the apostle, to do the same. We again see Him commanding and controlling the elements. We are bound to start with this, because we cannot begin to consider the question of faith nor can we have a true understanding of faith if we are not clear about Him. We are not talking about any sort of faith, we are talking about the Christian faith, and the essential preliminary to any consideration of that is to be clear about the Person of our Blessed Lord. There is no Christian message apart from that which starts by saying that Jesus of Nazareth is the only begotten Son of God, that He is the Lord of Glory, the Lord Jesus Christ; and here you see Him standing out in this effulgence of His glory, the Master of the Universe, the Lord of the elements. He manifests it, He demonstrates it. We start with that because the whole purpose of these Gospels is to portray Him. It is also absolutely vital in any consideration of our subject to·demonstrate that it is a failure in some shape or form to realize what He is that accounts for all our troubles.

However, it is equally clear that the special object of recording this incident is to call attention to this thing which happened to Peter. We see our Lord everywhere in the Gospels in His glory and in His deity, but each separate incident brings out something peculiar, something special of its own; and clearly the special thing here is the incident as it affects particularly the Apostle Peter.

Peter starts off so well, so magnificently. Then he gets into trouble and ends up so badly. Now that is the picture—Peter, who at first seems to be full of faith, ends up by being a miserable failure, crying out in desperation. How quickly it all happened! We are told of this particular sea that one of its chief characteristics is that storms come down upon it suddenly. It may be calm at one moment and the next moment there is a raging storm. That happened to the sea on this occasion, and it also happened to Peter—that sudden change in the whole position.

Now as I understand this incident, the vital thing is to observe closely what happened, and the point that must be emphasized is this, that the big difference between the miracle of stilling the storm and this present incident, is that there, the storm came in as a fresh factor to upset the disciples—there our Lord fell asleep and then the storm came—but here in this incident, as it concerns Peter, that is not the case at all. There is nothing new, there is nothing fresh. The storm had already started and was raging before our Lord came anywhere near the disciples or near the boat. The ship, we are told, was in the midst of the sea, tossed with the waves, and our Lord was praying, alone on the mountainside. That is the point we must stress—that here the disciples are in the boat without our Lord and the storm is raging, then He suddenly appears and this incident takes place. The thing to remember is that Peter had no new factor to contend with after he stepped out of the boat. It was not that he stepped out on to smooth water and that then the storm came; the storm was there before the Lord appeared near the boat at all. That is a very important point as I understand it. There was no new factor as there was on the other occasion, and yet Peter got into trouble and became unhappy and frightened and desperate. The question is: Why? And the answer is that the trouble was entirely in Peter. Our Lord gives us a precise diagnosis—it was little faith. 'O thou of little faith wherefore didst thou doubt?' It is little faith leading to the entry of doubt. Here, then, it seems to me there are a number of important lessons which we can learn, and, if we but learn them, and grasp them, they will save us from many an attack of spiritual depression.

First and foremost I must call attention to what I am constrained to describe as the Peter mentality, or if you prefer it, the Peter temperament. Many times we have had to emphasize the fact that when we are converted and saved and become Christian our temperaments do not change; they remain exactly what they were. You do not become somebody else, you are still yourself. We may all say: 'I live; yet not I, but Christ liveth in me', and while we go on to add, 'and the life which I now live in the flesh I live by the faith of the Son of God', yet that 'I' is always the same. You are always yourself, and, though you become Christian, you are still yourself. You have your own peculiar temperament, your own peculiar characteristics, and the result is that we all have our special problems. There are certain problems that are fundamental and common to us all, and even our particular problem comes under the general category of sin and the results of the Fall, but it comes to us in different ways, in several ways. We are all familiar with this fact. All members of the Church are not the same, all members of any group, however small, are not the same; we all have certain things about which we have to be particularly and exceptionally careful. Other people are not troubled by these things at all. Ah, yes, but they have other things about which they have to be careful. The hot-tempered person has to watch that temper very closely, and equally the phlegmatic and lethargic person has to be careful, because he is so flabby in his whole mentality that he tends not to stand when he should stand. In other words, we all have our particular difficulties and they generally arise from our own peculiar temperament which God has given us. I can indeed go further in this context and say that probably the thing we have to watch most of all is our strength, our strong point. We all tend to fail ultimately at our strongest point.

Now I believe that was very true of Peter. Peter's great characteristic was his energy, his capacity for quick decision, his active personality. He was enthusiastic and impulsive, and that was the thing that was constantly leading him into trouble. It is a very good thing to have an energetic nature. Some of the greatest men the world has ever known, if I understand them rightly as I read their biographies, are to be explained mainly by their energy, not by their intellectual capacity, not by their wisdom, but by their sheer energy. Notice this as you read the lives of many of the so-called great men. Energy is a great quality and the thing that generally comes with it is a capacity for decision. But this was the thing that was constantly bringing Peter into trouble. It often leads to an unsteady Christian life, a Christian life that lacks balance. What a perfect illustration we have of it here. Look at Peter as he recognizes the Lord at the beginning of this incident. There he is in the boat in the midst of a storm. He has sufficient faith to say to our Lord: 'If it be Thou, bid me come unto Thee on the water', and out he steps. How magnificent! Yes, but just look at him a few moments later, and there he is crying out in fear. Now that was always characteristic of Peter. When our Lord was talking about His death and how He was going to be forsaken, Peter does not hesitate to say: 'Though all men shall be offended because of Thee, yet will I never be offended'; and in no time at all he is denying with oaths and curses that he ever knew Him! Now that is what I call the Peter mentality —unsteady, the kind of person who is either on top of the mountain or down in the deepest depths, either full of enthusiasm and excitement and making us all feel that we are doing nothing at all, or utterly despondent and threatening to go out of the Christian life altogether. You know the type.

What is this due to, what is the cause of this alternation between ecstasy and miserable failure? The answer is that it is due to temperament. The trouble with this kind of person is that he tends to act without thinking; his faith has not been based upon sufficient thought. The difficulty with him is that he does not think things right through, he does not work them right out. Now that was the trouble with Peter. In the Gospels he is always the first man to volunteer. Take for example that incident in the twenty-first chapter of John. The disciples had been out fishing all night and had caught nothing and then our Lord appears on the seashore. At John's words 'It is the Lord', Peter girds his fisher's coat about him and jumps into the sea to go to Him. He is the first always, always first in everything, and that was his trouble. You have indeed a perfect illustration of it even after

Pentecost, in the second chapter of the Epistle to the Galatians. He was still the same impulsive man and Paul had to rebuke him over the fact that he did not work out the question of justification by faith only, as he should have done. He had no excuse, because he was the first man to admit the Gentiles into the Christian Church. You remember the Cornelius incident. As you read the account in the tenth chapter of Acts you will see Peter rising to a magnificent height. It was a tremendous thing for a Jew to bring a Gentile into the Christian Church. But he went back on that at Antioch and when those messengers came down from James, he dissembled, and Paul had to withstand him to the face. What was the matter with Peter? It was the old trouble, he accepted a position without working out all its implications. Now that is invariably the trouble with this type — this energy, this capacity for decision, this impulsiveness tends to make them do things intuitively instead of thinking them right through and understanding and grasping them; and the result is that there are these violent alternations in their spiritual life; now this is a very common cause of spiritual depression and that is why we are dealing with it.

That brings me to the second point which I want to emphasize, and that is the teaching of this incident concerning doubts: 'O thou of little faith, wherefore didst thou doubt?' This is important teaching—thank God for it. The first thing we learn here is that we ourselves sometimes produce our own doubts. None can dispute but that that was the trouble with Peter at this point. He produced his own doubts by looking at the waves. He led himself into difficulties which need not have arisen. It was not as though our Lord had said to Peter: 'Peter, be careful! Do you realize what you are doing?' No, not a word was said by anybody; Peter by looking at the waves himself produced the doubts. Let us be very careful here. We often lead ourselves into depression, we lead ourselves into doubts by dabbling with certain things which should be avoided. I am referring to certain types of literature, or to the folly of venturing into certain arguments which will take us beyond our depth. How important this is. There are people who are foolish enough to enter into an argument about science, though they know little or nothing about it. Instead of refusing to do so because they do not know enough, they have plunged in, and I have known people who have been shaken in their faith through doing so. In other words they should stand on the truth as they know it and not attempt to deal with scientific questions with which they are not competent to deal. We thus sometimes lead ourselves into doubts, and we must always be careful not to do so.

The second thing—and this is a thing for which I thank God — is that doubts are not incompatible with faith. I have many times in my pastoral experience found people who have been made very unhappy because they have not grasped that principle. Some people seem to think that once you become a Christian you should never be assailed by doubts. But that is not so, Peter still had faith. Our Lord said to him: 'O thou of little faith'. He did not say: 'Peter, because you have doubts you have no faith at all'. That is what many people ignorantly think and say, and it is very wrong. Though you have faith, you may still be troubled by doubts and there are examples of this not only in Scripture but also in the subsequent history of the Christian Church. Indeed, I would go as far as to say, at the risk of being misunderstood, that if anyone has never been troubled by doubts in his or her Christian life, such a person would do well to examine the foundations again and make certain that they are not enjoying a false peace or resting in what I would call a presumptuous believism. Read the lives of some of the greatest saints that ever trod this earth and you will find they have been assailed by doubts. Our Lord here surely gives the final word on this — doubts are not incompatible with faith. You may have doubts and still have faith, a weak faith.

To put it another way, and this would be my next principle, if doubts again control us, it is an indication of a weak faith. That was what happened to Peter. His faith had not gone, but because it was weak, doubt mastered him and overwhelmed him and he was shaken. If you had asked Peter certain questions at the very moment when he was in that state of terror and alarm, he would have given orthodox answers every time. If you had questioned him as to the Person of the Lord, I am certain he would have given you the right answer, but for the time being these doubts mastered him. His faith was still there, but, according to the teaching of our Lord here, whenever our doubts do master us, it is indicative of the fact that ours is a weak faith. We should never allow this to happen. Doubts will attack us, but that does not mean that we are to allow them to master us. We must never allow that.

How do we avoid it? The antidote is —great faith. It is little faith that allows men to be mastered by doubts, the antidote must, therefore, be a great faith, a big faith. That is the thing that is emphasized here above everything else. What are the characteristics of this great faith? The first is this—it is a knowledge of the Lord Jesus Christ and His power, with a steady trust and confidence in that. Now Peter, as we have already seen, starts off well and that is of the essence of true faith. Here was a man with the other disciples in the boat and with the storm raging round them. The sea and the wind were contrary and the boat was being tossed by the waves, and the position was becoming rather desperate. But suddenly our Lord appeared and when they saw Him they said: 'Is that a man walking on the water? It is impossible—it must be some kind of a ghost, it is a spirit'. They cried out for fear, and straightway Jesus spoke and said: 'It is I, be not afraid'. And then we have this magnificent exhibition of the essence of true faith by Peter. Peter answered Him, and said: 'Lord, if it be Thou, bid me come unto Thee on the water'. Now that is an indication of true faith for you see what it means; it means that Peter was saying in effect to our Lord: 'If you really are the Lord, well, then, I know there is nothing impossible to you. Give proof of it by commanding me to step out of this boat in this raging sea and enabling me to walk on it'. He believed in the Lord, in His power, in His person, in His ability. And he did not believe in it merely theoretically. He tried it! We are told here: 'And when Peter was come down out of the ship, he walked on the water.' Now that is the essence of faith—'Lord, if it be Thou. . . .' That is what faith says: 'If it is indeed You, well then I know You can do this: command me to do it'. And he did it. Here again is the great principle that we must always take hold of very firmly. The Christian faith begins and ends with a knowledge of the Lord. It begins with a knowledge of the Lord— not a feeling, not an act of will, but a knowledge of this Blessed Person. There is no value in any feeling unless it is based upon this. Christianity is Christ, and Christian faith means believing certain things about Him and knowing Him, knowing that He is the Lord of Glory come down amongst us, knowing something about the Incarnation and the Virgin Birth, knowing why He came, knowing what He did when He came, knowing something about His atoning work, knowing that He came, as He said Himself, not to call the righteous, but sinners to repentance, knowing that He says: 'They that are whole need not a physician but they that are sick', knowing that 'His own self bare our sins in His own body on the tree, that we, being dead to sins, should live unto righteousness; by whose stripes ye were healed'.

I find almost invariably when people come to me in a state of spiritual depression, that they are depressed because they do not know these things as they should. They say: 'I am such a miserable sinner, you do not know what I have been or what I have done'. Why do they say that to me? They do so because they have never understood what He meant when He said: 'I came not to call the righteous, but sinners to repentance'. The very thing they are saying in self-condemnation is the very thing that gives them the right to come to Him and to be certain that He will receive them. Where there is a failure to learn and believe these things, faith is weak. So strong faith means to know them. I am constantly having to say these things, I am constantly having to write them. I had to write a long letter on this very point to a man I had never seen. The poor man was miserable and held in bondage. Why? Because he did not see that Christ is the Friend of publicans and sinners and that He came to die for such people. He was not clear about the Person, he was not clear about the work of this Blessed Person. His faith was weak and the doubts were there because of that. There are many who go through life miserable and unhappy because they do not truly understand these things. If only they did understand them they would find that their self-condemnation in itself is an earnest of their repentance and the way to their ultimate release.

In other words, the great antidote to spiritual depression is the knowledge of Biblical doctrine, Christian doctrine. Not having the feelings worked up in meetings, but knowing the principles of the faith, knowing and understanding the doctrines. That is the Biblical way, that is Christ's own way as it is also the way of the apostles. The antidote to depression is to have a knowledge of Him, and you get that in His Word. You must take the trouble to learn it. It is difficult work, but you have to study it and give yourself to it. The tragedy of the hour, it seems to me, is that people are far too dependent for their happiness upon meetings. This has been the trouble for many years in the Christian Church, and that is why so many are miserable. Their knowledge of the Truth is defective. That, you remember, is what our Lord said to certain people who had suddenly believed on Him. He said:

'If ye continue in My word then are ye My disciples indeed. And ye shall know the truth and the truth shall make you free' (John 8. 31, 32). Free from doubts or fears, free from depression, free from things that get you down. It is the truth that frees—the truth about Him, in His Person, in His work, in His offices, Christ as He is.

Let us hurry to the second thing. Having started with that first thing as Peter so rightly started with it, do not forget the second as Peter unfortunately did. This is to refuse after-thoughts. 'Ah, but', you say, 'it is a good thing to think again.' Not with this Christian faith; it is folly. Doubts are very foolish, and it is good for us to see how foolish and ridiculous they are. So the next time we are tempted let us remember this man Peter, who should never have looked at the waves at all. Why not? For this reason, that he had already settled that question before he went out of the boat! Now you see why, earlier on, I emphasized the important detail that the storm was raging before the Lord ever came near the boat. It would have been entirely different if Peter had stepped out on to a calm sea and the storm had then come. Then there would have been some excuse for Peter. But it was not so, for Peter, when he said to our Lord: 'If it be Thou, bid me come to Thee on the water', had really dealt with the question of the waves. He had been struggling with them in the boat for some time already. He knew the boat was tossing, and so, when he made that statement to our Lord it means that he said to Him: I don't care what the sea is doing. He had got above it, he had solved that problem, and so he had gone out of the boat and was walking on the sea. There was nothing new about the waves, there was no new factor. He was not confronted by any sort of new problem. The Lord Jesus Christ was actually enabling him to walk on the turbulent waves. Well, why then look at them? What reason was there for doing so? None at all. It was ridiculous, it was foolish.

That is always the trouble with weak faith, it comes back again to questions which it has already solved and answered. If you have ever believed on the Lord Jesus Christ, you must, in some shape or form, have met with and dealt with the difficulties or you would not have arrived at faith. Well, why go back? It is sheer folly. Not only is it a matter of unbelief, it is a question of conduct and behaviour. Why sit down and face troubles again that you have already met and solved before you stepped out of the boat? I would repeat that this negative aspect of faith is very important. Having believed on Him you must shut the door to certain things and refuse to look at them. If you have dealt with them already, do not go back over them. How often have I had to say that in these studies! How often is our trouble due to the fact that we will go back. Peter should never have looked at those waves. There was no excuse for him, there was nothing new for him to consider. It is of the essence of faith to refuse after-thoughts. Reject them, have nothing to do with them. Say to them, 'I have already dealt with you!'

That brings me to the next principle. The next characteristic of faith is that it persists steadily in looking to Him and at Him. Let me divide it up in this way by giving you two or three simple principles. Faith says: 'What He has begun to do He can continue to do. The beginning of the work was a miracle, so if He can initiate a miraculous work He can keep it going; what He has already begun He can continue'. 'Being confident of this very thing,' says Paul, 'that He which hath begun a good work in you will perform it until the day of Jesus Christ' (Philippians 1. 6). Yes, says Toplady,

'The work which His goodness began
The arm of His strength will complete'.

That is an unanswerable argument.

Secondly, you and I can never doubt while we look at Him and are clear about Him. Without Him we are utterly hopeless. It does not matter how long you have been in the Christian life, you are dependent upon Him for every step. Without Him we can do nothing. We can only conquer our doubts by looking steadily at Him and by not looking at them. The way to answer them is to look at Him. The more you know Him and His glory the more ridiculous they will become. So keep steadily looking at Him. You cannot live on an initial faith—that is what Peter seems to have been trying to do. He started off with great faith and then instead of going on with faith he tries to live on it. You cannot live on an initial faith. Do not try to live on your conversion. You will be done before you know where you are. You cannot live on one climactic experience, you must keep on looking to Him every day. 'We walk by faith' and you live by faith in the Lord Jesus Christ. You need Him as much on your death-bed as you did on the night you were converted; you need

Him all the time. The Bible is full of examples of this. One of the most perfect illustrations is the way the Children of Israel had to collect the manna each day but the sabbath. That is the Lord's method. He does not give us enough for a month. We need a fresh supply every day, so start your day with Him and keep in touch with Him. That was Peter's fatal error; he looked away from Him. It is 'the fight of faith', you are walking on turbulent waves and the only way to keep walking is to keep looking at Him.

May I say a final word of consolation? It is all in this one incident, and it is that He will never let you sink. Peter cried out in terror and alarm, 'Lord,' he said, 'save me'. And immediately Jesus stretched forth His hand and caught him and said unto him: 'O thou of little faith, wherefore didst thou doubt?' 'And when they were come into the ship, the wind ceased.' Thank God for this consolation. He will never let you sink, because you belong to Him. You may fail Him, you may feel you are on the point of going down once and for ever, finally. Never—'no man shall pluck them out of My hands'. 'For I am persuaded', says Paul, 'that neither death, nor life, nor angels, nor principalities, nor powers, nor things present, nor things to come, nor height, nor depth, nor any other creature, shall be able to separate us from the love of God, which is in Christ Jesus our Lord' (Romans 8. 38, 39). Never. When you think you are lost His hand will be there and He will hold you. Just look to Him and say with John Newton:

> 'His love in time past
> Forbids me to think
> He'll leave me at last
> In trouble to sink;
> Each sweet Ebenezer
> I have in review,
> Confirms His good pleasure
> To help me quite through'.

Cry out in your desperation. Do not trade on that—but if you are alarmed cry out, and He will hear you and take you up.

But I do not end with that. I must end by saying that in a sense the great lesson of the whole incident is that He can keep us from falling. We will never need to cry out like that if we only keep on looking at Him. Believing in Him we shall never fall but keep straight on. If Peter had looked at Him he would have gone on walking on the sea, he would never have become distressed.

He is so great, He is the Lord of the Universe, He can not only walk on the sea Himself, He can enable Peter to walk on the sea. Nothing is impossible to Him. 'All things are possible with God', and He is God. So faith looks at Him and says with Charles Wesley:

> 'Faith, mighty faith, the promise sees
> And looks to that alone,
> Laughs at impossibilities
> And cries: It shall be done'.

That is faith. 'Faith, mighty faith, the promise sees (in Him), and looks to that alone', and to nothing else. It laughs at impossibilities—these boisterous waves—and cries: 'It shall be done'. 'Unto Him', therefore, 'that is able to keep you from falling, and to present you faultless before the presence of His glory with exceeding joy, to the only wise God our Saviour be glory and majesty, dominion and power, both now and ever, Amen' (Jude 24 and 25).

For ye have not received the spirit of bondage again to fear; but ye have received the Spirit of adoption, whereby we cry. Abba, Father. The Spirit itself beareth witness with our spirit, that we are the children of God. And if children, then heirs; heirs of God, and joint heirs with Christ; if so be that we suffer with Him, that we may be also glorified together.

Romans 8. 15-17

XII

THE SPIRIT OF BONDAGE

NO greater words than these have ever been written. They stand out even in a great chapter like this as an expression of truth which is quite unique. It is one of the most magnificent statements that is found anywhere in the whole realm and range of the Scriptures, and yet there is nothing more important about a statement like this than that we should realize exactly why it was the Apostle ever made it. The danger with some of these resounding phrases is that we tend to content ourselves with the words, or with some general impression which they make upon us; we enjoy them so much that we do not realize their significance, and therefore we do not truly appropriate to ourselves the teaching which they are meant to convey.

Take this great statement. Why did Paul ever make it, what was the object, what was his reason for doing so? The answer is given in the fifteenth verse: '*For*', says the Apostle, 'ye have not received the spirit of bondage again to fear'. In other words the statement is linked up with something that has gone before, and the Apostle has a very definite object in view in writing these words, and it is that he is anxious to save these Roman Christians from a spirit of discouragement—from a spirit of despondency or depression. They may have been actually suffering from that, but even if they were not at the moment, he is concerned that they never should suffer from it, and his one object is to provide them with an antidote against this depression, this spirit of bondage, this spirit of defeat, this spirit of discouragement that, as we have seen, is always threatening us in the Christian life. The Apostle does not throw out a magnificent statement like this without any context, it is not simply some wonderful truth that is suddenly uttered. It comes—as such statements almost invariably come in the writings of this great Apostle—as he is dealing with some very practical problem. These Epistles which we have in the New Testament are full of doctrine and of theology and yet it would be very wrong to say that the collection of New Testament Epistles is a text book of theology. It is not. The astounding thing is this, and it is important to bear in mind, that these pronouncements and doctrines are always introduced with some practical object in view, with the pastoral element right in the very forefront. These letters are pastoral letters written primarily because the Apostle was concerned to help people to an actual enjoyment and out-living of the Christian faith which they had believed and accepted.

It is very important, therefore, to notice exactly how he came to make this particular statement. What is the cause of the discouragement in this case? It is nothing less than the problem of living the Christian life, the problem, if you like, of dealing with sin. Paul has been dealing with that problem from the beginning of the sixth chapter of this mighty Epistle, and he is still dealing with it here. These people to whom he is writing have been converted and have believed on the Lord Jesus Christ, but now they are up against the problem of living this new life which they have received, in a world that is antagonistic and utterly opposed to them. They have to live it also in the face of certain things that they find within their own nature. It is a fight, it is a battle; there is sin without and within, and here are people who are now concerned about following the Lord Jesus Christ and living their lives as He lived His life in this world. Now it is very often face to face with that particular question and problem that discouragement and depression tend to come in. We have already considered many examples of the various means which the devil in his subtlety uses to discourage us. This again is a very common one, and particularly so with the conscientious type of person, who takes the Christian faith very seriously, the type of person who says, not, 'Now I am converted, all is well', but rather, 'This is a great and glorious life, and I must live it'. We are considering here the peculiar temptation that comes to such people.

What is the essence of this problem? It is that there is a failure on their part to realize certain truths concerning the Christian life, a failure to realize what is possible for us as Christians. It is, ultimately, a failure to understand doctrine, or, if you prefer it, it is, ultimately, another failure in the realm of faith. We have seen a number of things concerning faith; we have seen, for example, that it is to be an activity. Many people forget that and get into trouble, because they fail to realize that they have to apply their faith. Then we have seen that others get into trouble because they do not see that they have to continue and persist with the application of faith, that it is not enough to start well, but that we have to go on and that we cannot relax for a moment. But here the difficulty seems to be that of failing to realize that faith must be appropriated. Here is the Truth set down before us, but if we do not appropriate it, it will not help us. Failure to grasp that is one of the most remarkable things about man as the result of sin. We must all have noticed it. Have you not found yourself reading a passage of Scripture which you have read many times before, and which you thought you knew, and suddenly finding that it becomes alive to you and speaks in a way in which it has never done before? We must all have had this kind of experience many times. How easy it is to read the Scriptures and give a kind of nominal assent to the Truth and yet never to appropriate what it tells us!

I believe that that is the very essence of this particular problem which we are considering now, for it always tends to produce what the Apostle calls 'a spirit of bondage'—'you have not received the spirit of bondage again to fear'. What does he mean by this 'spirit of bondage'? He means the danger of having a 'servant spirit,' a serf-like spirit and attitude. The slave attitude generally arises from the tendency to turn the Christian life and the living of the Christian life into a new law, into a higher law. I am thinking of people who are quite clear about their relationship to the law—the Ten Commandments, or the moral law—as a way of salvation. They have seen clearly that Christ has delivered them from that, and that He alone could do so; they know that their own efforts will never enable them to fulfil the law. They see that Christ has redeemed us from the curse of the law; they are quite clear about their justification. However, they now begin to look positively at the Christian life, and in a very subtle way—quite unconsciously to themselves—they turn it into a new kind of law, with the result that they get into a spirit of bondage and of serfdom. They think of the Christian life as great task which they have to take up and to which now they are to apply themselves. They have read the Sermon on the Mount and realize that it is a portrayal of the Christian life, the life they desire to live. They turn to other teachings of our Lord recorded in the Gospels and they find it there. They then go through the Epistles and see there those detailed injunctions that are given by the apostles and they say: 'That is the Christian life'. And having thus found it they regard it as something which they have to take up and put into practice in their daily life and living. In other words, holiness becomes a great task to them, and they begin to plan and organize their lives and introduce certain disciplines in order to enable them to carry it out. This attitude is seen in a classic manner in the Roman Catholic Church and her teaching, in the whole idea of monasticism, which is nothing but a great exhibition of this very thing. There you have men and women who, having been confronted by the Christian truth, say: 'Obviously, the Christian life is a high and exalted life and if anybody is to live that life successfully it must become a whole time matter'. Going even further they say: 'You cannot do that and continue in business or in some profession or indeed in the world at all. You must segregate yourself from the world, you must go out of it'. And they do. Now that is the extreme form of this idea that holiness, and the cultivation of holiness and the spiritual life, is a whole-time occupation, and that you must devote yourself exclusively to it and have your rules, etc., to enable you to live it.

That, according to the Apostle Paul, is nothing but a spirit of bondage. But I need scarcely say that this is not confined to the Roman Catholics, nor to others who call themselves 'Catholics' —it can be quite common, and is quite common, among evangelical Christians. We can easily impose upon ourselves a new law. Of course we do not call it a law, and if we realized that we were putting ourselves under a law we would not do it; but still there is a tendency to do so. I can prove that by the frequent references which are made to this in the various New Testament Epistles. Take Paul's argument in writing to the Colossians where he has a specific passage dealing with this matter. Listen to him putting it like this at the end of chapter two: 'Let no man therefore judge you in meat, or in drink, or in respect of an holy-day, or of the new moon, or of the sabbath days; Which are a shadow of things to come; but the body is of Christ. Let no man beguile you of your reward in a voluntary humility and worshipping of angels, intruding into those things which he hath not seen, vainly puffed up by his fleshly mind, And not holding the Head, from which all the body by joints and bands having nourishment ministered, and knit together, increaseth with the increase of God. Wherefore if ye be dead with Christ from the rudiments of the world, why, as though living in the world, are ye subject to ordinances. (Touch not; taste not; handle not; Which all are to perish with the using); after the commandments and doctrines of men? Which things have indeed a shew of wisdom in will worship, and humility, and neglecting of the body; not in any honour to the satisfying of the flesh'. Now that gives us an insight into what was happening in the early Church. A kind of monasticism was coming in, in a most insidious manner. It is no longer present among us in that particular form, but the tendency, the temptation, is still there. Again, Paul writing to Timothy has to warn him against exactly the same thing. Listen to him in the First Epistle to Timothy, fourth chapter: 'Now the Spirit speaketh expressly, that in the latter times some shall depart from the faith, giving heed to seducing spirits, and doctrines of devils; speaking lies in hypocrisy, having their conscience seared with a hot iron; Forbidding to marry, and commanding to abstain from meats, which God hath created to be received with thanksgiving of them which believe and know the truth'. That is something, surely, which is quite common still. I remember very well the case of a thoroughly evangelical Christian lady who had ceased to eat meat. She believed that she could demonstrate quite clearly that a Christian should not eat meat for the reason that the animal had first of all to be killed, and that was a violation of the spirit of love. Now, there was a lady who imposed upon herself a law. What was her object? It was, as she thought, to live the Christian life truly. She took Christianity very seriously, she was an evangelical Christian, she was quite clear about justification by faith, but unconsciously she was turning Christian life and living into a new law which she had imposed upon herself. That passage which I have just quoted about seducing spirits that forbid to marry and forbid to eat meats should suffice to show what the Apostle means by this 'spirit of bondage again to fear'.

Let us try to interpret this in terms of certain things which are to be seen in the country at the present time, this tendency to impose new laws on Christian people. Later in this series I hope to come back to deal with this more in detail, but here it is in principle. This 'spirit of bondage' always brings with it and in its train, a spirit of fear. 'God hath not given us a spirit of bondage,' says Paul, in writing to the Galatians, but here he puts it: 'Ye have not received the spirit of bondage again to fear'.

Well, in what sense does this produce a spirit of fear? In the first place, it tends to produce a wrong fear of God. There is a right fear of God, and we neglect and ignore that at our peril; but there is also a wrong fear of God and that is a craven fear, 'a fear that hath torment'. These people, I suggest, tend to develop this kind of wrong fear. They regard God as a task-master, they regard Him as Someone who is constantly watching to discover faults and blemishes in them, and to punish them accordingly. Others think of God only as a stern Law-giver far away in the distance. This is very obviously true of that Catholic tendency to which I have already referred, but it is equally true in every manifestation of this particular trouble—God as Some-one far away in the distance and as the great Law-giver only.

But it is not only a fear of God, it is also a fear of the greatness of the task. Having outlined the task to themselves, they now begin to fear it. That is why they think it can only be lived if one segregates oneself from the world, and that a man cannot possibly be in business, or engaged in any profession and live the Christian life. Thus it becomes a kind of dread and terror; they are afraid of it. That is their attitude towards the Christian life. They have no joy in it because the gigantic nature of the task is something that fills them with a spirit of fear, and they are in trouble about themselves and the possibility of ever really living this life as it should be lived.

Then another way in which this spirit of fear manifests itself is that they tend to be afraid in a wrong way of the power of the devil. Now I have to qualify every one of these statements. There is a right fear of the devil. You will find that mentioned in the Epistle of Jude, you will find it also in the Second Epistle of Peter. There are flippant, spiritually ignorant people, who make jokes about the devil simply because they are utterly ignorant of him and of his power. But, on the other hand, we must not be subject to a craven fear of the devil. These people are, because they are aware of his power. They are spiritually-minded people—this is a peculiar temptation to some of the best people—and they see this mighty power, the power of the devil set against them, and they are afraid.

Then they are equally afraid of the sin which is within them-selves. They spend their time in denouncing themselves and in talking about the blackness and darkness of their own hearts. Again we must keep the balance. The Christian who does not know his own sinfulness and the blackness of his own heart is the merest child in the Christian faith, indeed, unless he has some knowledge of it, I query whether he is in the Christian faith at all. Clearly, according to the Scriptures, people who are not aware of indwelling sin, are either the merest tyros or else are unregenerate. But that is very different from having this spirit of fear, from being in this condition in which they simply live a life of 'scorning delights and living laborious days'. Now this is not so common today. I am tempted to say, alas, that modern Christians are much too healthy. Our peculiar problem is that we are much too healthy and lighthearted. If you go back to the last century, and if you go back to the century before and to the century before that, you will find this other tendency, this tendency to be mourning, and always mourning and never rejoicing at all. Indeed, some of them almost went so far as to say that if you did rejoice there was something wrong with you. Now that again is to be guilty of the spirit of fear because of an acute awareness of the power of indwelling sin.

In other words I can sum it up like this, the spirit of fear which results from the spirit of bondage in this type of Christian is ultimately a fear of themselves and a fear of failure. They say: 'I have come into this Christian life, yes, but the question is, can I live it? It is so marvellous and so wonderful and so exalted. How am I to live such a life, how can I rise to such heights?' And with this consciousness of their own weakness, of the greatness of the task and of the power of the devil, they enter into this spirit of bondage and are held down and troubled, worried and full of fears.

It is to people in that condition that the Apostle turns and says: 'Ye have not received the spirit of bondage again to fear', as if to say, 'You were in this spirit of bondage and fear but you have been brought out of it—why go back to it?' What is the antidote to this condition? The Apostle gives an outline in this magnificent statement. What is the answer? It is that we must realize the truth concerning the doctrine of the Holy Spirit and the indwelling of the Holy Spirit in the Christian.

That is the message, and that, according to the Apostle, works out in two ways. The first is that as I confront this mighty, glorious task of denying myself and taking up the cross and following the Lord Jesus Christ I realize that I am to walk through this world as He walked. As I realize that I have been born again and fashioned by God according to the image of His dear Son, and as I begin to ask: 'Who am I ever to live so? How can I ever hope to do that?'—here is the answer, the doctrine of the Holy Spirit, the truth that the Holy Spirit dwells within us. What does it teach? It first of all reminds me of the power of the Holy Spirit that is within me. The Apostle has already said that in verse 13 where he deals with the question of how to stop living after the flesh—'If ye live after the flesh ye shall die: but if ye through the Spirit do mortify the deeds of the body, ye shall live'. Here he comes back to that same teaching. 'For God hath not given us the spirit of fear'. 'You must realize that you are not living by yourselves—he says in effect to these Romans—'You have been thinking of this task of yours as if you alone, by yourself, had to live the great Christian life. You realize that you are forgiven, and you can thank God that your sins are blotted out and washed away, but you seem to think that that is all and that you are left to live the Christian life on your own. If you think like that,' says Paul, 'it is not surprising that you are in a spirit of fear and bondage, for the whole thing is entirely hopeless. It means that you just have a new law which is infinitely more difficult than the old law. But that is not the position, for the Holy Spirit dwells within you'.

In reality he has been dealing with that right through this eighth chapter. Take what he says in the third verse for instance: 'For what the law could not do, in that it was weak through the flesh, God sending His own Son in the likeness of sinful flesh and for sin, condemned sin in the flesh'. What does he mean by 'what the law could not do in that it was weak through the flesh'? He means that the law could not save anybody, the law could not enable anybody to live the Christian life, for the reason that the law is weak, because of the weakness of my flesh. 'What the law could not do in that it was weak through the flesh.' There is no flesh in the law, you obviously cannot talk about the weakness of the flesh of the law. What it means is, that the law was given, but that man in and of himself is asked to keep it. The weakness of the flesh is in the man, not in the law. The law is not weak, it is the man who has to carry it out who is weak. I heard an old preacher put that very well. He gave us a picture of a man digging a garden with a spade and as he kept on digging, the handle of the spade kept on breaking. He pointed out that there was nothing wrong with the spade as such, it was all right, but the handle was too weak. The actual spade itself was strong and made of iron, the failure was in the handle which was made of wood and therefore weak. That is the picture and is it not equally true that if we impose upon ourselves in this Christian life a new law which you and I have to keep in our own strength, we are doomed to failure? But we must not do that, because the Spirit now dwells in us. 'Ye are not in the flesh but in the Spirit.'

Observe how that is worked out from verse 5 to verse 14. The essential difference between the natural man and the Christian is that the latter has the Spirit of Christ in him. Whatever experiences a man has had if he has not the Spirit of Christ he is not a Christian—'But ye are not in the flesh, but in the Spirit, if so be that the Spirit of God dwell in you. Now if any man have not the Spirit of Christ, he is none of His'.

Here he comes back to that same argument. He says: 'You need not be in that spirit of bondage'. Why not? Because the Holy Spirit is in you and He will empower you and strengthen you. Paul is always repeating that message. Listen to him again in Philippians 2 verse 13: 'It is God which worketh in you both to will and to do of His good pleasure'. 'Work out your own salvation'. How? 'With fear and trembling.' Today we are much too healthy. 'Work out your own salvation with fear and trembling.' People do not fear at the point of conversion and they do not fear afterwards; they do not know the meaning of trembling —'Work out your own salvation with fear and trembling for it is God that worketh in you both to will and to do of His good pleasure'. That is the Spirit again. This is the way to get rid of the spirit of bondage and that false spirit of fear. We are to realize that the Spirit of God is in us. We must look to Him, we must seek His aid, we must rely upon Him. That does not mean that we are to be passive. It means we believe, that as we are wrestling, He is empowering us. We would not even have bothered to exert ourselves unless He had prompted us to do so. He works in us and we work it out, and as we realize this, the task is not impossible. Paul in the parallel passage in the fourth chapter of Galatians says: 'God hath sent forth the Spirit of His Son into our hearts'—the Spirit of His own Son. Do we realize that as Christians we have within us the self-same Holy Spirit that was in the Son of God when He was here on earth? The Father gives the Spirit and it is the same Spirit that was in the Son that is given to us. The Spirit that enabled Him will enable us. That is his argument.

Let me hurry to the second principle—the presence of the Holy Spirit in us reminds us of our relationship to God. This is a wonderful thing. 'Ye have not received the spirit of bondage again to fear; but ye have received the spirit of adoption, whereby we cry, Abba, Father.' The presence of the Holy Spirit within us reminds us of our sonship, yes, our adult sonship. We are not infants, the very term means that we are grown sons and have reached full age. We are sons in the fullest sense and in the possession of all our faculties. The clear realization of this gets rid of the spirit of bondage again to fear. It does not do away with 'reverence and godly fear', but it does away with the fear that the spirit of bondage brings.

How does it do so? Well, it enables us to see that our object in living the Christian life is not simply to attain a certain standard, but is rather to please God because He is our Father—'the spirit of adoption whereby we cry, Abba, Father'. The slave was not allowed to say 'Abba' and that slave spirit does not regard God as Father. He has not realized that He is Father, he regards Him still as a Judge who condemns. But that is wrong. As Christian people we must learn to appropriate by faith the fact that God is our Father. Christ taught us to pray 'Our Father'. This eternal everlasting God has become our Father and the moment we realize that, everything tends to change. He is our Father and He is always caring for us, He loves us with an everlasting love, He so loved us that He sent His only begotten Son into this world and to the Cross to die for our sins. That is our relationship to God and the moment we realize it, it transforms everything. Henceforth my desire is not to keep the law but to please my Father. We know something about that by nature. Filial love, filial reverence, filial fear is so different from that old servile fear. It is based upon the desire to please our father, and the moment we grasp that we lose the spirit of bondage. Our Christian living is not a matter of rules and regulations any longer, but rather our desire to show Him our gratitude for all He has ever done for us.

That, however, does not exhaust the matter. 'The Spirit itself beareth witness with our spirit, that we are the children of God: And if children, then heirs; heirs of God, and joint-heirs with Christ.' You see the argument, the inevitable logic. If we are children of God, we must be related to the Lord Jesus Christ. He is 'the first born of many brethren' and we are related to God as children and heirs. Have you ever noticed the amazing thing which John says in chapter 17, verse 23?—Listen to our Lord as He prays to the Father—'I in them, and Thou in Me, that they may be made perfect in one; and that the world may know that Thou hast sent Me, and hast loved them, as Thou hast loved Me'. Our Lord says there that God the Father loves us as He loved Him, the only begotten Son. So we begin to realize this, that we are now sons of God, children of God. We have this new dignity, this new standing, this new status, this glorious position in which we find ourselves. Go back again to that High Priestly prayer and notice how our Lord says that we are to glorify Him in this world exactly as He glorified His Father. Have you realized that? That is the Christian life, that is the reason for living the Christian life; it is to realize that I belong to God and that I must glorify Him. That is how I am to look at it. What a wonderful position. And the Spirit is in me and is enabling me to do it. He transforms my outlook and I lose the spirit of bondage again to fear.

Again I realize it in this way, I realize that the Holy Spirit is dwelling within me. That is Paul's argument in the sixth chapter of the First Epistle to the Corinthians: 'Know ye not that your body is the temple of the Holy Ghost?' That is the way to overcome the sins of the flesh. Constantly I find myself having to ask people this question—they come to me about some problem or difficulty and they say: 'I have been praying about this', and I say: 'My friend, do you realize that your body is the temple of the Holy Ghost?' That is the answer. I say it again at the risk of being misunderstood, but such friends in a way need to pray less and to think more. They must remind themselves that their bodies are 'the temples of the Holy Ghost which dwelleth in us'. Prayer is always essential, but thought is essential, too, because prayer can be just an escape mechanism, almost at times a cry in the dark by people who are desperate and defeated. Prayer must be intelligent, and it is only to those who realize that their bodies are the temples of the Holy Ghost that the answer will be given and the power will come.

Then, finally, of course, the Holy Spirit within us reminds us of our destiny. 'If children, then heirs; heirs of God, and joint heirs with Christ.' That is the way to look at the Christian life. Paul constantly uses this argument and frequently ends up by saying what he says so gloriously in the last two verses of Romans 8. The Christian is absolutely certain of his destiny, he is persuaded beyond any doubt that 'neither death, nor life, nor angels, nor principalities, nor powers, nor things present, nor things to come, nor height, nor death, nor any other creature, shall be able to separate us from the love of God which is in Christ Jesus our Lord.' It is not a question of keeping to a standard, it is not a question of vainly striving to do something; it is a question of getting ready for the place to which you are going. The way to get rid of the spirit of bondage and fear, is to know that if you are a child of God, you are destined for heaven and for glory, and that all the things you see inside yourself and outside yourself cannot prevent that plan from being carried out. So the Christian life is a matter of preparing for that. 'This is the victory that overcometh the world, even our faith.' Faith in what? Faith in my ultimate destiny. Or take it as John puts it in his First Epistle and third chapter, verse 2: 'Beloved, now are we the sons of God, and it doth not yet appear what we shall be: but we know that, when He shall appear, we shall be like Him; for we shall see Him as He is'. What does that lead to? It leads to what we read in the next verse: 'Every man that hath this hope in him, purifieth himself even as He is pure'. There is nothing that is so calculated to promote holiness as the realization that we are heirs of God and joint heirs with Christ, that our destiny is certain and secure, that nothing can prevent it. Realizing that, we purify ourselves even as He is pure, and we feel that there is no time to waste. That is the Apostle's argument in these three verses and it is all practical. That is the way to live the Christian life! Do not turn it into a law, but realize that you have received the Holy Spirit. Then work out this theme. Your Father is watching over you. He is looking after you—yes, let me use scriptural language—He is jealous concerning you because you belong to Him. You belong to Christ, you are His brother. The Holy Spirit is dwelling in your very body and you are destined for glory. Well, then, what of it? As you contemplate such a destiny say:

> 'Take my soul thy full salvation,
> Rise o'er sin and fear and care,
> Joy to find in every station,
> Something still to do or bear.
> Think what Spirit dwells within thee,
> What a Father's smile is thine,
> What a Saviour died to win thee,
> Child of Heaven, should'st thou repine?'

How wrong it is to be in a spirit of bondage and of fear. 'Child of Heaven, should'st thou repine?' Never! 'Think what Spirit dwells within thee, what a Father's smile is thine, what a Saviour died to win thee, Child of Heaven, should'st thou repine?' That verse of that hymn is a good exposition of these three verses. Lay hold of it, appropriate it, practise it. Do not worry about what you feel. The truth about you is glorious. If you are in Christ, rise to it 'o'er sin and fear and care'. Take your full salvation and triumph and prevail.

Where is then the blessedness ye spake of? for I bear you record, that, if it had been possible, ye would have plucked out your own eyes, and have given them to me.

Galatians 4. 15

XIII

FALSE TEACHING

I CALL your attention to that question addressed by the Apostle to the members of the churches in Galatia in order that we may consider together another cause of spiritual depression, or unhappiness in the Christian life. The whole of the Epistle to the Galatians really deals with this one question. These Galatians had listened to the preaching of the gospel by the Apostle Paul. They had been typical Gentile pagans. They were outside God, they had no knowledge whatsoever of Him or of His Son, or of the great Christian salvation, but the Apostle Paul had come and preached to them and they had received the message of the gospel with great joy. He describes, even in detail, their joy when they had first met him, and when he had first preached to them. It is quite clear that the Apostle, when he was among them, was not well physically. There can be very little doubt but that he was suffering from some sort of eye trouble, because he reminds them that when he was with them they would have plucked out their own eyes and given them to him if that could have helped him. One gathers that this painful inflammatory condition of his eyes was offensive and unpleasant to look at. There was nothing pre-possessing about the appearance of the Apostle. As he reminds the church at Corinth his presence was 'weak'. He did not have, what is called today, a commanding presence. He was a very ordinary man to look at without the additional disfiguration caused by this eye trouble. But, as he reminds them here, they were not offended in him in any way. He says 'my temptation which was in my flesh ye despised not', indeed they had received him 'as an angel of God, even as Christ Jesus', and they had rejoiced in this wonderful salvation. But they were no longer like that, they had become unhappy and he is constrained to ask them, 'Where is then the blessedness ye spake of'. They had become unhappy in themselves and they had almost turned against the Apostle. Their condition was one which was so depressed that he could even use this kind of language: 'My little children of whom I travail in birth again until Christ be formed in you'.

Now the question which he puts to them about their former blessedness is most striking. Indeed he has been putting it in other forms in the earlier parts of his letter to them. In the sixth verse of the first chapter he says: 'I marvel that ye are so soon removed from him that called you into the grace of Christ unto another gospel'. Then he puts it again in the third chapter and the first verse: 'O foolish Galatians, who hath bewitched you, that ye should not obey the truth, before whose eyes Jesus Christ hath been evidently set forth, crucified among you?' Now without adducing further evidence I think it is clear that these Galatian Christians who had been so happy, so rejoicing in their new found salvation, had now become spiritually unhappy and depressed.

The question confronting us is this: What was the cause of this change? What had happened to them? And the answer is perfectly simple, and can be put in one phrase—it was all entirely due to false teaching. That was the trouble with the churches in Galatia; all their problems emanated from a certain false teaching which they had believed. Now this is something which is dealt with very frequently in the New Testament. There is scarcely an Epistle where you will not find this matter dealt with somewhere. These infant churches had been much troubled by certain types of teachers who followed the Apostle Paul and imitated his message and preaching in many respects, but added to it their own particular teaching. The result was that it not only caused confusion in the churches but, further, led to this depressed and unhappy condition in the lives of so many Christian people. This was, of course, the work of the devil. The Apostle does not hesitate to say so, and reminds us the devil can even 'transform himself into an angel of light'. He attacks Christian people and insinuates various false ideas into their minds with the result that, for the time being, he may wreck their Christian testimony and rob them of their happiness. The history of the Christian Church since the New Testament canon is full of the same thing. It began at the very beginning and it has continued more or less ever since, and there is a sense in which it is true to say that the history of the Church is the history of the rising of many heresies and the battle of the Church against them, and the delivery of the Church by the power of the Spirit of God.

This is obviously a very great subject which I can but introduce and touch upon. False teaching can appear in many different forms; but we can divide them into two main sections. Sometimes it takes the form of a blatant denial of the Truth and of the cardinal principles and tenets of the Christian faith. Let us be quite clear about the fact that sometimes it can take that form. It may represent itself as being Christian but in actual fact be a denial of the Christian message. There have been, and still are, teachings which call themselves Christian which even deny the deity of the Lord Jesus Christ, and other cardinal and basic tenets of our faith.

But false teaching does not always take that form. There is another form, and that is the one to which I am now directing particular attention. In a sense this second one is even more dangerous than the first, and this is the form it had taken amongst the churches of Galatia. Here it is not so much a denial of the faith, not so much a contradiction of the cardinal elements, as a teaching which suggests that something else is required in addition to what we have already believed. That was the peculiar form which it took in the case of Galatia. Certain teachers had gone around to the churches there and said, in effect: 'Yes, we believe the gospel and we agree with Paul's preaching. It is perfectly right, everything he said was right, but he did not go far enough. He left out something that is absolutely vital and that vital something is circumcision. Hold on to everything you believe but if you want to be a true Christian you must in addition be circumcised'. That was the essence of their teaching.

Now it is not at all difficult to see how that particular teaching came in. The first Christians after all were Jews. You can read the history in the Gospels, and in the Acts of the Apostles. Let us be quite fair to them. It is very easy to understand their situation. They knew that their old religion had been given by God and they knew that it was true. Their difficulty was how to understand the new teaching in the light of their old and traditional teaching. They knew that circumcision had been given by God to Abraham and had been continued ever since; but here now was a new teaching which said that circumcision was no longer necessary, that that old distinction between Jew and Gentile had been abolished, that circumcision, together with the whole of the ceremonial law, had served its purpose and was no longer incumbent on the people of God. Now many were unhappy about this. They were not now unhappy about the

Gentiles coming in as such. At first that had been a difficulty to them (you remember that even the Apostle Peter found that rather difficult, and that it was only when God gave him the vision from heaven that he was prepared to receive Cornelius and other Gentiles into the Christian Church). But they could still not quite see how a Gentile could become Christian unless at the same time he became a Jew also. They could see that Christianity was the logical outcome of their old religion but they could not see how a man could come into it without entering via circumcision. So they had gone to these Christian Gentiles in Galatia and had suggested to them that if they were to be real Christians they must also submit to circumcision, they must put themselves under the law.

Now that is the theme with which the Apostle deals in this Epistle to the Galatians. You cannot read it without being moved, without being gripped. He is writing with passion. He is so concerned about this matter that he even leaves out the customary preliminary salutation, and having opened his letter he plunges into his theme and asks his question. Why does he feel this passion, why is he so moved? The answer is, of course, that he felt that the very Christian standing and position of these people was at stake, and that unless they saw the truth of this matter, their whole Christian position might very well be in jeopardy. There is no letter, therefore, in which the Apostle speaks with such vehemence. Listen to this: 'But though we, or an angel from heaven, preach any other gospel unto you than that which we have preached unto you, let him be accursed'. You could never read anything more vehement than that. And he repeats it: 'As we said before, so say I now again, If any man preach any other gospel unto you than that ye have received, let him be accursed'. That is the way in which he silences any tendency to say: 'It doesn't matter that these people do not see what I see, we are all Christians together'. Not at all, there is a definite intolerance here because, as he suggests and teaches, the whole Christian position is involved in this matter.

I am calling attention to this not because of any particular interest in the history of the Galatians as such, but because of its relevance to us. That is the glory of the New Testament. It is not an academic Book, it is the most up-to-date Book. There is not a single problem or heresy described in the New Testament that you will not find in some shape or form in the Church at this moment. We are not engaged in a mere academic discussion of spiritual depression, we are talking about ourselves and we are talking to one another; and it is because these things are still with us and because the Galatian heresy in a modern form is still with us that I am calling your attention to it. There are many Christian people who have passed through this experience. When they encountered the Truth for the first time they were amazed at it. They said: 'I never knew that that was Christianity'. They received it with joy and they experienced amazing blessing; but subsequently they were confronted by some other teaching. They may have read about it, or somebody may have preached on it, or it may have been suggested to them by a friend, and so they were introduced to another kind of teaching. At once this other teaching appealed to them because it appeared to be so spiritual and because it promised such unusual blessing if they but believed it, and so they took it up. But then they began to find themselves unhappy and confused. Others who do not actually take up and accept the teaching are still made unhappy and confused by it, because it disturbs them, and because they cannot answer it. Their joy seems to go and they are in perplexity. Whichever it is they lose their first happiness.

There is scarcely any need to mention any particular teaching as such, as I am sure you are familiar with what I have in mind. Yet I must mention certain things just by way of illustration and not with the intention of dealing with them in detail. Apart from the obvious examples, in heresies such as the Jehovah's Witnesses or Seventh Day Adventists, you find it inherent in Roman Catholicism with its insistence on obedience and conformity to things not taught in the Scriptures. It appears in the teaching that adult baptism by immersion is essential to salvation. Again it is often met in terms of the absolute necessity of speaking with tongues if you are to be sure that you have received the Holy Spirit, and sometimes it is met in connection with physical healing in the teaching that no Christian should ever be ill. Those are but some illustrations. There are many others, I simply mention these in order that we may realize that this is a very practical matter and not merely a theoretical question. We are all confronted by these things and, as I hope to show, they all partake of the character of the heresy that we are considering.

Here, it seems to me, the Apostle has laid down once and for ever a great principle which we must ever carry in our minds if we want to safeguard ourselves against these dangers, and to make sure that we are 'standing fast in the liberty wherewith Christ has made us free' and not being 'entangled again with the yoke of bondage'. It was his love of these people that made him write in this way. As he tells them here, he felt as a father does to a child. It was not that the Apostle was pedantic or narrow, intolerant or self-centred. On the contrary, his only concern was the spiritual life and welfare of these people, 'My little children,' he says. He is like a mother, 'I travail again in birth until Christ be formed in you'. And it is in that spirit I would direct attention to this subject. God knows I would prefer not to deal with it at all. We are living in an age which does not like this sort of thing. The tendency is to say: 'What does it matter?' And this tendency is apparent not only in those who are outside the Church but also in those who are inside the Church. I approach it therefore with reluctance and simply because I feel that I should be betraying my calling by God into the Christian ministry, if I did not expound the true teaching of the Word of God whatever modern opinion may chance to be.

How then do we face this kind of position? The first thing the Apostle lays down is the question of authority. That must of necessity come first. These perplexities and problems are not a matter of feeling or of experience, and they must never be judged merely by results. False teaching can make people very happy. Let us be quite clear about that. If you judge only in terms of experience and results you will find that every cult and heresy the world or the Church has ever known will be able to justify itself. What, then, is the authority? The Apostle tells us plainly in the first chapter. Indeed the question of authority is the very thing he deals with in the first two chapters. Here the Apostle's own personal position was involved and that is why he has to say so much about himself. He takes up a position in which he defies anyone to preach any other gospel but his. He says: 'But though we, or an angel from heaven, preach any other gospel . . . let him be accursed'. Why? What is the test? It is: 'I certify you, brethren, that the gospel which was preached of me is not after man; for I neither received it of man neither was I taught it but by the revelation of Jesus Christ'. And then he goes on to tell them of how he came into the ministry. He says: 'Ye have heard of my conversation in time past in the Jews' religion how that beyond measure I persecuted the Church of God and wasted it;

and profited in the Jews' religion above many my equals in mine own nation, being more exceedingly zealous of the traditions of my fathers', etc. He had lived in that way until that moment on the road to Damascus when the Lord Jesus Christ had set him in the ministry, to which, he now knew, he had been separated from his mother's womb. He was given his commission and his message by the Lord Jesus Christ Himself. Ah, yes, but Paul knew even more than that. Though he had come into the ministry in this unique way and was able to describe himself to the Corinthians as 'one born out of due time' he nevertheless says that the gospel that was given to him was exactly the same gospel as that given to the others also, the other Apostles who had been with the Lord in the days of His flesh. When he spoke to the other apostles at Jerusalem he found he was preaching exactly the same gospel as they were preaching. Though it had come to him in this individual way as a direct revelation, the others were preaching exactly the same thing as he was preaching himself.

There, then, is the basis of authority and that is the authority that the Apostle pleads here and on which he argues. He says that it is not a question of one man saying this and another man saying that. He asserts that he was not preaching merely what he thought. It was given to him as it was given to the other apostles, and so they were all saying the same thing. The test of Truth is its Apostolicity. Is it, and does it conform to, the apostolic message? That is the test and that is the standard. The gospel of Jesus Christ as announced and taught in the New Testament claims nothing less than that it comes with the authority of the Lord Jesus Christ Himself Who gave it to these men who, in turn, preached it and caused it to be written. Here is the only standard. And it is still the only standard.

We have no standard at all apart from the New Testament, and therefore we must take every point of view and bring it to, and hold it in, the light of this. As we do so we shall find that these false teachings are always guilty along one of two lines. The first is that they may contain less than the apostolic message. Let us be perfectly clear about the fact that there is an apostolic message, a positive Truth agreed upon by all the apostles and preached by them—there is that definite message. Now false teaching may be guilty of stating less than that message, of leaving out certain things. This is something which misleads so many Christians today. If a man says something flagrantly

wrong they can see at once that he is wrong, but they are not so
quick to see that a teaching may be wrong because it is less than
the apostolic message, because it does not say certain things.
It may be less than the true teaching on the Person of the Lord
Jesus Christ. It may be denying His Incarnation, it may be
denying the two natures in the One Person; it may be denying
the Virgin Birth, it may be denying the miraculous in His life,
it may be denying the literal physical resurrection. It calls itself
Christian, but it is less than the Truth. Again it may deny at
some point the work of Christ. It may deny the fact that 'God
made Him to be sin for us who knew no sin that we might be
made the righteousness of God in Him'. It may describe the
death of Christ as being nothing but a marvellous exhibition of
love. It may deny that God punished our sins 'in His own Body
on the Tree'. That is what the apostles preached, that Christ
'died for' our sins. If, therefore, a teaching leaves that out it is
less than the Apostolic Truth. It is the same with the rebirth.
So often this doctrine is not taught and its absolute necessity is
not emphasized. Again we find the same thing even with respect
to conduct and behaviour although the New Testament emphasizes conduct and behaviour. People may say they believe on
Christ, but then they tend to deduce that if you believe in Christ
you are safe and it does not matter what you do. But that is the
terrible error of antinomianism. The New Testament teaches
the importance of works saying that 'faith without works is dead'.
Now to leave out anyone of these things is to come short of the
apostolic message.

The second danger, as we have already seen, is the exact
opposite, namely, the danger of adding to the Truth and, while
acknowledging the apostolic message to be right, of suggesting
that there must be something added on to it. Now that is the
thing we are dealing with in particular. Once more we must
remember our first principle, that every teaching is to be tested
by the teaching of the New Testament, not by feelings, not by
experience, not by results, not by what other people are saying
and doing. Here is the test, Apostolicity—the New Testament
teaching.

Another very good test is this: always be careful to work out
the implications of a teaching. That is what the apostle does in
the second chapter of this Epistle to the Galatians. This new
teaching appeared not to be denying Christ at all, and yet the

apostle is able to show very plainly that it denies Him at the most vital point. He even had to do that with the Apostle Peter at Antioch. Peter, who had been given a vision in connection with Cornelius (Acts 10) and had apparently seen these things very clearly, was influenced subsequently by the Jews and felt that he could not eat with the Gentiles but with Jews only. But Paul had to withstand him to the face and to tell him plainly that in doing this he was denying the faith. Now Peter did not want to do that, he did not want to deny his salvation by Christ through faith alone. But Peter had to be made to see his real position clearly and to understand that by his actions he was announcing that something in addition to faith in Christ is necessary. Let us then always work out the implications of what we say and do. Let me give an illustration of what I mean. A Christian woman with whom I was once discussing this matter was in difficulty about this point. She could not see how certain unbelieving people who live very good lives are not really Christian. She said: 'I cannot see how you can say they are not Christian, look at their lives'. A good Christian herself, she was really in trouble about it. But I said: 'Wait a minute, don't you see what you are implying, don't you see what you are saying? You are really saying that those people are so good and so excellent and so noble that the Lord Jesus Christ, the Son of God, is unnecessary in their case, that the coming of the Son of God from heaven was unnecessary to them. He need not have died upon the Cross, they can reconcile themselves to God by their works and good living. Cannot you see that that is denying the faith; indeed, that by that argument you are really saying that Christ Himself and His death are unnecessary?' And she saw it by working out the implications of the things she was saying. Do not look at things at their face value only, but see what they really imply.

The third thing which it seems to me is the special character-istic of this particular heresy as it is expounded in the Epistle to the Galatians is that it is always an addition to revelation. 'This preaching about circumcision is not a part of Christ's message,' says Paul in effect. 'These people preach that but they did not get it from Christ. Christ when He gave me the message did not say all people must be circumcised. It is something apart from His revelation, it is an addition to the apostolic message'. You will find that this is always the characteristic of the type of heresy with which we are dealing. Take for instance the Roman Catholic claim. The Roman Catholic Church claims that she is as much inspired today as those first apostles were, but she has no basis in Scripture for saying that. She says it herself, and she herself makes the claim that this subsequent revelation has been given to the Church. This claim is made quite openly; there is no subtlety about it, and it means that the Church herself is as authoritative as the Word. They say the pronouncements of the the Pope speaking 'ex cathedra' are as inspired as the New Testament Epistles, and are an addition to this revelation. But this is true not only of the Roman Catholic Church, there are others who make a like claim.

Before you accept any one of these teachings always take the trouble to read about their origins. Almost invariably you will find that somebody or other had a 'vision'—in the vast majority of the cults it is a woman. Read the histories and you will find that the teaching is based upon the authority of a woman. The apostle says that 'he suffers not a woman to teach'. But that does not matter to them. Not only that, the woman has had a vision and been given some special revelation. 'Ah,' they say, 'you don't find that in the Scriptures, but it has been given directly to this person from God and by God.' They are adding something to the revelation, it is something further, it is something more advanced. They claim that their founders were as inspired as were the apostles of Jesus Christ, and they base their authority on that. Apply that test to most of these movements and you will find it is true. But remember that it is also true of many who are still within the ranks of the Christian Church and who yet take this view of the Scriptures. 'Ah, yes,' they say, 'those men were inspired, but men are still inspired. We do not deny inspiration, but we say that you can add to the Truth. The first centuries did not exhaust the revelation of the Truth and special things are being revealed to us through our greater knowledge and learning in this twentieth century.' That is adding to the revelation. That means that the Scriptures are no longer sufficient; the findings of modern scholarship must be added. But in allowing the additions of the modern mind and modern outlook you are really claiming a further revelation.

Another invariable characteristic is that this teaching always emphasizes some one thing in particular and gives great prominence to it. Here in the case of the Galatians it was circumcision. But whatever it may be it is this one thing that has led to the special teaching, this one thing is the mainspring of the entire movement. They allow that you are a true believer, but in addition you must have this one thing—the seventh day, or the immersion of believers, or tongues, or healing or something else. This one thing is essential. That is the big thing. It is always in a prominent position, at the centre, and you are more conscious of that one thing than you are of Christ because the emphasis is on that. You cannot account for the Movement apart from that one thing, circumcision or whatever else it may happen to be.

The third point is that all these things are an addition to Christ. The Roman Catholic says, 'Of course we believe in Christ, but you must also believe in the Church, you must believe in the Virgin Mary, you must believe in the saints, you must believe in the priesthood in addition'. From the sheer standpoint of orthodoxy and doctrinal beliefs I find myself nearer to many a Roman Catholic than to many within the ranks of Protestantism, but where I part company and must part company with them is that they add these vital pluses—Christ, plus the Church, plus the Virgin Mary, plus the priests, plus the saints, and so on. Christ alone is not enough and He does not stand in all His unique glory at the centre. And it is the same with all the others. You must have some special experience, you must have some special belief about 'observing days' as the apostle puts it, you must go through some special rite or sacrament. So it is always 'Christ plus' something, and you must have this essential addition.

Then we must show in the fourth place that this wrong doctrine always leads in some shape or form to the conclusion that faith alone is not enough. The apostle puts that plainly in the fifth chapter and the sixth verse, 'For in Jesus Christ neither circumcision availeth anything nor uncircumcision, but faith which worketh by love'. These false teachings are always telling us that we must do something ourselves; we must add on some plus, some action on our own part, or allow something to be done to us. Faith is not enough. We do not stand by faith, and justification is not by faith only. We have to do some certain work, we have to do something special before we can get this great experience of salvation. But according to Paul, to say such things means that we are 'fallen from grace'.

But lastly let me point out this. And I thank God for this last test because it has been such a help to me. To believe in such teaching always leads to denying former Christian experience.

'Where is the blessedness ye spake of?' You know what he means
by that. He says, in effect: 'Foolish Galatians, beloved Galatians,
are you really telling me that what you experienced when I
first came among you was of no avail, was all useless? Where is
the blessedness ye spake of? O foolish Galatians, who hath
bewitched you? You know that as many as are of the works of
the law are under the curse. You know that you have received
the Spirit. Come back, remember that you have received the
Spirit. Did you receive Him by the works of the Law? Of course
you did not. Cannot you see that you are denying your own past
experience?'

These false teachings are all guilty of that. That is what the
apostle points out in his account of his argument with Peter.
He told Peter that he was going back on his own life and experience. That is the meaning of his whole argument about Abraham
also. Abraham was blest, not after circumcision but before circumcision, therefore you cannot say that circumcision is essential.
Abraham had his great blessing before and not after circumcision. To say that circumcision is essential is therefore to deny
this experience. How often have I had to use this argument!
These wrong teachings are subtle and attractive and you feel that
that is what you need, that it must be right. Then you suddenly
remember this argument about experience and it holds you.
You remind yourself for instance, of men like George Whitefield
and John Wesley who were undoubtedly filled with the Spirit
in an astounding, amazing, mighty manner by God, outstanding
saints of God and among God's greatest servants; yet you find
that they observed the first day of the week and not the seventh,
you find that they were not baptized in a particular manner,
you find that they never spoke with tongues, you find that they
did not hold healing meetings and so on. Are we to say that all
these men were lacking in knowledge and insight and understanding? Cannot you see that these new teachings which claim
so much are denying some of the greatest Christian experience
throughout the ages and the centuries. They are virtually saying
that truth has only come by them and that for 1,900 years the
Church has dwelt in ignorance and in darkness. The thing is
monstrous. We must realize that these things are to be tested in
this way—'where is the blessedness ye spake of?'

That brings me to the last word, and the final test, which is
just this. Having gone through all these tests you are ready to

join with me in saying what the apostle said in the seventeenth verse of the last chapter of this epistle to the Galatians: 'From henceforth let no man trouble me for I bear in my body the marks of the Lord Jesus'. What does he mean? This is what he means—'God forbid that I should glory save in the Cross of the Lord Jesus Christ by whom the world is crucified unto me and I unto the world'. Stop talking to me about circumcision, I am not interested. Stop talking to me about the observers of the Seventh Day, or any other particular sect. Stop talking about all these things that are held to be absolute essentials if I am to be a complete Christian. I do not want them. 'God forbid that I should glory', I will make my boast in nothing and in no one, nor in any special teaching 'saving in the Lord Jesus Christ' and Him alone. He is enough, because by Him 'the world has been crucified to me and I am crucified unto the world'.

Let me put it plainly, I will not make my boast, I will not glory, even in my orthodoxy, for even that can be a snare if I make a god of it. I will glory only in that Blessed Person Himself by whom this great thing has been done, with whom I died, with whom I have been buried, with whom I am dead to sin and alive unto God, with whom I have risen, with whom I am seated in the heavenly places, by whom and by whom alone the world is crucified unto me and I am crucified unto the world. Anything that wants to come into the centre instead of Him, anything that wants to add itself on to Him, I shall reject. Knowing the apostolic message concerning Jesus Christ in all its directness, its simplicity and its glory, God forbid that any one of us should add anything to it. Let us rejoice in Him in all His fulness and in Him alone.

And let us not be weary in well doing: for in due season we shall reap, if we faint not.

Galatians 6. 9

XIV

WEARY IN WELL DOING

THE Bible is a Book which has been written in order that God's people may be helped in this world. That is especially true of the New Testament Epistles, which were all written because of some situation that had arisen in the churches, and the way to understand their message is not to think of a man writing a thesis in his study. On the contrary, the Apostle Paul was an evangelist, a man who travelled about, and he generally wrote because of some trouble that had arisen, and in order to help people to understand the cause of their trouble and the way to overcome it. So he dealt with the possible causes as they arose, and we can be quite certain that there is no cause of spiritual depression today that is not dealt with in the Epistles. The ills of the spiritual life are always the same, they never vary. The appearances differ, the particular guise in which the trouble may appear may vary, but the cause of it all is the devil and he never varies in his ultimate objective.

Here we find another cause of this condition of spiritual depression, and at once it reminds us of something that we have to underline again, as we have done several times before, namely the terrible subtlety of our adversary. We have been looking at the way in which the devil tempts Christian people and makes them miserable by suggesting false teaching. We have observed his very clever way of putting certain things at the centre which should not be there, or of giving us some new kind of religion which is a mixture of various religions. But now we are in quite a different climate altogether. At this point the apostle is not concerned about the danger of our going astray through heresy and error, or by taking up some particular cult and believing it to be the true faith. That is not what he is concerned about here. Here, the devil does something much more subtle, in that there is apparently nothing wrong at all. What happens is that people just become weary and tired, while still going in the right direction. Here we have the case of those who are on the right road and facing the right way. They are moving in the right direction but the trouble is that they are shuffling along with drooping heads and hands and the whole spectacle and picture they present is the very antithesis of what the Christian is meant to be in this life and world.

Now perhaps the best way of looking at this tendency to weariness on our part is to look at it first of all in general. This is what we may call the danger of the middle period. It is something which is true not only in the Christian life as such, it is true of the whole of life. It is the problem of middle life, and, if you like, of middle age. It is something which is evident on all hands, it is something we all have to face sooner or later as we grow older. Great attention is being paid to young people today, and a considerable amount of attention is being paid to old people; but I am perfectly convinced that the most difficult period of all in life is the middle period. There are compensations in youth and there are compensations in old age which seem to be entirely lacking in this middle period. It is something we all have to encounter. As we get older, our resilience and our vigour tend to go and we are aware of a slowing down and a slackening in our powers. This is something with which we are all familiar by hearsay, if not in actual experience. It is true also, is it not, in connection with a man's work or profession? That is what constitutes a problem to so many people. It means that they have got beyond that stage of developing and building up and have attained to a certain level. For many reasons it is impossible to develop further. There they are on the level, and the difficulty is to keep going on that level while lacking the stimulus that took them there. This has often happened to a man in business, and he may sometimes find it much more difficult to maintain a business than it is to build it up. Everything seems to be with him in a sense when he is building it up, but it is when he arrives at that point and loses certain stimuli, that he finds it extremely difficult to hold the position. I could illustrate this almost endlessly taking it purely from the standpoint of natural life and from our experiences in work and in professions and various other callings. If you read the biographies of the most successful men the world has ever known in any particular branch, you will find that they are all agreed in saying that that level or plateau was the most difficult period in their lives.

Now this is equally true in the religious or the spiritual life. This is the stage which follows the initial experience, that initial

experience in which everything was new and surprising and wonderful and clear, the stage in which we were constantly making
new discoveries which never seemed to come to an end. But
suddenly we are conscious of the fact that they do seem to have
come to an end, and now we have become accustomed to the
Christian life. No longer are we surprised at things, as we were
at the beginning, because we are familiar with them and know
about them. So that all that thrill of new discovery which ani-
mated us in the early stages suddenly seems to have gone.
Nothing seems to be happening, there does not seem to be any
change or advance or development. Now this may be true of us
individually, it may be true of our work, it may be true of our
church, it may be true of a whole collection of people, it may be
true of a country, or of society. I am given to understand, and I
know it is true, that this particular phenomenon happens to be
one of the major problems in connection with foreign mission
work, and missionaries who have spent time abroad will know
exactly what I mean by the things I am saying. It is something
that always tends to happen when we have got over the newness
and the thrill and excitement of doing something that we have
never done before, and we settle down into our routine, doing
the same thing day after day. Then this trial arises, and we are
no longer carried over it by that initial momentum which seemed
to take us through it all in the early stages at the beginning.

This is the condition with which the apostle deals here. Perhaps, to make it all worse, there may be troubles and difficulties,
caused by other people, which may add to our troubles. They
may do things they should not do and offend in various ways.
As the result of such trials and difficulties and troubles at a time
when we ourselves are in this critical period, we become weary
in well doing. Thus, frequently, there comes a point at which
development and advance seem to have come to an end and we
are in some kind of doldrums when it is difficult to know whether
the work is moving at all, either backwards or forwards. All
seems to be at a standstill and nothing seems to be taking place.
Now there is no doubt at all but that some of these Galatian
Christians had arrived at that particular point. The position
revealed by our analysis in the previous chapter—the false
teaching, the heresies and so on, undoubtedly had something to
do with this.

We may say then that we are considering people who are not

so much tired of the work as tired in it: 'be not weary in well-doing'. That is the condition. What shall we say about it and what shall we do about it? Let me say at the outset that there is no aspect of this great problem of depression in which negatives are more important than they are on this particular occasion. Whenever we are found in this position of weariness, before we begin to do anything positive, there are certain negatives that are absolutely all-important. The first is this: Whatever you may feel about it do not consider the suggestion that comes to you from all directions—not so much from people, but from within yourself, the voices that seem to be speaking around and about you—do not listen to them when they suggest that you should give up, or give way, or give in. That is a great temptation that comes at this point. You say: 'I am weary and tired, the thing is too much for me'. And there is nothing to say at that point but this negative—do not listen. You always have to start with these 'don'ts' on the very lowest level; and that is the lowest level. You must say to yourself: 'Whatever happens I am going on'. You do not give in or give way.

But that perhaps is not the greatest temptation. The greatest is the one I am going to put in the form of my second negative injunction. Do not resign yourself to it. While there are people who hand in their resignations and say, 'I am quitting', that is not so with the majority. The danger of the majority at this point is just to resign themselves to it and to lose heart and to lose hope. They will go on, but they go on in this hopeless, dragging condition. To put it more particularly, the danger at this point is to say something like this: 'Well, I have lost that something which I had, and obviously I shall not get it back again. But I am going on, and out of loyalty I will go on, as a sheer duty. I have lost the enjoyment I once had, that is gone and it is undoubtedly gone for ever. I just have to put up with it, I will resign myself to my fate, I won't be a quitter, I won't turn my back on it, I will go on, though I go on feeling rather hopeless about it all, just shuffling down the road, not walking with hope as I once did, but keeping on as best I can'. That is the spirit of resignation, stoicism if you like, putting up with it.

Now that is the greatest danger of all; and again, I suggest, it is something which is dangerous not only on the spiritual level, about which we are most concerned, but also on every level in life. We can work like that in our profession, we can live our lives

like that, in a sense. We are really saying to ourselves: 'The
golden hours have gone, the great days belong to the past. I may
never know that again but I will just keep on'. There is something, of course, which seems wonderful about this, something
that seems heroic about it. But you notice that I put it as a
negative. Indeed I say that it is a temptation of the devil. If he
can get God's people to lose hope, he will be content indeed. And
as I see things today, this is perhaps the greatest danger of all
confronting the Christian Church, the danger of doing a thing in
a formal spirit and as a matter of duty. Going on, it is true, but
wearily trudging along instead of walking as we ought to walk.

That brings me to my third and last negative, and this again
you will recognise as a very dangerous thing. This third danger
is, that when we thus become weary and tired, we will resort to
artificial stimulants. You know the temptation. It has been the
ruin of many a man who has built up a profession or a business
and then gets into this weary state. He is conscious that he has
not the vigour and the vim that he once had, and he does not
feel, as the phrase puts it, on top of his job. He does not know
what to do about it himself and then somebody suggests to him
that what he needs is some kind of a tonic. The whole danger in
connection with the drinking of alcohol comes in at that point.
Many a man has ended as a drunkard who started by taking a
little alcohol to help him to carry on; and people take to drugs
and various other things in precisely the same way.

But this has a very important and vital spiritual application.
I have seen people in the church dealing with this general
spiritual weariness in that very way. They work up some kind of
excitement or they adopt new methods. They say that they must
rouse themselves out of this, so they put on some new programme.
Have you not seen it sometimes in the advertisements outside
church buildings? Can you not think of certain churches that are
always putting out some fresh announcements or finding some
new attraction? Such churches are obviously living on artificial
stimulants and it is all being done with this idea in mind. The
pastor or some other responsible person has said: 'We are just
in a rut, we are becoming rather dead. What can we do about it?
Well, let's do this, or that. It will provide work and activity, it
will be a new interest'. Now that sort of thinking in the spiritual
life and in the life of the Church is comparable to one thing only
on the natural level, and that is to the man who takes to drink

or drugs in order to give himself some excitement or to work himself up. Obviously this is an extremely subtle temptation and a very subtle danger. It seems to be so plausible, it seems to be just the thing we need, and yet, of course, the terrible fallacy behind it all is that, in a scientific sense, what you are really doing is to exhaust yourself still more. The more a man relies upon alcoholic drink or drugs, the more he is draining away his natural energy. Moreover, as he becomes more exhausted, so he will need to have still more drink and still more drugs; and so the process goes on in a cumulative manner. And it is exactly the same in the spiritual realm.

There, then, are three negatives which are of supreme importance. Let us now turn to the positive. We must avoid these dangerous pitfalls, but is there nothing else we can do? Here we are, weary in well doing, but what can we do? The first thing must be self-examination. Start by examining yourself. Do not just say that your dreary state cannot be helped. Do not take to the stimulants. Sit down and say to yourself: 'Well, now, why am I weary, what is the cause of my weariness?' It is surely an obvious question. You must not treat the condition before you diagnose it; you do not apply the remedy before you know the cause. It is a dangerous thing to rush to treatment before you know the cause; you must diagnose first. You must therefore ask yourself why you are weary, and why you have got into this condition.

There are many possible answers to the question. You may be in that condition simply because you are working too hard physically. You can be tired in the work and not tired of the work. It is possible that a man has been over-working—I do not care in what realm, whether natural or spiritual—and has been over-taxing his energy and his physical resources. If you go on working too hard or under strain you are bound to suffer. And of course if that is the cause of the trouble, the remedy you need is medical treatment. There is a striking example of this in the Old Testament. You remember that when Elijah had that attack of spiritual depression after his heroic effort on Mount Carmel, he sat down under a juniper tree and felt sorry for himself. But the real thing he needed was sleep and food; and God gave him both! He gave him food and rest before He gave him spiritual help.

But let us assume that it is not that. Something else may be the cause of the trouble, and very frequently it is that we may have been living the Christian life, or doing Christian work, by means of carnal energy. We may have been doing it all in our own strength instead of working in the power of the Spirit. We may have been working with mere carnal, human, and perhaps even physical energy. We may have been trying to do God's work ourselves; and of course if we try to do that there will be only one result, it will ultimately crush us because it is such high work. And so we must examine ourselves and see if there is something wrong with the way in which we are doing this work. It is possible for a man to preach with carnal energy, and if he does, he will soon be suffering from this spiritual exhaustion and depression.

But then a still more important and much more spiritual question arises. I must ask myself why I have been doing this work and what has really been my motive. I have been active and I have enjoyed doing the work, but now I find it has become a burden. And now comes this question. Why have I really been doing it the whole time? It is a terrible question that, because it may be the first time we have ever asked it. We have taken all for granted and assumed that our motive was pure. But we may find that it was not. Some people work for the sake of the thrill and excitement. There is no question about it at all. I have seen people very actively engaged in Christian work because there was a certain amount of excitement in it. There are some people who are not happy unless they are always doing something, and they do not always realize that what they are out for is the thrill and the excitement of the activity. As certainly as we live in that way we will get exhausted, we will become tired, and equally certainly our greatest enemy will come in, and that is self. We have really been doing all that we have been doing, to satisfy self, in order to please ourselves, in order to be able to say to ourselves: 'How wonderful you are and how much you do'. Self says that we are important. We have to admit that it has not all been for the glory of God, but for our own glory. We may say that we do not want the praise and that 'to God be the glory', but we like to see results and we like it to appear in the papers and so on—self has come in and self is a terrible master. If we are working to satisfy and please self in any shape or form, the end is always going to be weariness and tiredness. How important it is to ask ourselves about the motive in connection with our work!

Lastly, and a very important question this—has this work, I wonder, kept me going? Instead of being God's work, has it been a sort of mainspring of my life? I am sure there are many persons who know what I mean by that. One of the greatest dangers in the spiritual life is to live on your own activities. In other words, the activity is not in its right place as something which you do, but has become something that keep you going. Some of the greatest tragedies I have seen have been in such men, who did not realize that they had been living for years on the force and strength of their activities. These kept them going, and then when they were taken ill or grew old, and could no longer do what they used to do they became depressed. They did not know what to do with themselves, because they had been living on their own activities. I suppose it is one of the most obvious tendencies in our civilization. It is certainly one of the greatest causes of neurosis at the present time. Unfortunately the world has become so mad that we are kept going by this terrific momentum and rush of life, and instead of our being in control, the thing is controlling us. And ultimately it exhausts us and depresses us.

Here, are some of the main elements in this vital process of self-examination. Let me emphasize the principle. If in any respect in your life at this moment you are weary, I beseech you to stop and ask yourself: 'Why am I weary, how am I being carried along?' Examine your whole attitude towards your life and the thing in particular that you are doing, and discover how you feel about the Christian life. Why did you ever come into it, what is it, and so on? Stop, and ask yourself those questions.

But let me put the matter positively. There are certain great principles, according to the teaching of the apostle here, which we must recognize if we are to be cured of this condition. In the first place, there are phases in the Christian life as in the whole of life. The New Testament talks about being babes in Christ, it talks about growing. John writes his first epistle to little children and young men and old men. It is a fact, it is Scriptural. The Christian life is not always exactly the same, there is a beginning and a continuing and there is an end. And, because of these phases there are many variations. Feelings, perhaps, are the most variable. You would expect to have most feeling at the beginning, and this is what usually happens. Very often Christian people become weary because certain feelings have gone. They do not realize that what has happened is that they have grown older. Because they are not as they once were they think that they are all wrong. But as we grow and develop spiritually, changes must take place and all these things obviously make a difference in our experience. Let me put it in the form of an illustration. I happened to see, the other day, a little child, about four years old I should think, coming out of her house with her mother, and I could not help being attracted by the way she came out of that house. She did not walk, she jumped out, she skipped out, she gambolled out like a lamb; but I noticed that the mother walked out. Very well, let us be sure that we are not failing to realize that there is something like that in the spiritual life. The child is abounding in energy and has not yet learned how to control it. The mother actually had a great deal more energy than the child, although looked at superficially it would seem that she had much less because she walked out quietly. But we know that that is not so. The energy is actually much greater in the adult though it appears to be greater in the child; and it is because they have misunderstood this experience of slowing down, that so many people think they have lost something vital and so become weary and depressed. Let us recognize that there are phases; let us recognize that there are these stages of development in the Christian life. Sometimes the realization of that fact alone will solve the whole problem.

But come to the second principle. 'Let us not be weary in well doing.' It is 'well doing' remember. Now that is the thing we tend to forget. 'Ah,' we say, 'the same old thing week after week.' That is our attitude towards our life, and because that is our attitude towards it we become weary. But Paul says, let me remind you, that you are in the Christian life, and the Christian life is a life of well doing. If you regard the Christian life as a dreary task you are insulting God. What is our Christian life? The question is all important and we, too often, answer that it is to avoid the things other people do. That it is to walk this straight and narrow road, it is to say no to this and to engage in that. It is to go to church. It is an awful task, it is a hard life in which we find ourselves! Is not that our attitude far too frequently? And the reply to that is, that we are engaged in 'well doing'. If you and I come to regard any aspect of this Christian life merely as a task and a duty, and if we have to goad ourselves and to set our teeth in order to get through with it, I say we are insulting God and we have forgotten the very essence of Christianity. The Christian life is not a task. The Christian life alone is worthy of the name life. This alone is righteous and holy and pure and good. It is the kind of life the Son of God Himself lived. It is to be like God Himself in His own holiness. That is why I should live it. I do not just decide to make a great effort to carry on somehow. Not at all, I remind myself that it is a great and good life, it is 'well doing'. How have I got into this life—this life that I am grumbling and complaining about, and finding hard and difficult? Let me press this question. How did you get into this Christian life? Here we are in the narrow way, how did we come from the broad way? What has made the difference? These are the questions; and there is only one answer. We have come from that to this, because the only begotten Son of God left heaven and came down to earth for our salvation, He divested Himself of all the insignia of His eternal glory and humbled Himself to be born as a babe and to be placed in a manger. He endured the life of this world for thirty-three years: He was spat upon and reviled. He had thorns thrust into His head and was nailed to a cross, to bear the punishment of my sin. That is how I have come from that to this, and if I ever, even for a fraction of a second, question the greatness and the glory and the wonder and the nobility of this walk in which I am engaged, well then I am spitting upon Him. Out upon the suggestion! 'Be not weary in well doing.' My friend, if you think of your Christian life in any shape or form with this sense of grudge, or as a wearisome task or duty, I tell you to go back to the beginning of your life, retrace your steps to the wicket gate through which you passed. Look at the world in its evil and sin, look at the hell to which it was leading you, and then look forward and realize that you are set in the midst of the most glorious campaign into which a man could ever enter, and that you are on the noblest road that the world has ever known.

But let me go further. The next principle is that this life of ours on earth is but a preparatory one. 'Be not weary in well doing for in due season we shall reap if we faint not.' You are tired and weary and you feel at times it is too much for you? Go back and look at your life and put it into the context of eternity. Stop and ask yourself what it all means. It is nothing but a preparatory school. This life is but the ante-chamber of eternity and all we do in this world is but anticipatory of that.

Our greatest joys are but the first fruits and the foretaste of the eternal joy that is coming. How important it is to remind ourselves of that. It is the sheer grind of daily life that gets us down. You may say: 'Here is another day to get through', or a preacher may say: 'Another Sunday, and I have to preach twice today'. What a terrible thing to say. The sheer grind sometimes almost gets us down to that. But the answer is to look at it all and to put it all into its great context and to say: 'We are going on to eternity and this is but the preparatory school'. What a difference that makes. 'Keep on,' says Paul, 'with your well doing, because of the certainty of the harvest that is coming.' 'Be not weary in well doing for in due season we shall reap if we faint not.' The moment you realize something of the truth about the harvest you will not faint.

'The world is too much with us', that is our trouble. We are too immersed in our problems. We need to look ahead, to anticipate, to look forward to the eternal glories gleaming afar. The Christian life is a tasting of the first-fruits of that great harvest which is to come. 'Eye hath not seen, nor ear heard, neither have entered into the heart of man the things which God hath prepared for them that love Him.' 'Set your affection on things above and not on things on the earth.' Realize something in mind and heart of the glory of the place to which you are going. That is the antidote, that is the cure. The harvest we shall reap is certain, it is sure. 'Therefore,' says Paul to the Corinthians, 'be ye steadfast, unmovable, always abounding in the work of the Lord for as much as ye know that your labour is not in vain in the Lord.' Go on with your task whatever your feelings; keep on with your work. God will give the increase, He will send the rain of His gracious mercies as we need it. There will be an abundant harvest. Look forward to it. 'Ye shall reap.'

And above all let us consider the Master for Whom we work. Let us remember how He endured and how patient He was. Take that mighty argument in the twelfth of Hebrews again. 'You have not yet resisted unto blood.' He did. He came down and endured it all, and how patient He was. How humdrum His life was, most of His time was spent with ordinary petty people who misunderstood Him. But He went steadfastly on and did not complain. How did He do it? 'For the joy that was set before Him He endured even the cross, despising the shame.' That is how He did it. It was the joy that was set before Him, He knew about the crowning day that was coming, He saw the harvest that He was going to reap, and, seeing that, He was able not to see these other things but to go through them gloriously and triumphantly. And you and I have the privilege of being like Him. 'If any man would be My disciple, let him deny himself, take up his cross'—that is it—'and follow Me'. We may even have the honour of suffering for His Name. Paul says a most extraordinary thing in writing to the Colossians (1. 24). He says that he is privileged to make up in his own body what remains of the suffering of Christ. What if you and I as Christians are having the same privilege without knowing it? Well, remind yourself of your blessed Master and look to Him and ask Him to forgive you for ever having allowed yourself to be weary. Look at your life again in this way, and as certainly as you do so, you will find that you are filled with a new hope, a new strength, a new power. You will not need your artificial stimulants or anything else, for you will find that you are again thrilled with the privilege and joy of it all, and you will hate yourself for having grumbled and complained, and you will go forward still more gloriously, until eventually you will hear Him saying: 'Well done, thou good and faithful servant, enter thou into the joy of thy Lord', 'Come, ye blessed of My Father, inherit the kingdom prepared for you from the foundation of the world'.

And beside this, giving all diligence, add to your faith virtue; and to virtue knowledge; and to knowledge temperance; and to temperance patience; and to patience godliness; and to godliness brotherly kindness, and to brotherly kindness charity.

2 Peter 1. 5-7

XV

DISCIPLINE

HERE, in this first chapter of his second epistle, the Apostle
Peter deals with yet another cause of spiritual depression.
Indeed his object in writing the letter at all was to deal with it.
He writes to encourage people who had been discouraged, and
discouraged to such a degree that they seem to have been doubt-
ing the Faith which they had believed and accepted. That is
something that may arise as a very real danger in this state of
spiritual depression; if the condition persists and continues, it
invariably leads to doubts and uncertainty, and to a proneness
to look back to the old life from which we have been delivered.

Fortunately for us the apostle in this instance gives us a very
perfect description of the condition. He tells us indirectly a number
of things about the people to whom he is writing. For instance he
puts it like this. Having given his exhortation he says in verse 8:
'For if these things be in you and abound, they make you that
ye shall neither be barren nor unfruitful in the knowledge of our
Lord Jesus Christ'. He says: 'For if these things be in you and
abound'—you will then become what you are not at the moment.
And what is that? 'They make you that you will be neither barren
nor unfruitful in the knowledge of our Lord Jesus Christ', implying
that their condition was 'barren and unfruitful'. But not only
that, he says that they were 'blind and could not see afar off and
that they had forgotten that they had been purged from their old
sins'. Indeed, there is a further suggestion that they were falling,
for he tells them that if they do these things they shall 'never
fall', and not only that, but if they do these things they will
'make their calling and election sure'. It is clear that at
that time, they were not very sure about these things.

There is no doubt about their being Christian. That is something we have to go on repeating because there are some who have
such false and unscriptural notions of the Christian, that they
will hold that a person who can be described as Peter describes
these people is not really Christian at all. But obviously they are
Christians otherwise he would not be writing to them. There is

a false idea of a Christian held by many as of a man who is always walking on the mountain top, and there are some who think that if one is not always there, one is not a Christian at all. That is a thoroughly unscriptural view to take of the Christian man. These people are Christians, but they are unhappy, they are most definitely ineffective, their lives do not seem to lead to anything and they are not helpful to other people. Not only that but they are not very productive as far as they themselves are concerned and their faith does not fill them with joy and with certainty. They are 'barren and unfruitful'. The words really describe them—ineffective in helping others and also lacking in knowledge and understanding. They are not growing in the knowledge of the Lord. Here is this tremendous knowledge and understanding that is available but they have not got it, they have not advanced in it, they have not grown, they are unfruitful in that respect. In fact though they are definitely and specifically Christian they seem to have very little to show for it. Also they seem to be failing to understand the meaning of their conversion, they seem to have forgotten the fact that they have been 'cleansed from their old sins', and they are living as if that had not happened. Now all these things always and inevitably go together. When there is a lack of understanding and fruitfulness in this matter of comprehension you will generally get a corresponding failure in the life, both with respect to its own holiness, and its usefulness and value to other people.

Now that is the description which the apostle gives of these people and of course we are all, alas, quite familiar with the type. It is the kind of man that you cannot deny is a Christian, though there is little in his life to show for it. He seems to be 'bound in shallows and in miseries', he does not give the impression of being as our Lord said a Christian would be when he received the Holy Spirit: 'Out of his inward parts shall flow rivers of living waters'. No, the impression he gives is one of barrenness and unfruitfulness, nothing is being fructified by him, he seems to be passing nothing on to others. And as regards himself his life is weak and it does not seem to be increasing and developing. The whole life seems utterly ineffective, and he is downcast and unhappy and shaken by doubts. He does not seem to be able to give 'a reason for the hope that is in him'. He says he believes and yet he is always in this position in which the very foundation of his faith seems liable to be shaken. Now that is the condition which the apostle deals with here and which we are now considering.

The first thing we have to consider is the cause of the condition. Why is it that anybody ever gets into such a state? There are Christians who correspond to this description—why are they like that, why are they unlike other Christians who are fruitful, and whose lives are effective and living and life-giving—what is the difference? That is the question we must consider, and it seems to be perfectly clear that the apostle here tells these people very plainly that there is only one ultimate cause for all the manifestations of this depression, and that is a lack of discipline. That is the real trouble, it is a sheer absence of discipline and order in their life. But, fortunately again for us, the apostle does not leave it at a general statement. The New Testament writers never stop at generalities, they always go further and bring out the details, they consider the problem point by point; and fortunately the apostle does that in this particular instance.

Why are these people lacking in discipline in their lives, why is this slackness, this indolence so apparent in their lives? The first cause seems to be that they have a wrong view of faith. Now this I find in the beginning of the fifth verse, where he says: 'And beside all this—for this very cause—giving all diligence add to your faith'—supplement your faith, furnish out your faith with the things which he then proceeds to mention. Now there, surely, is a suggestion that they have a wrong view of faith. This is something which is very common. They seem to have had a kind of magical view of faith; the idea, in other words, that as long as you have faith all is well, that your faith will work automatically in your life, and that all you need to do as a Christian is just to believe the truth. You must accept the faith and having done that all the rest will happen to you; you just take one step, you make a decision, or whatever it may be called, and that is all that is necessary. I describe it as almost a magical view of faith, or an automatic conception of faith. But perhaps I can put it in a different form. Very often there is what we must needs describe as a mystical view of faith. This certainly accounts for the trouble in many people. By a mystical view I mean a conception of faith which always thinks of it as a whole. Putting it negatively I mean that such people do not realize that faith needs to be supplemented by virtue, knowledge, temperance, patience, godliness, brotherly kindness and charity, as the apostle shows here. They have one formula only and the one formula is that you must always be 'looking to the Lord', and as long as you 'look to the Lord' there is nothing else to do. They say that any attempt to do anything else is dropping back to the 'salvation by works' position. So if you have a problem in your Christian life they say to you: 'Just look to the Lord, abide in the Lord'.

This is a very common error. You will find it in a most interesting form in the case of expositors who hold this view. In expounding certain passages of Scripture where much emphasis is put upon details they are obviously in difficulty, because from their standpoint you must not be concerned about details. There is only one thing to do, you 'abide in the Lord and look to Him' and as long as you do that there is nothing more to be done. This is a most productive cause of this kind of spiritual depression and lethargy with which we are dealing. Such people spend their time in this unhappy condition. All along they are trying to apply this exhortation to 'just abide in the Lord', and to 'look to the Lord', and for a while all seems to be well, but then somehow or another something seems to go wrong and they do not seem to be 'abiding' and they are unhappy once more. The problem returns, and so the whole of their life is spent in trying to maintain this one position which they recognize. Now this is clearly a very important matter, and we must be sure that our view of faith is the New Testament view, and that we realize what the apostle means here when he goes on to say that we have to 'add' to our faith, to 'supplement' our faith, with certain other things.

The second general cause of this condition is undoubtedly nothing but sheer laziness or indolence, nothing but slackness, or, to use the apostle's language, a lack of diligence. He says: 'Beside this, giving all diligence'. He is very concerned to impress that upon us, and so he repeats it in the tenth verse. I think we all know something about this. There is a kind of general indolence or laziness which afflicts us all and is undoubtedly produced by the devil himself. Have we not all noticed that when it comes to things in the spiritual life, we do not seem to have the same zeal and enthusiasm, nor do we apply the same energy as we do with our secular calling or vocation, our profession or business, our pleasure, or something we happen to be interested in? Have we not all noticed when we have been working quite well that somehow if we turn for a season of prayer, we suddenly feel tired and fatigued? Is it not curious that we always become tired and sleepy when we want to read the Bible? We are fully persuaded that it is something purely physical, and that we really cannot help ourselves, but it is as certain as anything can be that the moment we begin to apply ourselves to spiritual things we shall immediately come face to face with this problem of indolence and the laziness that afflicts us, however alert and energetic we may have been previously.

Or take it as it assumes the form of procrastination. We desire to read the Bible, we want to study it, we want to read a Commentary; but we do not feel like it at the moment, we think it is a bad thing to try to do these things when we do not feel at our best, and we had better put it off until we feel better, there will be a more appropriate opportunity later on. Or we have not the time, or we lack the opportunity. How often have we all passed through this kind of experience. Then when the time does come, in a strange manner we still find we cannot apply ourselves. It is beyond dispute that most of us are living lives which are seriously lacking in discipline and in order and in arrangement. Never perhaps has life been quite so difficult for the Christian as it is at the present time. The world and the organizations of life round and about us make things almost impossible; the most difficult thing in life is to order your own life and to manage it. The reason for this is, not that these external things really compel us but that if we do not realize the danger of drifting and put up a stand against it, we will have failed without knowing it. There are so many things that distract us. You start with your morning newspaper (many people start with two rather than one), and then in a few hours come your evening paper or papers. Now these things are thrust upon us. Of course we are not bound to buy a paper but it is there and everybody else does so. Perhaps it is delivered at the door. The thing is put in front of us and without our realizing it there is something occupying our time. I need not waste time in detailing all these things, the wireless, the television and the things we have to do, meetings to attend, incidents here and there, various problems that arise. The fact is that every one of us is fighting for his life at the present time, fighting to possess and master and live our own life. All pastors will agree with me when I say that there is nothing that one is being told more frequently today than just this: 'I do not know what to do, I do not seem to have time to read my Bible and to meditate as I would like'.

Now the simple answer to that is, that it is sheer lack of discipline, it is a sheer failure to order our life. It is no use complaining about circumstances. It simply comes back to this, and there is no need to argue about it—we all have time! If we have time to do these other things, we do have the time, and the whole secret of success in this respect is to take that time and insist that it is given to this matter of the soul instead of to these other things. That is the second cause of the trouble—a sheer lack of discipline in the life, a failure to order our lives, to command and to control our lives as we know in our heart of hearts we should.

That being the cause, let us turn to the treatment. What is the treatment prescribed by the apostle for this condition? It is just the reverse of the cause of the trouble. First and foremost he emphasizes 'all diligence'. 'Make every effort'—according to another translation. That is it—'make every effort'—'beside this', 'for this cause', 'in the light of these things'—the exceeding great and precious promises that are given, with all the things that appertain to life and godliness, and because you have escaped the corruption that is in the world through lust— because of all these things make every effort, give all diligence, or as it is translated in the tenth verse, be more zealous than ever before to do these things. Here is the treatment then, the exercise of discipline and of diligence.

Perhaps the best way of putting this matter is to put it in a simple historical manner. I defy you to read the life of any saint that has ever adorned the life of the Church without seeing at once that the greatest characteristic in the life of that saint was discipline and order. Invariably it is the universal characteristic of all the outstanding men and women of God. Read about Henry Martyn, David Brainerd, Jonathan Edwards, the brothers Wesley, and Whitfield—read their journals. It does not matter what branch of the Church they belonged to, they have all disciplined their lives and have insisted upon the need for this; and obviously it is something that is thoroughly scriptural and absolutely essential. 'For he that cometh unto God must believe that He is', says the author of the Epistle to the Hebrews (11. 6), yes, and also 'that He is a rewarder of them that diligently seek Him'. We must be diligent in our seeking. 'But,' says someone, 'your preaching, is it not an inculcation of justification by works?'

You see how subtle the devil is! 'Surely you are going back to the Roman Catholic heresy and the whole Catholic type of devotion?' The answer to that argument is that it is the Apostle Peter, the inspired apostle, who goes out of his way to remind us that all these Scriptures are inspired, it is he who tells us that we must 'add' to our faith these various other things and to give all diligence in the doing of it. Be more zealous, be still more active, he says. And, of course, there is no contradiction at all. The error of justification by works is in trusting to the discipline of your own soul to save your soul; but the opposite to trusting to your works is not to do nothing, it is to do everything but not to put your trust in any of it. It is not the works that are wrong, it is the faith in your works, trusting in your works. But what a subtle danger this is. It seems to me that one of the chief dangers in Protestantism today, and especially in evangelical circles is that, in our fear of the error of justification by works, we have been saying that works do not matter at all. We argue that faith alone counts, and because I am a man of faith it does not matter what I do and my life can be thoroughly lacking in discipline. Out upon the suggestion! The opposite to a false trust in works is not indolence, lack of discipline and doing nothing, it is to be diligent and more diligent, to be zealous, and to add to your faith. But all the time you must realize that your action alone will never be enough, but that God is certainly a rewarder of them that diligently seek Him. So many people say that they would give anything to have but a vestige of the knowledge that the saints had, 'If only I had that joy, I would give the whole world for that—why cannot I have the experience of the warm heart?' they say. The answer is that they have never really sought it. Look at the lives of those men and the time they gave to Scripture reading and prayer and various other forms of self-examination and spiritual exercises. They believed in the culture and the discipline of the spiritual life and it was because they did so that God rewarded them by giving them these gracious manifestations of Himself and these mighty experiences which warmed their hearts.

So we put first the sheer necessity of discipline and order. Indeed I am tempted at this point to deal with the matter in detail. If we agree about the importance of claiming time and of ordering our daily lives we must insist at all costs that certain things must be done. In other words if I really believe that the

Bible is more important to me than the daily newspaper, I must read my Bible before I read the newspaper. Whatever I may leave undone, I must see to it that this is done. My prayer time must be insisted upon, I must have my time for meditation; whatever else is not done, I must do these things. That is the beginning, that is an illustration of an element of order coming back into life. So many people fail and become miserable and depressed simply because they have not taken themselves in hand. You will have to do it yourself it will never be done for you, indeed, nobody else can do it for you. If you do not attend to these things in detail I assure you that you will remain a depressed Christian. 'Give all diligence', 'make every effort', 'be more than zealous', see to it at all costs.

The second principle is that we have to supplement our faith. 'Add to your faith', says this authorized version, 'supplement it', says another, 'furnish it out', says another. The authorities tell us that this word 'furnish' is a Greek word that was used in con- nection with the performance of a drama. It means the providing of a kind of orchestra or chorus. You furnish the performance with this orchestra, this chorus, so that it may be complete. It was something that rounded off the performance and made it a perfect performance. That is the meaning of the word, add to it, furnish it, supplement it, make the thing complete, let it be a full-orbed faith.

What do you add to faith? The apostle gives us this list. I must just note them. The first thing he says is: 'Add to your faith virtue'. What does he mean by that? Here again is a word the meaning of which has changed since this authorized version was produced. It does not mean virtue in the sense in which we commonly use it at the present time, for each item in the list is a virtue in that sense. Its meaning here is energy, moral energy, it means power, it means vigour. Now, this is very important. The condition that the apostle is dealing with is this languid, undisciplined, slack kind of Christian life and he begins by reminding them that: 'Now you have faith, you believe the truth, there is no doubt about that, you have like precious faith with us'. Well, what more need they do about it? He tells them that in addition to the faith which they have, they must cease to be languid. In other words, add to your faith moral energy, pull yourself together, don't shuffle through your Christian life, walk through it as you should do with vigour, add to it that kind of strength and of power. Do not be a languid Christian who always gives the impression that he or she is on the point of swooning and fainting and might fail at any moment. Do not be languid, says the apostle, furnish your faith with manliness and power—virtue.

How necessary is this exhortation. Compare and contrast the typical average Christian with the typical average person of the world. The Christian claims that he is interested in spiritual things, and in the Kingdom of God and in a knowledge of God and of Christ. This is his claim. He says that he has faith and that is what faith means. Yet compare him with the average person who is interested in various games and the things that happen in the world of sport. You see the difference, there is nothing languid about the person who is interested in these things. Look at their excitement, and their energy. Then look at the Christian by contrast, how languid he is, how apparently apologetic he is. And the reason is that this type of Christian has failed to add to his faith. He says that he is a Christian and believes the Truth but he fails to 'furnish out' his faith.

'Add to your faith virtue and to virtue knowledge.' This does not simply mean knowledge of doctrine. We have that in a measure otherwise we would not have faith. This means a kind of insight, it means understanding, it means enlightenment. We do not know everything the moment we believe in Christ, we do not understand fully then, that is only the beginning. There are constant appeals and exhortations in the New Testament epistles to growth in understanding—'that your love may grow', says Paul, 'in understanding'. That is the thing the Apostle Peter is saying at this point. He says that they must not stop at believing. They are already Christians but they have to understand the Christian life. They must come to see the subtle dangers that surround them, they must understand something of the ingenuity of Satan. They need understanding: so 'add to your faith', strive for this insight, this apprehension, this enlightenment. How essential it is that we should give ourselves to a diligent reading of the Scriptures and of books on the Scriptures and on the doctrines of the faith. You will never understand the faith truly unless you apply yourself to these things. It is a painful process sometimes and it certainly needs all the discipline we can ever apply. The student never becomes proficient in any subject without hard work. The talk about that brilliant type of man who never does any work at all and then comes out first in the examination is sheer myth. It just does not happen, it is a lie. Without knowledge—and you will never have knowledge without applying yourself—a man can never have this true understanding, this true knowledge. It needs discipline and application; it is indeed supremely hard work to furnish out your faith with knowledge.

The next thing is temperance, which means self-control, and here it does not simply mean that you control your life in general. This temperance is a much more detailed and particular thing than that. It means that you will have to control every single aspect of your life. It may mean you will have to control even your eating and your drinking. The authorities are constantly telling us that many people are in a poor state of physical health because they eat and drink too much. There is no doubt that that is true and that there is an increasing tendency to it in the modern world. It is thrust upon us. it is made attractive; and there are people who suffer from tiredness and lethargy very often simply because of lack of temperance or self-control. They do not control their appetites, their lusts, their passions, their desires; they eat too much, or drink too much, or even sleep too much. The way to get an insight into that is to read the lives of the saints, to read their diaries, to read what they did with themselves and how they controlled their lives. How fearful they were of these very things, and how clearly they realized that they had to avoid them at all cost.

Patience means patient endurance, to keep on though everything discourages you. You have to do that, you, yourself. You must add this to your faith. It does not just mean passively 'looking to the Lord'; you yourself have to exercise patience and go on steadily doing this, day by day.

And then godliness which at this point undoubtedly means concern about and carefulness in maintaining our relationship with God. Then in the last two items in the list he is concerned about our attitude towards our fellow men. Brotherly kindness means our relationship to our fellow Christians. Charity means love towards men even though they are outside the faith. We have to watch these things in detail.

The apostle having taken us through these various steps and stages now gives us encouragement to do all that he has told us to do. What is the encouragement? First of all he reminds us of what we are. He tells us that we have become 'partakers of the

Divine Nature'. If you feel that I have been preaching a hard doctrine, and that this is reducing the Christian life to a hard task, if you are at all hesitant or doubtful, let me ask a few questions. Do you realize what you are, as a Christian? Do you realize that you are a 'partaker of the Divine Nature', do you realize that the Son of God came from heaven to earth and went even to the Cross of Calvary to save you, to deliver you from the world and its lusts? 'Having escaped the corruption that is in the world through lust.' Lust is the cause of that corruption. Are you going to remain in that condition? Do you not want to escape from it? Realize, he says, that Christ has died that you may be taken out of it, and that you have been taken out of it. For this very cause then 'give all diligence'. 'Surely,' Peter argues, 'you have not forgotten that "you have been purged from your old sins", surely you have not forgotten that you died with Christ and are therefore dead unto the law and dead unto sin?' 'How shall we that are dead unto sin live any longer therein' —that is Paul's way of putting it. That is Peter's argument. We have to realize that, and what a tremendous encouragement it is as we face the fight of faith.

But you do not stop at that. Realize further, says the apostle, that if only you do these things you will have great joy and happiness in the present. 'Wherefore, brethren, give diligence to make your calling and election sure'; and you can make your calling and election sure by doing these things. You will never be happy if you do not. It is not enough to say: 'The Word of God says "whosoever believeth", and I believe—therefore. . . .' That is true but it does not always satisfy. It is right that we should reason so, that is a part of our assurance, but if we think assurance stops at that we are making a profound mistake. If we want to make our calling and election sure we have to give diligence to do all these things that the apostle lists, and as we do so we shall have great joy and peace and happiness. We shall know where we stand and we shall reap these first-fruits of the glory that awaits us.

'If you do these things you shall never fall.' Nothing is more discouraging than our various fallings. We fall and then we are miserable and unhappy and down comes depression which tends to make us feel utterly hopeless about everything. Well the thing to do is to avoid falling, and if you do these things you shall never fall. It does not mean that you are being kept and that you are doing nothing. He says, do these things and you will not fall. So give all diligence to all these things so that you may not fall.

And finally—and how glorious it is—'for so', he says, 'an entrance shall be ministered unto you abundantly into the everlasting kingdom of our Lord Jesus Christ'. He is not talking about salvation here because these people are already saved; he is talking about the ultimate entrance into glory. Notice the word 'ministered'. For so, he says, an entrance shall be 'ministered' unto you. That is exactly the same word as the word previously translated 'add'. You minister these things to your faith, and an abundant entrance shall be ministered to you. It works reciprocally. In other words, 'if you do these things,' says Peter, 'if you discipline your life, if you order your life and furnish out your faith in this way and with these various other qualities,' he says 'you will never fall' in the present, you will have great joy and happiness resulting from your assurance, and when the end comes you will go out of this life into the next with your sails filled with the glorious breezes of Heaven. There will be no hesitation about it, it will not be an entrance with torn sails; rather an 'abundant entrance' will be ministered unto you. You will not need to say with Lord Tennyson:

> 'And may there be no moaning of the bar
> When I put out to sea'.

For it will not be a putting out into some unknown sea, but rather an ending of the storms of life and a triumphant entry into the haven of our eternal rest and glory in the presence of God.

If we are unhappy and depressed Christians it is more than likely that it is all due to that lack of discipline. Let us therefore be up and doing, and giving all diligence, let us supplement our faith and not be afraid. Let us get our ideas clear and then put them into practice, and supplement our faith with this strength and vigour, with this knowledge, with this temperance, with this patience, godliness, brotherly kindness and love. Let us begin to enjoy our Christian life and to be useful and helpful to others. Let us grow in grace and knowledge and so be an attraction to all who know us to come and join with us in the like precious faith, and to experience the blessedness of these exceeding great and precious promises which never fail.

Wherein ye greatly rejoice, though now for a season, if need be, ye are in heaviness through manifold temptations: That the trial of your faith, being much more precious than of gold that perisheth, though it be tried with fire, might be found unto praise and honour and glory at the appearing of Jesus Christ.

1 Peter 1. 6, 7

XVI

TRIALS

HAVING considered many reasons why Christians may
suffer from spiritual depression, we come to the particular
reason with which the Apostle Peter deals in this section. There
can be no question but that his only object in writing this letter
was to deal with this very state. So he starts by reminding these
people of certain things, and then he comes at once to his theme.
He introduces the matter by talking about the great salvation:
'Blessed be the God and Father of our Lord Jesus Christ which
according to His abundant mercy hath begotten us again unto
a lively hope by the resurrection of Jesus Christ from the dead.
To an inheritance incorruptible and undefiled and that fadeth
not away . . . Wherein', he then says, 'ye greatly rejoice, though
now for a season if need be ye are in heaviness through manifold
temptations'. That is his description of these people. They
'greatly rejoice' in this blessed hope, and yet they are 'in heaviness through manifold temptations'. Here again, as we have found
in so many instances, the description seems to be quite contradictory. He is describing people who at one and the same time
are greatly rejoicing and yet are in heaviness. But we have seen,
again so often, that there is nothing contradictory about this.
You may if you like call it paradoxical, but it is not contradictory. Indeed the condition of the Christian as described in the
New Testament seems always to include these two elements and
at one and the same time we find that these Christian people
of whom the apostle writes are 'greatly rejoicing' and are also
'in heaviness'.

This is something about which we must be very clear before
we proceed any further. There is a superficial view of Christianity
which would regard this as quite impossible, the kind of view of
the Christian life which simply says that all the problems have
gone and now 'I am happy all the day'. Such people cannot
accept Peter's description for a moment and would say of any
Christian who is 'in heaviness' that it is doubtful whether he is a
Christian at all. There is that teaching concerning the Christian

life which gives the impression that once one has arrived at a decision, or once one has been converted, there are no more troubles, no ripples on the sea of life. Everything is perfect and there are no problems whatsoever. Now the simple answer to that view is that it is not New Testament Christianity. That is the kind of thing which the cults have always offered and which modern psychology is also offering. There is nothing for which one should thank God so much as the honesty of the Scriptures. They give us the simple truth about ourselves and about our life in this world.

We have to start therefore by realizing that this is something which is postulated of the Christian. Now let us make no mistake about this word 'heaviness'. Heaviness means to be grieved, it means we are troubled. It is not merely that we have to suffer certain things, but that the suffering of these things does grieve us. We are troubled by them and are really made unhappy by them. So Peter describes these people as showing these two characteristics at one and the same time, a great rejoicing and yet being grieved. You will find that so frequently in the Scriptures. Take as a perfect example of it the series of paradoxes which the apostle uses to describe himself in 2 Corinthians 4. 'We are troubled on every side and yet not distressed; we are perplexed but not in despair; persecuted but not forsaken; cast down but not destroyed; always bearing about in the body the dying of the Lord Jesus'—and so on. These statements appear to be mutually exclusive at first, but they are not. They are just a part of the paradox of the Christian life. This is the amazing thing about the Christian that at one and the same time he does experience these two things. 'If that is so,' says someone, 'where is the problem?' The problem lies here, that we fail to maintain the balance and that we tend to allow this heaviness, this grief to overwhelm us and really cast us down. The danger is not merely that we are temporarily upset by it, but that it really may become a prevailing mood which we can never get rid of, and that, as a result, people looking at us are more conscious of this 'grievous heaviness' than they are of the 'great rejoicing'.

What we are really saying and what we have to realize and to remember is that the Christian is not one who has become immune to what is happening round and about him. We need to emphasize this truth because there are certain people whose whole notion and conception of the Christian life makes the Christian quite unnatural. Grief and sorrow are something to which the Christian is subject, and there is a sense in which I am prepared to argue that the absence of a feeling of grief in a Christian in certain circumstances is not a recommendation for the Christian faith. It is unnatural, it goes beyond the New Testament, it savours more of the stoic or of the psychological state produced by a cult rather than of Christianity. There is nothing which is more instructive and encouraging as you go through the Scriptures than to observe that the saints of God are subject to human frailties. They know grief and sorrow, they know what it is to feel lonely, they know what it is to be disappointed. There are abundant examples of this in the Scriptures. You see it in the life of the Apostle Paul perhaps more than in anyone else. He was subject to these things and he does not conceal that fact. He was still a very human person though he had such amazing faith and though he had had such wonderful experiences in his communion with his blessed Lord. Very well, these things may be found at one and the same time, and the Christian must never regard himself as one who is exempt from natural feelings. He has something that enables him to rise above these things, but the glory of the Christian life is that you rise above them though you feel them. It is not an absence of feeling. This is a most important dividing line.

Having laid down that postulate let us consider why it is that a Christian should thus be in heaviness and in this condition of grief. The answer is, of course, these 'manifold temptations'. The word translated temptations really means 'trials'. These people were like this because they were passing through manifold trials. Now that is an interesting word, the Greek word here translated 'manifold'. It is obviously a favourite word of the Apostle Peter, and he uses it later on to describe the grace of God. It means 'many-coloured', like the various colours in the spectrum. The poet Shelley had the same idea when he wrote:

'Life like a dome of many-coloured glass
Stains the white radiance of eternity'.

That is the meaning of the word used here, and the apostle says that they were troubled because they were experiencing these manifold trials. They come in different ways and colours, in different shapes and forms and there is no end to the variety.

What are these trials? In this Epistle Peter makes it quite clear what he has in mind. Many of these Christians were being persecuted. In the second chapter we read: 'I beseech you as strangers and pilgrims, abstain from fleshly lusts, which war against the soul; having your conversation honest among the Gentiles: that, whereas they speak against you as evildoers, they may by your good works which they shall behold, glorify God in the day of visitation'. The Christian, because he is a Christian, is subject to this kind of thing in the world. Because he is a new man, because he is born again, he is inevitably bound to be misunderstood. He is a pilgrim and he is like a stranger in a strange land. He lives a different type of life, he has different ideas and customs. The other people looking on, notice the difference and they do not like it, in fact they make it very plain that they dislike it. These early Christians were subject to persecution and trials that came in that way.

We get many accounts of these trials in the Bible, and the saints of God have always had to meet this kind of thing. The Apostle Paul, indeed, in writing to Timothy (2 Timothy 3. 12) goes so far as to say: 'Yea, and all that will live godly in Christ Jesus shall suffer persecution'. It is a law, according to the Scriptures that the more we approximate to the Lord Jesus Christ in our life and living, the more likely we are to meet troubles in this world. Look at Him. He did no evil, neither was any guile found in His mouth. He spent His time in healing people, doing good and preaching; and yet look at the opposition, look at the trials He had to endure. Why? Because He was what He was. The world in its heart of hearts hates Christ and it hates the Christian, because such holy living condemns it. The man of the world does not like it because it makes him feel uncomfortable. The apostle knew what these people were experiencing at the hands of evildoers, and he goes on in the fourth chapter to put it still more specifically: 'For the time past of our life may suffice us to have wrought the will of the Gentiles, when we walked in lasciviousness, lusts, excess of wine, revellings, banquetings, and abominable idolatries; wherein they think it strange that ye run not with them to the same excess of riot, speaking evil of you'. The world was annoyed with these people because they had given up that sort of life and were living the Christian life. As soon as they became Christian they got into trouble with the world. People who had been friendly before now began to ignore them and to criticize them and to speak unkindly—and worse— about them to others.

That was one of the things that was causing them grief. They were in heaviness because of this, and it is something the Christian has had to endure throughout the centuries. Nothing is more trying than this misunderstanding on the part of other people, and it becomes still more difficult if it happens to be someone who is near and dear to you. How trying it is when a Christian finds himself, perhaps, the only Christian in a family. This kind of trial does happen, and for a Christian never to meet it in some shape or form suggests that there is something radically wrong with his Christianity. The Apostle Paul experienced this constantly. You remember how he says, 'Demas hath forsaken me'. That was not a light thing to Paul; he was troubled by it. He had to stand his trial absolutely alone; people on whom he thought he could rely suddenly ran away from him, and there he was, alone. 'No man stood with me.' That is the kind of thing that grieves a Christian, and you have but to read the lives of the saints to find this kind of thing constantly. Read the journals of John Wesley and you will find he was frequently in this condition because of misunderstandings. This, on a big scale, is to be found in the life of Charles Haddon Spurgeon in connection with the famous 'Down grade' controversy. Men whom he had regarded as friends, and some of whom he had trained in his own college at his own expense, suddenly fell away from him. You have but to read his account of it to see how he was hurt and grieved. He was in heaviness because men whom he thought he could rely on suddenly failed him. It undoubtedly shortened his life. I was reading in the journals of George Whitefield recently, an account of this very thing. Whitefield had had a season of exceptional nearness to Christ and he was rejoicing in it, but he makes a note in his journal to remind himself of the fact that in some strange way such experiences were often followed by grievous trials, and, no doubt, he says: 'I shall be subject to that again'. He knew it, it was his experience, it is almost an inevitable law in the life of the man of God in a world of sin.

Here, then, were these Christians suffering manifold trials. The term is comprehensive, it means anything in this life that tends to trouble you, something that touches you in the most sensitive and delicate part of your being, in your heart, in your mind, the things that tend to cast you down. How does the apostle deal with the situation? It is most interesting, and it is what you and I must do if we are to maintain this two-fold aspect of our Christian life. If we are to go on rejoicing in spite of the things that grieve us, we must approach them and face them all in the way in which the apostle instructs us.

What is his teaching? The first thing he does is to lay down a great principle, which is that we must understand why these things happen to us. That is the first thing and how often do we need to say this to ourselves and to one another. I sometimes think that the whole art of the Christian life is the art of asking questions. Our danger is just to allow things to happen to us and to endure them without saying anything apart from a groan, a grumble or a complaint. The thing to do is to discover, if we can, why these things are taking place. To try to discover the explanation, and in this connection the apostle uses the following terms. 'Wherein,' he says, 'ye greatly rejoice, though now for a season if need be. . . .' 'If need be!' Ah, that is the secret. What does he mean by that phrase? There is no uncertainty about the answer to that. It is a conditional statement, which you can translate if you like: 'though now for a season if such proves needful'. 'If such proves needful.' It is not merely a general statement to the effect that in a world like this these things must happen. It is much stronger than that. He does not say: 'Well, you are greatly rejoicing in this blessed hope though in a world like this you may have to endure certain things'. That is all right, that is perfectly true; but the apostle does not merely leave it at that. His is a positive statement. He says: 'You are at the moment enduring this grief, because it has proved needful for you that you should do so'. Now, there then, is our principle; there is a definite purpose in all this. This does not happen accidentally, this is not something that just takes place because of the whole organization of life. That does come into it, but it is not the main reason. These things happen, says the apostle, because they are good for us, because they are part of our discipline in this life and in this world, because—let me put it quite plainly—because God has appointed it.

That is the apostle's doctrine as it is the doctrine of the whole of the New Testament, and as it certainly is the doctrine of the saints of the centuries. In other words, we must look at the Christian life in this way. We are walking through this world under the eye of our Heavenly Father. That is the fundamental thing, the Christian must think of himself as in a pecular relationship to God. This is not true of any one who is not a Christian.

There is a very definite plan and purpose for the whole of my life, God has looked upon me, God has adopted me and put me into His family. What for? In order that He may bring me to perfection. That is His objective—'that ye may be made (more and more) conformable to the image of His dear Son'. That is what He is doing. The Lord Jesus Christ is bringing many sons unto God, saying: 'Behold I and the children that Thou hast given me'. If we do not start with that fundamental conception of ourselves as Christians, we are bound to go astray, and we are certain to misunderstand these things.

The doctrine of the Scriptures is, at the very lowest, that God permits these things to happen to us. I go further, God at times orders these things to happen to us for our good. He may do it sometimes in order to chastise us. He chastises us for our slackness and for our failure. We were looking in the previous chapter at the failure of the Christian to discipline himself. Peter exhorts the Christians to discipline themselves, to add to their faith, to furnish out their faith, not merely to be content with a bare minimum but to let it be a full-orbed faith. We may not pay heed to that exhortation, we may persist in our slackness and in our indolence. Well, as I understand the New Testament doctrine, if we do that we must not be surprised if things begin to happen to us. We must not be surprised if God begins to chastise us. The argument in Hebrews 12 is as strong as this: 'Whom the Lord loveth He chasteneth'. If you have not known chastisement I doubt whether you have ever been a Christian. If you can say that since you have believed you have never had any trouble at all, your experience is probably psychological and not spiritual. There is a realism about Christianity, as I said at the beginning and it goes so far as to teach that God, for our good, will chastise us if we pay no heed to the exhortations and the appeals of the Scripture. God has other methods also. He does not do these things to those who are outside the family, but if they are His children He will chastise them for their own good. So we may be experiencing manifold trials as a part of our chastisement. I am not saying it is inevitable, I say it may be so.

But then sometimes God does this to us to prepare us for something. It is a rule of the Scriptures, and a rule which is confirmed by and exemplified in the long history of the Church and her saints, that when God has a particularly great task for a man to perform, He generally does try him. I care not which biography you pick up, you may take the life of any man who has been signally used by God and you will find that there has been a severe time of testing and of trial in his experience. It is as if God would not dare to use such a man unless He could be certain and sure of him. So one may have to pass through this kind of experience because of some great task ahead. Look at Joseph, and at the things that happened to him. Can you imagine a more dismal kind of life. Everybody seemed to be against him. His own brethren were jealous of him and got rid of him. He was taken to Egypt and there people turned against him. He had done nothing wrong but because he was what he was things went against him. But in all this God was only preparing the man for the great position that He had in store for him. And it is the same with all the great men of the Bible. Look at the suffering of a man like David. Indeed look at any one of them and you will find that their lives were full of trials and difficulties. The Apostle Paul was no exception. Look at the list of his sufferings and trials in the Second Epistle to the Corinthians, chapters 11 and 12. It has always happened like that.

It seems also from the teaching of the Scriptures and the lives of saints, that God sometimes prepares a man for a great trial in this way. I mean that He prepares him for a great trial by giving him some lesser trials. It is there that I see the love of God shining out so gloriously. There are certain great trials that come in life, and it would be a terrible thing for people suddenly to be plunged into a great trial from the undisturbed and even tenor of their ways. So God sometimes, in His tenderness and love, sends lesser trials to prepare us for the greater ones. 'If need be'— if such proves needful, if God, in looking upon us as our Father, sees that this is just what we need at that moment. So we start with this great principle, that God sees and knows what is best for us and what is needful. We do not see, but God always does, and, as our Heavenly Father, He sees the need and He prescribes the appropriate trial which is destined for our good.

But let us come to the second principle which is the precious character of faith. Peter says in the seventh verse that these things had happened—these manifold temptations—in order 'that the trial of your faith, being much more precious than of gold that perisheth, though it be tried with fire, might be found unto praise and honour and glory at the appearing of Jesus Christ'. How important this is—the precious character of faith. He brings that

out in his comparison with gold. Look at gold, he says in effect,
Gold is precious but not as precious as faith. How does he establish
that? He shows that gold is something that ultimately is going to
vanish. It is only temporary. there is nothing permanent about it,
though it is wonderful and very precious. But faith is eternal.
Gold perishes but faith does not. Faith is something that is everlasting and eternal. The thing by which you live, says the apostle,
is the thing which accounts for your being in the Christian life.
You are in this faith position and you do not realize, he continues,
what a marvellous and wonderful thing it is. We walk by faith,
the whole of our life is a matter of faith, and you see, says the
apostle, this is so precious in the sight of God, it is so marvellous,
it is so wonderful that God wants it to be absolutely pure. You
purify your gold by means of fire. You get rid of the alloy and all
the impurities by putting gold in the crucible and applying
great heat to it, and so these other things are removed and the
gold remains. His argument, therefore, is that if you do that with
gold that perishes, how much more does it need to be done with
faith. Faith is this extraordinary principle which links man to
God; faith is this thing that keeps a man from hell and puts him
in heaven; it is the connection between this world and the world
to come; faith is this mystic astounding thing that can take a
man dead in trespasses and sins and make him live as a new
being, a new man in Christ Jesus. That is why it is so precious.
It is so precious that God wants it to be absolutely perfect. That
is the apostle's argument. So you are in these manifold temptations because of the character of faith.

But let me put that in a slightly different form. Our faith, we
see, needs to be perfected. There must therefore be degrees of
faith. There are differences in the quality of faith. Faith is many-
sided. There is generally at the beginning a good deal of ad-
mixture in what we call our faith; there is a good deal of the
flesh that we are not aware of. And as we begin to learn these
things, and as we go on with the process, God puts us through
His testing times. He tests us by trials as if by fire in order that
the things which do not belong to the essence of faith may
fall off. We may think that our faith is perfect and that we can
stand up against anything. Then suddenly a trial comes and we
find that we fail. Why? Well that is just an indication that the
trust element in our faith needs to be developed; and God
develops the trust element in our faith by trying us in this way.

The more we experience these things, the more we learn to trust God. We naturally trust Him when He is smiling on us, but a day comes when the clouds are blackening the heavens and we begin to wonder whether God loves us any longer and whether the Christian life is what we thought it to be. Ah, our faith had not developed the element of trust, and God so deals with us in this life as to bring us to trust Him in the dark when we can see no light at all, and to bring us to the point where we can confidently say:

> 'When all things seem against us,
> To drive us to despair,
> We know one gate is open
> One ear will hear our prayer'.

That is true faith, that is real trust. Look at a man like Abraham. God had so dealt with him that he could 'hope against hope'. He trusted God absolutely when every appearance was to the contrary. And that needs to be developed in us. We do not start like that, but as we go through these experiences we find that 'behind a frowning providence He hides a Father's face', and the next time the trials come we remain calm and collected. We can say: 'Yes, I know, I do not see the sun but I know it is there. I know that behind the clouds the Face of God is looking upon me'. It is by means of these trials that that element of trust is developed.

It is exactly the same with the element of patience or patient endurance, the sheer capacity to go on and to keep on in spite of discouragement. That is one of the greatest tests a Christian can ever have. We are not patient by nature. We start as children in the Christian life and we want everything at once, and if it does not come, we become impatient and grumble, we complain and we sulk like children. That is because we are lacking in patience and patient endurance. There is nothing more emphasized in the New Testament Epistles than this quality of just keeping on whether things go well with us or not. We are to go on saying: 'God knows what is best for me. I will trust in God'. 'Even though He slay me yet will I trust Him.' That is patient endurance, keeping on, and it is as we are tried and tested that all these other elements which go to furnish out our faith become developed and are perfected.

Let me then put it in a final general principle in this form. These trials are essential, says Peter, in order to show the genuineness of our faith. His actual phrase is—'that the trial of your faith'. Now 'trial' there means 'the attestation of it'. The picture he has in his mind is of a test being applied to something, and then after it has been tested a certificate is given. For instance the report on a ring might be, 'Yes, it is 18 carat gold'. That is what is meant by trial. He is not interested in the process as such; trial is the certificate of attestation, declaring the genuineness of our faith. The approved character of our faith is thus manifested. That is why these things happen to us.

Surely this is quite obvious. It is the way in which we endure trials that really certifies our faith. You remember how our Lord, in the parable of the sower depicts the seed falling amongst thorns. There seemed to be a marvellous harvest coming but it did not come because these other things choked the Word. Our Lord interprets that as being comparable to the way in which trials come and crush and choke the Word so that it never comes to fruition. At first it seems so wonderful, but it does not last. The trials prove that it was a spurious faith, that it was not a real faith, not a genuine faith. There is nothing which so certifies the genuineness of a man's faith as his patience and his patient endurance, his keeping on steadily in spite of everything. That is the teaching of our Lord, and it is the teaching of the whole of the New Testament.

There is nothing that is so wonderful in the life of the greatest saints as just that, the way in which they stood like rocks when others fell away round and about them. It is the glorious story of the Martyrs and the great Confessors. They had trials, but they just stood on what they knew to be God's truth without regard to the consequences, and they went on with their faith shining out gloriously. Now these things are happening to you, says Peter, that the genuineness of your faith may be perfectly evident to all. Christians that fall away are no recommendation; those who start well but who do not continue disgrace the faith. The thing that shows the difference between the spurious and the real is the capacity to stand the test 'All that glitters is not gold'. How do you prove it? You put your material in a crucible and you put a flame underneath. You find that dross will burn while the gold remains, and is purer than it was before. These things happen to us in order that the genuineness of our faith may be revealed. That is the most important thing after all.

Let me add just a word on what Peter says for our encouragement. Let me remind you of it. What is the consolation? It is that although these things happen to us, yet they only happen 'for a season'. 'Wherein ye greatly rejoice, though now for a season if need be.' Do not get the impression that I am teaching that this state of trial is the perpetual condition of the Christian. It is not. These things come and go as God deems fit. We shall never be tried and tested except it be for our good, and as we respond to the teaching, God will withdraw the test. He does not keep us permanently under trial. As Whitefield said, these things alternate, and God knows exactly how to send them and when. And we can be sure with the Apostle Paul, that: 'There hath no temptation taken you but such as is common to man: but God is faithful, who will not suffer you to be tempted above that ye are able; but will with the temptation also make a way to escape that ye may be able to bear it' (1 Corinthians 10. 13). He is your loving Father, He knows how much you can take and stand. He will never send too much for you. He knows the right amount, and He will give the right amount, and when you have responded He will withdraw it. It is only 'for a season'. Do these words come to some downcast, heavy-laden Christian? Does all seem blackness and darkness? Are you not having the liberty you once had in prayer? Have you almost lost the faith you once had? Do not be troubled. You are in the hand of your Father. There may be a glorious period coming for you, He may have some unusual blessing for you, He may have some great work for you to do. Do not be downcast, it is only 'for a season'. You are in the hands of your loving Father, so trust Him and go on. Keep on and say: 'I am content only to be in Thy hands. "Only to do Thy will, my will shall be".'

The second thing is this. As you are experiencing this heaviness, remind yourself also of the things 'wherein ye greatly rejoice'. Now that is something you and I have to do. The trouble is that when these trials come we tend to see nothing but the trials, or nothing but clouds. At such a time just go back to the third verse of this chapter. When you can see nothing at all just open your Scriptures and start reading this. Though you see nothing but darkness at the moment, read this and say: ' "Blessed be the God and Father of our Lord Jesus Christ". I know that is always true'. 'Which according to His abundant mercy hath begotten us again unto a lively hope by the resurrection of Jesus Christ from the dead, to an inheritance incorruptible, and undefiled, and that fadeth not away, reserved in heaven for you, who are kept by the power of God through faith unto salvation ready to be revealed in the last time'. Remind yourself of that and say: 'Yes, these things are happening, these trials are falling around me thick and fast. They are coming from all directions, but I will not sit down under them and say "alas, alack", I will stand up rather and say: "I know God is good, I know Christ died for me, I know I belong to God, I know my inheritance is in heaven, I cannot see it now but I know it is there, I know God is keeping it and that no one will ever take it out of His mighty hands".' Say that to yourself. Remind yourself of the things in which you greatly rejoice, though now for a season if need be you are in manifold temptations.

Then go on to the ultimate statement which is this—'That the trial of your faith being much more precious than of gold that perisheth, though it be tried with fire, might be found unto praise and honour and glory at the appearing of Jesus Christ'. It is coming, I know not when, but I know it is coming—'the day of Jesus Christ'—and I shall be there. I know therefore that all that happens to me in this life and world has that as its ultimate objective. It is going to be a 'great day'. You remember how Paul in writing about preachers—himself and Apollos and others in 1 Corinthians 3 says that every man is building upon a foundation. Some are building with hay and wood and stubble; others are building very carefully with solid material and, says Paul, 'the day will declare it'. Every man's work shall be tried and tried by fire. There is a great deal that is going to go up in smoke. 'The day will declare it.' 'The day' will declare who has been building solidly and who has been rushing up his building with shoddy material. 'It is all right,' says Paul, 'with me it is a very small things that I am judged of you or of any man's judgment, yea, I judge not my own self'. He has committed the judgment to God and he knows that a declaration will be made on the day of the revelation of Jesus Christ (1 Corinthians 4. 1-5).

That, says Peter, that is the thing to look forward to. When the great day comes, the genuineness of your faith will be made manifest. There will be praise and honour and glory. Your little faith, the faith you think is so little, will stand out as something tremendous. It has stood the test and it is going to minister unto 'praise and honour and glory'. Whose honour and praise and glory? First of all His. I have used the quotation already. The

Lord Jesus Christ says: 'Here am I and the children that Thou hast given Me'. He will stand at that great day and look with a sense of satisfaction at Christian people, those whom He called. They have passed through great tribulation, but they have stood the test, they have not faltered, He will look at them and He will be proud of them. They will be to His glory and praise and honour at the great day that is coming.

But it will also be to our honour and glory and praise, yours and mine. We shall share in that glory, and we shall hear Him praising us and saying: 'Well done, thou good and faithful servant, enter thou into the joy of thy Lord'. He will clothe us with His own glory and we shall spend our eternity enjoying it with Him: and the greater and the more genuine our faith the greater will our glory be. 'We must all appear before the judgment seat of Christ and give an account of the deeds done in the body' (2 Corinthians 5. 10). There is to be a judgment of rewards, and it is according to our faith, and the way it has stood the test, that we shall be rewarded.

We may be in heaviness through many temptations and trials at this present time, and we may be weeping as we go along. It does not matter. We are promised that the day will come when 'the Lamb which is in the midst of the throne . . . shall lead us unto living fountains of water' and that God Himself 'shall wipe away all tears from our eyes', and we shall be with Him in glory everlasting.

That is the Christian way of facing trials. Thank God we are in His hands. It is His way of salvation and not ours. Let us submit ourselves to God, let us be content to be in His hands, and let us say to Him: Send what Thou wilt, our only concern is that we may ever be well-pleasing in Thy sight.

And ye have forgotten the exhortation which speaketh unto you as unto children, My son, despise not thou the chastening of the Lord, nor faint when thou art rebuked of Him: For whom the Lord loveth He chasteneth, and scourgeth every son whom He receiveth. If ye endure chastening, God dealeth with you as with sons; for what son is he whom the Father chasteneth not? But if ye be without chastisement, whereof all are partakers, then are ye bastards, and not sons. Furthermore we have had fathers of our flesh which corrected us, and we gave them reverence: shall we not much rather be in subjection unto the Father of spirits, and live? For they verily for a few days chastened us after their own pleasure; but He for our profit, that we might be partakers of His holiness. Now no chastening for the present seemeth to be joyous, but grievous: nevertheless afterward it yieldeth the peaceable fruit of righteousness unto them which are exercised thereby.

Hebrews 12. 5-11

XVII

CHASTENING

A MOST prolific cause of this condition of spiritual depression is the failure to realize that God uses varied methods in the process of our sanctification. He is our Father Who has 'loved us with an everlasting love'. His great purpose for us is our sanctification—'This is the will of God even your sanctification' (1 Thessalonians 4. 3) and 'that we should be holy and without blame before Him in love' (Ephesians 1. 4). God's great concern for us primarily is not our happiness but our holiness. In His great love to us He is determined to bring us to that, and He employs many differing means to that end.

Our failure to realize that often causes us to stumble and, in our sin and folly, at times even to misunderstand completely some of God's dealings with us. Like foolish children we feel that our heavenly Father is unkind to us and we pity ourselves and feel sorry for ourselves and feel that we are being dealt with harshly. That, of course, leads to depression and it is all due to our failure to realize God's glorious purposes with respect to us.

Now this is the matter that is dealt with in such an extraordinary and perfect manner in this twelfth chapter of the Epistle to the Hebrews where the theme is, that sometimes God promotes sanctification in His children by chastising them, and especially by enabling them to understand the meaning of chastisement. That is the theme to which I would call your attention. Nowhere, perhaps, do we see more clearly the fact that sanctification is God's work than in connection with this subject of chastisement. 'Look at the things you are suffering,' says the writer. 'Why are you suffering them?' The answer is that they are suffering these things because they are children of God. He tells them that God is doing these things to them for their good —'Whom the Lord loveth He chasteneth and scourgeth every son whom He receiveth'. And then you notice that, not content with putting it like that he puts it negatively as well. He says: 'If ye endure chastening, God dealeth with you as with sons; for what son is he whom the Father chasteneth not? But if ye be without chastisement, whereof all are partakers, then are ye bastards'—you are not truly children in the family, you are not sons. Now that is a very significant statement. Let me put it like this in the form of a principle. What this man is really saying is that the whole of salvation is God's work from beginning to end, and that God has His ways of producing it. Once God starts working He goes on with that work—'He that hath begun a good work in you will perform it until the day of Jesus Christ'. God does not start a work and then give it up or leave it in an incomplete condition—when God starts His work upon His people He is going to complete that work. God has an ultimate objective and purpose for them and that is that they might spend eternity with Him in glory. Much that happens to us in this world is to be understood and explained in the light of that fact; and it is as definite as this, according to this man's argument, that God will bring us to that condition, and nothing shall prevent our coming into that condition.

Now God has several ways of doing this. One is to give us instruction through the great doctrines and principles that are taught in the Bible. He has given us His Word. He caused men to write these words by the Holy Spirit for our instruction in order that we might be prepared and perfected. But if we become recalcitrant, if we will not learn the lessons that are presented to us positively in the Word, then God, as our Father, with the great end and object in view of perfecting us and preparing us for glory, will adopt other methods. And one of the other methods which He uses is this method of chastisement. Earthly parents that are worthy of the name—we are living in such flabby days that we can scarcely use the argument as this man was able to do—do this. They chastise their children for their own good, and if the child is not behaving properly as the result of positive instruction, then punishment must be meted out, discipline must be exercised. It is painful but necessary, and the good parent does not neglect it. This man says that God is like that, and infinitely more so. If, therefore, we will not be obedient to the positive lessons and instructions of God's Word, we must not be surprised if other things begin to happen to us. We must not be surprised if we begin to endure certain things which are rather painful. These things are done to us deliberately by God, says this man, as a part of the process of sanctification. And you notice how strongly he puts it. He says that we have to examine ourselves and to find out whether we are experiencing this at all, because he says here quite definitely, that if we have no experience of this kind of treatment, then it is very doubtful whether we are children at all. If we know nothing of this process we are not children, we are illegitimate, we do not belong to God, for 'Whom the Lord loveth He chasteneth'. There is a sense, therefore, in which we can say that the person who ought to be most unhappy about himself or herself is that Christian, or professing Christian, who is not aware of this kind of dealing at all. It is something about which we should be alarmed. Far from being annoyed by the process, we ought to thank God for it for He is giving us proof that we are His children, He is treating us as His children. He is punishing and chastising us in order to make us conform to the pattern and to be worthy of Him who is our Father.

This is something that is constantly taking place in the life and experience of the children of God. It is also something that is taught everywhere in the Scriptures. There are endless examples and illustrations that might be quoted. It is the great message of the seventy-third Psalm. It is the great message of the book of Job. You find the Apostle Paul deals with it in the fifth chapter of the Epistle to the Romans where he talks about rejoicing in tribulation, etc. It enters into the argument of the eighth chapter of Romans. You get it again in the first Epistle to the Corinthians and the eleventh chapter in the section that deals with the Communion Service. The apostle teaches that there were members of the Church who were sick and ill because they were not living the Christian life—'For this cause many are weak and sickly among you'. Indeed some had died because of that—'Many sleep'. Then read the first chapter of the Second Epistle to the Corinthians and you will find the apostle describing the experience that has happened to him. He says that it happened in order that he might learn not to trust in himself but in the living God. Another great classic statement of this teaching is to be found in the twelfth chapter of the Second Epistle to the Corinthians, where Paul talks about 'the thorn in the flesh' that was given to him, and his whole reasoning and argument about that. The purpose of it all, he says, was to keep him in the right spiritual condition lest he might be over-exalted. He was given a thorn in the flesh, and though he prayed and asked God three times to remove it, God did not do so, and he at last learned his lesson. So it promoted his sanctification. Read the first chapter of the Epistle of James: 'Count it all joy, my brethren, when ye fall into divers temptations, etc.' It is something to rejoice in. And then see it all summed up in the word of the risen Lord Himself as you find it in the third chapter of the Book of Revelation in the nineteenth verse: 'As many as I love I rebuke and chasten'.

So we see this great doctrine running right through the Bible. Indeed, all God's treatment of the Children of Israel under the old dispensation is but an extended commentary on this. It was because they were His people that He did those things unto them. 'Ye only have I known of all the families of the earth; therefore I will punish you for all your iniquities' (Amos 3. 2). It was because they were His children that He so dealt with them.

The question that obviously faces us therefore is, what is chastisement, what does it mean? It means to train. The fundamental meaning of the word is just that. It is the training through which a child is put, it is the method of training a child. We rather tend to confuse it with the word punishment. It includes correction, but it also includes instruction; it includes rebuke, indeed it may include a good deal of punishment, but the essential thing is, and the essential object of chastisement is, to train and to develop the child so as to produce a grown person. Well, now, if that is the meaning of chastisement let us consider for a moment the ways in which God does chastise.

How does God chastise His children? He does so very largely through circumstances, all sorts and kinds of circumstances. Nothing is more important in the Christian life than we should realize that everything that happens to us is of significance if we can but see it. Nothing happens to us accidentally—a sparrow 'shall not fall to the ground without your Father', says our Lord, and if that is true of the sparrow how much more so of us? Nothing can happen to us apart from our Father. Circumstances are constantly affecting us and their purpose is to produce our sanctification—pleasant circumstances and unpleasant circumstances. We should therefore be observant and always watching for lessons, seeking and asking questions.

Now let me particularize. The Bible teaches us very clearly that one particular circumstance which God often uses in this respect is some financial loss, a change in one's material position, the loss of goods, the loss of possessions, the loss of money. These are often used by God. You get descriptions of it in the Old

Testament, and it has often happened in the subsequent history
of God's people in the Church, that by means of some loss in a
temporal and material sense God has taught a man a lesson
which apparently he could not have learned in any other way.

Then take the question of health. I have already reminded you
of the First Epistle to the Corinthians, chapter eleven. The
apostle teaches quite specifically that there were some people
who were sick and ill because God had sent this upon them in
order to teach them and to train them. 'Let a man examine
himself and so let him eat of that bread, and drink of that cup;
For he that eateth and drinketh unworthily, eateth and drinketh
damnation to himself, not discerning the Lord's body. For this
cause many are weak and sickly among you, and many sleep.'
Now this is a method that God has often employed, so that those
who say that it is never God's will that any of us should be sick
or weak are simply denying the Scriptures. But let no one drop
into the trap and say: 'Are you teaching that every sickness is a
punishment sent by God?' Of course I am not, I am simply
saying that God at times uses that method in order to chastise
His children. If it is 'for this cause' that many are 'weak and
sickly', it is God's action. God allowed that to happen to them,
or God may have brought it upon them, for their own good.
God's will is more important than the health of man's body, and
if a man will not submit himself and subject himself to the
positive teaching of the Word, then God will certainly deal with
that man, and He may very well send an illness upon him and
lay him aside in order to make him think. May I remind you that
the great Dr. Thomas Chalmers always said that what really
brought him, under God, to understand the gospel truly was an
illness which confined him to his sick chamber for nearly twelve
months. He had been a brilliant 'scientific' and 'intellectual'
preacher, but he came out of that sick chamber as a preacher of
the gospel, and he thanked God for that visitation. There is a
parallel to that in the Second Epistle of Paul to the Corinthians,
first chapter and ninth verse where he tells us that he had 'the
sentence of death' in himself. And then there is the classic statement about the thorn in the flesh in chapter twelve. God did not
remove that thorn because He was anxious to teach the apostle
to say 'when I am weak then am I strong', and to rejoice in
infirmity rather than in health in order that God's glory might be
promoted. There is no doubt that God allowed this thing, God

perhaps even produced it, in order to chastise and train His servant in that particular way.

In the same way God has allowed persecution. These Hebrew Christians were being persecuted. That is why they were so unhappy. Their goods had been stolen, their houses had been destroyed because they were Christians, and they were asking: 'Why are we having this sort of treatment? We thought that if we believed the gospel all was going to be well with us, but we seem to be full of trouble, while those who are not Christian seem to be doing well and succeeding in everything. Why is this?' Here is the answer to them in this twelfth chapter.

The doctrine, however, goes further, it goes so far as to say that God seems to employ death at times in this way—'many are weak and sickly among you, and many sleep'. It is a mystery, no one can understand it, but it is the clear teaching of the Scripture, and therefore I say that we must realize that all these things have a significance. By means of circumstance, the things that happen to us in this life and world, in our career, by the passing or failing of examinations, by health or sickness, by all these things, God is bringing His purpose for us to pass. If you are a child of God all these things have a significance for you, and you must learn how to examine them in order to discover their message. And thereby your sanctification will be promoted.

Another way in which God chastens us, and I must put it in a category on its own, is this. God undoubtedly at times seems to withdraw His presence and to hide His face from us for this precise purpose. You will find that that is the great theme of the Book of Job. You will find it again in the Book of Hosea in chapters 5 and 6. God even tells the people there: 'I will go and return to My place till they acknowledge their offence, and seek My face'. God withdrew Himself and withdrew His presence, withdrew His face and His blessing in order to bring them to the place of repentance; it is a part of sanctification.

Then again one often finds in the Christian life that there are variations in feelings and in sentiments. That is a matter that often troubles and perplexes God's people. We have all known something about it. You find that for some reason or another the experience you have been enjoying, suddenly comes to an end and you say with Job: 'O that I knew where I might find Him'. You are not conscious of having done anything wrong, but God seems to have withdrawn Himself and you feel yourself to be deserted. These desertions of the Spirit, that seem to take place from time to time, are again but parts of God's way of chastising His children, part of His great process of training and preparing us for the grand end and object He has in view for us.

That brings me to my next question which is this. Why does God chastise? We have seen what chastisement is, we have seen how God chastises, we now ask the great question, why does God do this? And there are abundant answers to the question in this section of His Word. From verse 5 to verse 15 in this twelfth chapter of the Epistle to the Hebrews is really nothing but an extended answer to this question. It is because God loves us—'For whom the Lord loveth He chasteneth and scourgeth every son whom He receiveth'. That is the fundamental answer. It is all because of the love of God. It is because God loves us that He appears at times to be 'cruel to be kind'. It is all done for our good; that is the thing we must lay hold of, it is always for our good. Now look at the statement in verse 7. In the Authorized Version it says: 'If ye endure chastening, God dealeth with you as with sons'. But the Revised Version, and various other versions, are beyond doubt very much better at this point. It is not so much: 'If we endure chastening'; it should rather be put like this: 'It is for your chastening you endure'. Why are you enduring? That is the question; that is the question these Hebrew Christians were asking—if we are Christians why are we enduring? And the answer is that you are enduring because you are Christian, you are enduring for your chastening. In other words the purpose of your enduring is your growth, your training, your development; the things that you are enduring are part of your chastening. What is chastening?—Your training. So that we have to take hold firmly of that fact, that all the suffering and the enduring and all the unhappiness is with this great end and object in view, namely, our preparation and our training. But the author says it again—and you notice how he goes on repeating himself—in verse 10. 'For they'—earthly parents—'for a few days chastened us after their own pleasure, but He for our profit that'—in order that—'we might be partakers of His Holiness'. Now there it is stated in its most explicit form; quite definitely the teaching is that God chastens us in order that we might become partakers of His holiness, in order that we might be sanctified. It is all done, he says, 'for our profit', and the profit is sanctification. God sanctifies us through the truth by doing these things to us and then, by means of His Word, expounding to us what He is doing.

Now if that is the general object that God has in view in chastening us in this way, let us also look at some of the particular reasons which He has for doing so. One is that there are certain faults in us, certain faults in all of us, which need to be corrected. There are certain dangers confronting all of us in this Christian life against which we need to be protected. The fact that a man is a Christian does not mean that he is perfect. Alas, you do not immediately on belief in the Lord Jesus Christ arrive at a state of complete perfection. Indeed you do not arrive at that state at all in this life; there is imperfection remaining, the 'old man' remains. The result is that there are certain things that always need to be dealt with in particular, and in the Scriptures we are told very clearly how God uses chastisement in order to deal with some of these particular problems. What are they? Here is one. Spiritual pride, spiritual elation in a dangerous and in a wrong sense. Let me remind you of the classic words which put this so perfectly and which really need no exposition at all. The Apostle Paul in the twelfth chapter of the Second Epistle to the Corinthians says: ' . . . I knew such a man, whether in the body or out of the body I cannot tell; God knoweth; how that he was caught up into paradise, and heard unspeakable words, which it is not lawful for a man to utter; of such an one will I glory: yet of myself I will not glory, but in mine infirmities. For though I would desire to glory, I shall not be a fool; for I will say the truth: but now I forbear, lest any man should think of me above that which he seeth me to be, or that he heareth of me'—and listen—'And lest I should be exalted above measure through the abundance of the revelations; there was given to me a thorn in the flesh, the messenger of Satan to buffet me, lest I should be exalted above measure'. There it is perfectly. The apostle had been given some very rare, exceptional, unusual experience, he had been lifted up into the third heaven, he had seen and had heard and felt wonderful things, and the danger was spiritual pride, being exalted over-much. And he tells us that the thorn in the flesh was sent to him, was given to him deliberately in order to safeguard him. Spiritual pride is a terrible danger, and it is a danger that persists. If God does grant us in His mercy and love some unusual experience, we are in a position which the devil may exploit to our harm; and oftentimes men who have had such experiences have needed chastisement in order to keep them in the right and safe place.

Another danger is the danger of self-confidence. God has given gifts to man and the danger is for man to rely upon himself and his gifts and to feel in a sense that he does not need God. Pride and self-assurance are a constant danger. These are not sins of the flesh as such, these are spiritual dangers, and are therefore even more, dangerous and subtle.

Then there is always the danger of being attracted by the world and its outlook and its way. The point that is made by the Scriptures is that these things are so subtle. It is not that a man deliberately sits down and decides that he is going back into the world. It is something that happens almost imperceptibly. The world and its attractions are always there and a man slips into them almost without knowing it. So he needs to be chastised lest he comes to love the things of the world.

Yet another danger is that of resting on our oars, the danger of being satisfied with the position we have reached in the Christian life—smugness, self-satisfaction. We are not modernists, we do not believe the kind of thing so many believe today, we are orthodox, we cease to do certain things which we know are obviously wrong. We believe we are perfect in our belief, and that our lives are beyond reproach, and so we become smug and self-satisfied. We rest upon our oars, and so we do not grow. If we compare ourselves with what we were ten years ago, there is really no difference. We do not know God any more intimately, we have not advanced one step, we have not 'grown in grace and in the knowledge of the Lord'. We are resting in a state of self-satisfaction. Perhaps I can sum it all up by saying that it is the terrible danger of forgetting God and not seeking Him and His fellowship. It is the awful danger of thinking of ourselves in terms of experience, rather than constantly in terms of our direct immediate knowledge of Him and our relationship to Him. As we go on year by year, in the Christian life we ought to be able to say that we know God better than we used to, we should be able to say that we love Him more than we once did. The more you know any good person the more you like such a person, the more you love such a person. Multiply that by infinity and there is your relationship and mine to God. Do we know God better, are we really seeking Him more and more? God knows, the danger is to forget Him because we are interested in ourselves and in our experience. And so God in His infinite love chastises us in order to make us realize these things, in order to bring us back to Himself, in order to safeguard us against these terrible dangers that are constantly threatening us and surrounding us. Let me put it to your experience. Can you say that you thank God for things that have gone against you? That is a very good test of our whole profession. Can you see why certain things—things which were unpleasant and which made you feel very unhappy at the time they happened to you—can you look back and say, 'It is good for me that I was afflicted', like the Psalmist in Psalm 119. 71.

I say then that God chastises us for these particular reasons. But let me put it all positively. To be sanctified means that we display certain positive qualities. It is to be the kind of person who is exemplifying the Beatitudes and the Sermon on the Mount in his life, it is to be a person who is showing the fruits of the Spirit—love, joy, peace, etc. Now that is what sanctification means. God, in sanctifying us, is bringing us more and more into conformity with that condition. And it is very clear that in order to bring us there it is not enough that we be given the positive teaching of the Word; the element of chastisement is also necessary. The Word exhorts men to 'look to Jesus'. You notice that it does so in the chapter before it comes to the chastisement. The author's exhortation is: 'Let us run with patience the race that is set before us looking unto Jesus, . . .'. If we did that always nothing else would be necessary; if we always kept our gaze upon Him and tried to conform to Him, all would be well. But we do not, and therefore chastisement becomes necessary. And it is necessary in order to produce certain qualities in us. Here they are. Humility—it is in many ways the crowning virtue. Humility, the most priceless of all the gems, one of the most glorious of all the manifestations of the fruit of the Spirit—humility. It was the supreme characteristic of the Lord Himself. He was meek and lowly in heart. 'The bruised reed He will not break, the smoking flax He will not quench.' It is the last point at which we arrive, and, God knows, we all have to be humbled in order to arrive at humility. Failure can be very good for us there. It is very difficult to be humble if you are always successful, so God chastises us with failure at times in order to humble us, to keep us in a state of humility. Examine your life and see this kind of thing happening.

Then take heavenly-mindedness. The Christian is to be heavenly-minded. His great interest should be there not here. How difficult it is to be heavenly-minded, to keep 'our affections on things above', to 'set them there and not on things which are on the earth'. How often has it become necessary that God should chastise us in order to make us heavenly-minded. We so cling to the world that God has to do something which shows us very clearly that the things that bind us to this world are fragile and can be snapped in a second. And so we are suddenly awakened to the fact that we are only pilgrims in this world, and we are made to think of heaven and of eternity.

Meekness! How difficult it is to be meek in our attitude towards others and in our relationships with them—love to others, sympathy towards others. There is a sense, I suppose, in which it is almost impossible for us to be sympathetic unless we know something of the same experience. I know very well in my work as a pastor that I would not have been able to sympathize with people, indeed, I would not have been able to understand certain people and their problems, unless I had passed through the same experience myself. God has sometimes to deal with us in order to remind us of our need of patience. He says in effect: 'You know I am patient with you, go and be patient with that other person'.

These, then, are some of the things that show us clearly the need and necessity for chastisement. God, because He loves us, because we are His children, does chastise us in order that it may eventually lead to this marvellous and wonderful 'peaceable fruit of righteousness'.

So far we have looked at it all in principle. In our next study I hope to show how this same section applies all that teaching and how we are to apply it to ourselves. The great principle is that God deals with us in chastisement because we are children. If, therefore, you are not aware of something of this kind of dealing, I can but urge you to go back and examine yourself and make sure that you are a Christian at all because: 'Whom the Lord loveth He chasteneth and scourgeth every son whom He receiveth'. Blessed be God Who has undertaken our salvation and our perfection and Who, having started the work will go on with it, and Who so loves us that if we will not learn the lessons voluntarily, will chastise us in order to bring us into conformity with the image of His dear Son.

*And ye have forgotten the exhortation which speaketh
unto you as unto children, My son, despise not thou
the chastening of the Lord, nor faint when thou art
rebuked of Him: For whom the Lord loveth He
chasteneth, and scourgeth every son whom He receiveth.
If ye endure chastening, God dealeth with you as with
sons; for what son is he whom the Father chasteneth
not? But if ye be without chastisement, whereof all
are partakers, than are ye bastards, and not sons.
Furthermore we have had fathers of our flesh which corrected us, and we gave them reverence: shall we not much
rather be in subjection unto the Father of spirits, and
live? For they verily for a few days chastened us
after their own pleasure; but He for our profit, that we
might be partakers of His holiness. Now no chastening
for the present seemeth to be joyous, but grievous:
nevertheless afterward it yieldeth the peaceable fruit
of righteousness unto them which are exercised thereby.*
Hebrews 12. 5-11

XVIII

IN GOD'S GYMNASIUM

WE must now proceed to give further consideration to the Biblical teaching that God produces and promotes our sanctification partly by various things that He does to us. Over and above the positive instruction He gives us in the Scriptures, God deals with us in other ways also. If we do not respond to the teaching, if we are His people, and because we are, God will deal with us in chastisement. In this connection we have already seen that there are many places in Scripture where this particular doctrine is outlined and taught very plainly. But I think it will be generally agreed that there is no better statement of it than the one which we find here in the twelfth chapter of the Epistle to the Hebrews and especially from verse five to verse fifteen. Indeed, it can be said that the whole of the Epistle to the Hebrews is but an extended exposition of this great doctrine of the purposes of God with respect to His people, as revealed in chastisement. We have already seen, in our general consideration of the subject that God does undoubtedly use this particular method. Indeed the main argument of these verses is that if we do experience this treatment it is a proof that we are God's children; but that if we do not, then it raises very serious doubt, to say the least, as to whether we are truly the children of God at all. We have also considered the reason why God does chastise, and we came to the conclusion that He does it in order to safeguard us from certain temptations that are always threatening us. There are certain dangers round and about us in this earthly life and we need to be kept from them—the danger of pride, self-satisfaction, and smugness, the danger of drifting away and becoming worldly without realizing it, these horrible dangers that are constantly threatening the Christian in this life and this world. On the positive side we saw that He does it in order that He may stimulate within us the growth of the fruit of the Spirit. There is nothing so good for the promotion of humility as chastisement, and we need it if we are to be humble and meek and lowly. The teaching is that God as our Father, and in His infinite grace and kindness, does discipline us so, for 'He scourgeth every son whom He receiveth', and 'Whom the Lord loveth He chasteneth'. That is the doctrine, that is the teaching.

Now, having laid down that principle we must continue our consideration of this passage, because that is not all, that is not enough. Indeed, as I understand the argument of this man in the twelfth chapter of Hebrews we can put it like this: That chastisement, even chastisement by God, does not work in us automatically. The mere fact that we are chastised does not mean that, of necessity, we are going to benefit by it. The writer's argument is that it is only as we understand this teaching concerning chastisement, and apply it to ourselves properly and truly, that we shall derive any benefit from it. Now that is obviously, a most important point because if we think that this sanctification of ours is something that takes place almost automatically while we remain in an entirely passive condition, then we are just denying the very essence of this man's case and the whole point of his argument. Chastisement does not work automatically, it is not something mechanical, even this benefits us ultimately 'by the Word'. The whole of sanctification is as our Lord says in John 17, 'by thy truth', it is by the application of the Word in every step, in every aspect. And that is particularly true with regard to this whole question of chastisement.

Let me then put the argument to you as it is unfolded here, in this way. There is a wrong way of regarding chastisement, and there is a wrong way of reacting to chastisement. You remember that we have seen that chastisement may come in many forms. It may come through circumstances, it may take the form of some financial loss or problem in our business or profession; it may come as something that casts us down and that causes us to be troubled and perplexed; it may come through some personal disappointment—the treachery of a friend or the crashing to the ground of some great hope we may have had in life. It may come through illness. Here I must repeat and emphasize that I am not saying that all these things are of necessity always produced by God. I am not saying that. The Bible does not teach that everything everyone suffers is sent from God; the teaching is that illness may be sent by God and that God does chastise us sometimes by means of illness as well as by those various other circumstances. Let us be quite clear about that. God may use any one of these things, but obviously these things

happen to all and therefore we must never say that every un-
welcome happening is, of necessity, a chastisement from God.

There are, then, wrong ways of reacting to trials and tribulations and chastisement. What are they? This man notes three.
The first is this, the danger of despising. You find that in the
fifth verse: 'My son despise not thou the chastening of the Lord'.
That is the first wrong way of regarding chastisement, to regard
it loosely, to pay no attention to it, to shake it off as something
light, and not to take it very seriously—putting on a bold front,
as it were, and not allowing it to affect us at all. There we are,
going along somewhat thoughtlessly, and one of these things
happens to us, but instead of weighing and considering it and
allowing it to do its work, we do our utmost to shake it off and to
get rid of it, to laugh it away as it were. That is something that
surely needs no emphasis because it is perhaps the commonest
reaction to trials and tribulations at this present time. We are
living in an age when people are afraid of true feeling. It is a
very sentimental age, but there is a vital difference between
sentiment and emotion. A hardness has entered into life. We are
always trying to 'steel' our nerves and feelings and we regard
it as being old fashioned to feel things. The world has become
hard and the whole course of life today shows that very clearly.
Many of the things that are disgracing life today could not
happen if only people were sensitive—if they had even a little
sensitivity. But we steel ourselves and put on this bold front and
the result is that when things do go wrong and when God is
chastising us, we do not pay any attention to it. We regard it
lightly and instead of paying attention we deliberately ignore it,
and do not allow it to disturb us. Now the Scripture warns us
very definitely and very solemnly against this. There is nothing
so dangerous to the soul as to cultivate this impersonal attitude
towards life, which is so common today. It is because of this that
people become loosely attached to husband or wife, loosely
attached to their own family. It is because of this that they can
walk out on their responsibilities and trample upon the sanctities.
This impersonal attitude towards life is deliberately taught and
encouraged, it is regarded as the hallmark of the true gentleman
and the real gentlewoman—the kind of person who is surrounded by some case of steel, who never betrays any emotion
and who seems to be entirely lacking in any true sensibility. Now
that attitude can come into the Christian life and cause people

to despise even the chastening of the Lord. They throw it off and dismiss it, they refuse to pay attention to it.

The second false reaction to chastisement is this—'Nor faint when thou are rebuked of Him', in the same fifth verse. This, of course, is a quotation from the Old Testament, from the Book of Proverbs, and it refers to the danger of being discouraged by chastisement, the danger of fainting under it, the danger of giving up and giving in, the danger of feeling hopeless. We are all familiar with this. Something happens to us and we say: 'I really can't bear it'. The heart gives in, the thing is on top of us. We give up and give in, we faint under it all, we become utterly discouraged. That in turn leads to the tendency to wonder why it has happened and as to whether it is fair of God. We grumble and complain and have a sense of grudge. That was the condition of these Hebrew Christians. They said: 'We thought when we became Christian that we were going to enter into some marvellous life, but see what is happening to us. Why do these things happen to us? Is it right? Is this Christian faith true?' And they were beginning to turn back to their old religion. That is the reason why this man wrote this Epistle—it was because they were discouraged by their trials. They were fainting because the Lord had tried them. 'Faint not'—'nor faint when thou art rebuked of Him'. That sense of despair tends to come in and we say: 'Really things are too much for me, I cannot go on. "Oh, that I had wings like a dove for then I would fly away and be at rest!"' We all know it; we react like that far too frequently to the chastening of the Lord, instead of facing it as this man teaches us to do. We are all too ready to hold up our hands and say: 'No, I cannot, this is too much. Why, why am I being dealt with thus?' We are not the first to feel like that. Read the Psalms and you will find that the Psalmist often passes through that phase. But it is utterly wrong and a very false reaction to God's rebuke and chastisement and to God's fatherly dealings with us.

The third of the wrong reactions is the one he mentions in verse fifteen—'Lest any root of bitterness springing up trouble you, and thereby many be defiled'. Again we know, alas, what it means. Some people react to the trials and troubles and chastisements of life by becoming bitter. I know nothing that is so sad in life, certainly there is nothing sadder in my life and work and experience as a minister of God, than to watch the effect of trials and troubles upon the lives of some people. I have known people who, before the misfortunes befel them, seemed to be very nice and friendly, but I have observed that when these things happen they become bitter, self-centred, difficult—difficult even with those who try to help them and who are anxious to help them. They turn in upon themselves and they feel that the whole world is against them. You cannot help them, the bitterness enters into their souls, it appears in their faces and their very appearance. A complete change seems to take place. We often unconsciously proclaim what we are by the way in which we react to the things that happen to us. These things that happen to us in life test us, they test us to the very depths and they show whether we are truly children of God or not. Those who are not children of God are generally made bitter by misfortunes. Sometimes, temporarily, even the children of God may be, and they need to be warned against this particular reaction to chastisement and trouble—against a root of bitterness springing up.

If we are guilty of any one of these three reactions, the things which happen to us will not help us at all. Even the chastisements of God will do us no good if that is the way we react. If we shake it off lightly, if we faint under it, if we become bitter because of it, it will not benefit us. The very chastisement that may be sent to us by God, and be meted out by God Himself, will not profit us at all.

That is why this man exhorts the people to whom he writes, to face these things in the right way. What is the right way? Let us look at it positively. The first thing he tells us is that we must learn to behave as sons and not as infants. Now this is important at this point because the Authorized Version has unfortunately used a wrong word here: 'Ye have forgotten the exhortation which speaketh unto you as unto children'. It should be—'Ye have forgotten the exhortation which speaketh unto you as unto sons'. You may say that a son is a child and that therefore the word 'children' is perfectly correct but the man who wrote this chapter actually used a word that should be translated as 'son' and is translated as 'son' later on. It is an important distinction. What he is really saying is—'You have forgotten the exhortation that speaketh unto you as grown men —as sons. You are no longer children, you are no longer babes. you are no longer infants'. There was never a babe or an infant that did not misunderstand chastisement. When we are children we always think we are being dealt with harshly, that it is most unfair of our parent and that we do not deserve it. That is the child's reaction, and, spiritually, some of us remain children. But this man says: 'Now remember that you are not children. You are men, you are sons, you are adults'. And his exhortation is: 'Pull yourself together, do not behave as a child'. You notice the great sanity of the Scriptures, and the way in which they approach us. You are men, they say; very well, then, stop fainting, stop whimpering and crying, stop acting like a child and sulking. You say you are men but you show that you are still only babes by behaving in such a manner.

What are we to do, then, because we are men? In verse five we are given a number of exhortations. He begins with a negative in the form of rebuke. He says: 'You have forgotten the exhortation'. So, obviously, the right thing to do is to remember the word of exhortation. This author says in effect: 'Here you are, you Hebrew Christians, and all others like you, you are falling into these traps but you are entirely without excuse. If the Gentile Christians did that, there would be some excuse; but there is no excuse for you. You have the Old Testament. If you only read the Book of Proverbs alone and really considered it and applied it, you would never react in the way you do—"remember the word of exhortation".' Now, applying that to ourselves, we can take it that every time anything of a trying nature happens to us in this life and world we are never just to look at the thing in and of itself. As Christians we are to take everything and put it immediately into the context of the Bible. 'Remember the word of exhortation'. In a sense that is the one great difference between the non-Christian and the Christian. When anything goes wrong in the life of the non-Christian what has he to fall back upon? He has nothing but worldly wisdom and the way in which the world reacts, and that does not help. The Christian, however, is in an entirely different position. He has the Bible, and he should at once take any circumstance and put it right into this context. The Christian does not react to events as the world does. He asks: 'What do the Scriptures say about this?' 'The word of exhortation.' The Christian brings that in, and applies it. He puts everything into that context. What foolish creatures we are. How often are we guilty of acting as the world does and not as Christians at all. Let us remember that we are men, that we are sons of God, that we have God's Word. Put the thing whatever it may be, into the context of God's Word.

What next? The next part of his argument, still in the fifth verse is that we must listen to and follow the arguments of the Word of God. 'Ye have forgotten the exhortation which speaketh unto you as unto children.' Now that word 'speaketh' is not wrong but it is not quite strong enough. A better translation would be: 'Ye have forgotten the exhortation which reasoneth with you', 'reasoneth with you as sons'. That again is something that fascinates and thrills me. You see, the Word of God does not merely give us general comfort, what it gives us always is an argument. There is nothing that I so dislike and abominate as a sentimental way of reading the Scriptures. There are many people who read the Scriptures in a purely sentimental manner. They are in trouble and they do not know what to do. They say, 'I will read a Psalm. It is so soothing—"The Lord is my Shepherd I shall not want".' They make of it a kind of incantation and take the Psalms as another person takes a drug. That is not the way to read the Scriptures. 'The word of exhortation reasoneth with you', argues with you. And we must follow the logic of it, and bring intelligence to the Scriptures. We can never bring too much intelligence to our reading of them, they are not merely meant to give general comfort and soothing—follow the argument; let them reason it out with you.

The next step obviously is: What is the argument? Well, I need not stay with this because in a sense I have already dealt with it. Let me summarize briefly. The great argument is that it is God Who is doing this, and God is doing it to you because you are His child. This is put here in several forms, but nowhere is it put more clearly than in verses nine and ten: 'Furthermore we have had fathers of our flesh which corrected us, and we gave them reverence; shall we not much rather be in subjection unto the Father of spirits and life?' God is our spiritual Father, the Father of the new life that is in us, not the earthly, not the fleshly life any longer but the spiritual. So it is God doing this to you, and He is doing it because you are His child, He is doing it for your good because you are His child. Now that is the argument, that is the truth we have to grasp. So we do not merely react in general, we do not faint, we do not try to shake it off at once. Our whole attitude is changed. We say: 'God is in this and God is doing this to me because I am His child, because I do not belong to the world, because He sent His Son to die for me and has destined me for heaven. God is in this, and it is all being done for my good'.

It is imperative, however, that we follow the argument and the reasoning with respect to the way in which God thus deals with us. It is all here in the eleventh verse. 'Now,' he says, 'no chastening for the present seemeth to be joyous, but grievous; nevertheless afterward it yieldeth the peaceable fruit of righteousness. . . .' But he has not finished. He adds: 'Unto them which are exercised thereby'. The secret is all in this phrase 'exercised thereby'. The only people who are going to derive benefit from the treatment, says this man, are those who carry out the exercise—those who are exercised thereby, those who submit to God's treatment. If you shake it off, the treatment will do you no good; if you faint under it, it will do you no good; if you become bitter, it will do you no good. It only does you good if you submit to the process.

What is the process? to take this man's actual words it is this. He tells us that God is going to do these things to us by putting us into a gymnasium. That is the original meaning of the word which is translated as 'exercised' and this is a very wonderful picture. We are told that the very root of this word gymnasium is a word which signifies 'being stripped naked'. So the picture we have here is of ourselves being taken into a gymnasium and there we are told to strip.

Why are we told to strip? This is for two main reasons. Obviously, the first is that we may go through the exercises unhindered by our clothing. 'Let us lay aside every weight and the sin which doth so easily beset us.' But there is another reason why we should be stripped. We do not go into that gymnasium on our own to take our exercises. The Instructor takes us in and the Instructor looks at us and examines us. He is looking at us to see if there is balance and symmetry in our physical form. The Greeks were very interested in this. They went in for the culture of the body, and the symmetry of the physical proportions. So the Instructor strips us in order to see where a little extra exercise is needed to bring up a particular group of muscles or to correct a defective stance or posture. That is the picture that is presented here. We are in a gymnasium with the Instructor looking on, telling us what to do and putting us through the exercises.

I feel that there is here a kind of double picture, at least we can use this one picture in two different ways. We can think of it simply in terms of a man who needs to be exercised. He has been rather neglecting his body, he has been indolent and slack in a physical sense, so the Instructor takes him and puts him through his exercises in order that he may become a fine specimen of manhood. But I cannot help feeling, in view of the context, that there is also another suggestion. Listen to verses twelve and thirteen: 'Wherefore lift up the hands which hang down, and the feeble knees; And make straight paths for your feet, lest that which is lame be turned out of the way; but let it rather be healed'. I cannot myself avoid the conclusion that there is also a picture here of a person suffering from some kind of joint disease. You notice that the knees are feeble and that there is a lameness. This person has become somewhat diseased, troubled in the joints; and when such is the case you will generally find that not only is the knee itself weak but the muscles around it become flabby also. I see, therefore, here a wonderful picture of what we call physiotherapy. You need not only to treat the disease in the joint, you need to put the patient through various exercises and movements also. Massage alone is not enough, you must also get the patient to do his part in making active movements.

Let us hold these two ideas in our mind as we work out the teaching in detail. God, says this man, by doing the things that He is doing to you, is as it were putting you into that spiritual gymnasium. He has you stripped, He is examining you, He knows exactly what you need. Now all you have to do is to submit to Him and do exactly what He tells you. Listen to the Instructor, go through the exercises, and if you do so it will give you 'the peaceable fruit of righteousness. What does all this mean? Being interpreted it means this. The first thing we have to do is to examine ourselves or submit ourselves to the examination of God's Word. The moment any untoward event happens to us we must say: 'I am in the gymnasium. Something must be the matter. What has been going wrong? Where is my trouble?' That is the way the Christian should always react to any one of these things that happen. Is it illness, is it accident, is it a failure, is it a disappointment, is it someone's death? I do not care what it is, but on the basis of this teaching, the first thing I should say to myself is: 'Why has this happened to me, have I been going astray somewhere?' Read Psalm 119 and you will find the Psalmist says: 'It was good for me that I have been afflicted. . . .' 'Before I was afflicted I went astray: but now have I kept Thy word.' He had not realized that he had been slipping away but his affliction makes him think, and he says: 'I thank God for this, it is a good thing for me, I am a better man for it: I was going astray'. Therefore you and I should always in the first instance examine ourselves, and ask: 'Have I been negligent in my spiritual life, have I been forgetting God, have I become somewhat elated and self-satisfied, have I sinned, have I done any wrong?' We examine ourselves, we try to discover the cause, we do it thoroughly. None of this as this man tells us is 'joyous', but we must search our life and examine ourselves to the very depths, however painful it may be, to see if there is some respect in which we have been going astray without our knowing it. We must face it honestly.

Secondly, we must acknowledge it and confess it to God. If we find the sin, if we have found the fault, if we have found slackness or anything that is wrong or unworthy we must go at once and confess it honestly and completely to God. That is a vital part of the exercises, and we shall never get well until we carry it out. God commands us to do this, so let us do it. Let us go straight to Him. It may also involve going to somebody else, it may mean apologizing, it may mean confessing something. It does not always mean this, but if God tells us to do it we must do it. Listen to the voice within us (the voice of the Instructor in the gymnasium) the voice of God speaking to us; and as we examine ourselves, we must pay attention to it and say: 'I will do it, I will do it whatever it may cost'. We must carry out the exercise in detail. We must confess and acknowledge the fault, the failure, the sin to God.

What next? Well, having done that which is, if you like, a kind of loosening process, we now begin to take positive exercises. We come to verse twelve—'Wherefore'—you notice the logic of the argument—'lift up the hands which hang down and the feeble knees'. This is His way of telling us to pull ourselves together, to brace ourselves, to stand erect, to tone ourselves up. My illustration of the joints comes in in a most useful manner at this point. Anyone who has ever had rheumatism in any shape or form knows that instinctively we all tend to nurse and protect painful parts. If I have a pain in my knee I try not to bend it. We protect, we shield the painful parts. And we do exactly the same spiritually. What this man exhorts us to do therefore, in verse twelve, is to stop nursing our painful joints! Movement is the best thing for them at a certain stage. 'Wherefore lift up the hands which hang down, and the feeble knees.' 'But,' you say, 'I haven't the strength or the power to do it.' Says the Instructor:

'Lift them up, stand erect, be ready for the movement, the more
you move it the better it will be'.

This is something which is literally true on the physical level
and you will find that you will always be given that instruction
by one who knows his business. Keep moving, don't let yourself
get stiff, keep the joints moving, keep them as supple as you can.
And this is equally true in the spiritual realm. Have you not
seen people who when trials come adopt a kind of pose? They
are very sorry for themselves and they want everybody else to be
sorry for them. 'Get out of that pose,' says this man, 'shake it
off, lift up the hands which hang down, straighten the feeble
knees, hold yourself up. Realize you are a man, pull yourself
together.' This is the time to do this, not at the beginning. We
do it after we have received instruction and after we have gone
through the loosening up phase.

What else? The answer is in verse thirteen: 'And make straight
paths for your feet, lest that which is lame be turned out of the
way; but let it rather be healed'. 'Make straight paths for yourself.' Why? The argument is altogether reasonable. If the path
is not smooth and straight the diseased joint may be dislocated,
but if you make a straight and flat road for the lame to walk
along it will help him to be healed. You see the importance of
the straight road. What does it mean spiritually? It means that,
having done all we have considered, we just say to ourselves: 'Yes,
I have gone astray, I must come back to the straight and narrow
road'. So we map out again the way of holiness, we come back to
the highway of God, we realize once more, the need of discipline,
we decide to stop doing certain things, we make a straight path
for our feet. And then as we walk again along this road of holiness
we will find that our feeble knees are being strengthened and the
whole of our system braced up as by a tonic.

The last instruction is in verse fourteen—'Follow peace with
all men and holiness, without which no man shall see the Lord'.
This word 'follow' again is not strong enough. What the writer
actually said was 'pursue', 'pursue peace', 'pursue holiness', or,
even more strongly, he says 'hunt' for peace, 'hunt' after holiness,
'strive' after it. I cannot understand how any one who has read
the Scriptures can accept and adopt any idea of passivity with
respect to the way of holiness. Here is a man who tells us to
yearn after holiness with all our might until we have it, to follow
after it, pursue it, to hunt after it—peace and holiness, peace with

17

other people, yes, and all and everything that we can do to be holy and to be like God. Those are the exercises through which God puts us in the gymnasium; that is God's way of making us to be really His children.

Let me end with a word of encouragement. 'No chastening for the present seemeth to be joyous, but grievous; nevertheless afterward it yieldeth the peaceable fruit of righteousness.' This process is very painful at the time, but listen to the promise; 'afterward it yieldeth the peaceable fruit of righteousness'. Do not worry about the pain, keep on moving those stiff muscles and you will find that they will soon become supple. Keep on with the exercises for 'afterward it yieldeth the peaceable fruit of righteousness'. The more we are put through this training in the gymnasium the better, because God is preparing us, not for time only, but for eternity. Physical exercises are only for a while and a time and our earthly parents discipline us for a few days only while we are in this world; but this life of ours in this world is a preparation for eternity. It is not this world that matters, it is the next; it is not the here and now that are important, it is the eternal. God in this life is preparing us for everlasting bliss and glory.

Remember also in that connection the One to whom we are going—'without holiness no man shall see the Lord'. If we want to see God we had better do the exercises in the gymnasium very thoroughly. 'Without holiness, no man shall see the Lord'— verse fourteen—and God is putting us through these exercises in order to make us holy. If you and I, therefore, do not pay attention to this treatment that God is giving us, it just means that we do not realize who we are, or it means that we are not children of God at all. If we really want to go on to God and heaven we must submit and do exactly what He tells us, because He is putting us through all this treatment in order to promote our holiness. It is all for our profit and that we may become sharers and partakers of His own holiness.

Finally, and beyond all else for our encouragement, look at the One who subjected Himself to it all, though He need not have done so—'Looking unto Jesus the Author and Finisher of our Faith who for the joy that was set before Him endured the Cross, despising the shame'. He knew what it meant. He said: 'Father if it be possible let this cup pass from Me, nevertheless not My will but Thine be done'. He endured it all for the joy that was laid up for Him and for your salvation and mine. So when you may feel that the discipline is too much and that it is very painful, in addition to all that I have said, look unto Him, keep looking at Him and follow Him. And as certainly as we do so we shall find that this which for the moment is so painful and grievous will afterward yield, even in this life and world, and still more in glory, this wonderful fruit of health and righteousness, of peace and of the enjoyment of God. I do not know what you feel, but as I have meditated this last fortnight upon this great word, I say honestly and in the presence of God, that there is nothing that gives me greater comfort and greater solace than this, to know that I am in God's hands, and that He so loves me and is so determined upon my holiness and upon bringing me to heaven, that if I do not listen to His Word and follow it, He will deal with me in another way. He is going to bring me there. It is alarming, but it is also glorious. 'Nothing shall be able to separate us from the love of God which is in Christ Jesus our Lord.' Take the exercises, my friend, hurry to the gymnasium, do what He tells you, examine yourself, practise it all whatever the cost, however great the pain, and enter into the joy of the Lord.

Be careful for nothing; but in everything by prayer and supplication with thanksgiving let your requests be made known unto God. And the peace of God, which passeth all understanding, shall keep your hearts and minds through Christ Jesus.

Philippians 4. 6, 7

XIX

THE PEACE OF GOD

THIS is undoubtedly one of the noblest, greatest and most comforting statements which is to be found anywhere in any extant literature. One is tempted to say that about many passages in the Scriptures, and yet from the standpoint of our personal lives in this world, and from the standpoint of practical experience, there is nothing that has greater comfort for God's people than these two verses. In them the apostle is continuing what is not only the major theme of this fourth chapter, but the major theme of the entire Epistle. He is concerned about the happiness and the joy of the members of the church at Philippi. He has written the specific exhortation that they should 'rejoice in the Lord alway', and again he says, 'rejoice'. In his great desire that these people might maintain that constant rejoicing in the Lord, the apostle has been considering various forces and factors that tend from time to time to rob the Christian of that joy and to bring him down to a lower level of Christian living. He has said: 'Let your long suffering—your forbearance—be known unto all men for the Lord is at hand'. He has shown how an unquiet spirit, a grasping desire to have our own way so frequently robs us of our joy.

Here in these verses he goes on to consider another factor that is perhaps more problematical than any of the others which tend to rob us of the joy of the Lord, and that is what we may well describe as the tyranny of circumstances, or the things that happen to us. How many they are, and how often do they come! Here the apostle deals with this question in a final manner. It is remarkable as you read through the Bible, to notice how often this particular subject is dealt with. A very good case can be made out for saying that all the New Testament epistles face this particular problem, and were designed to help the first Christians to overcome the tyranny of circumstances. They lived in a very difficult world and had to suffer and to endure a great deal; and these men called of God wrote their letters in order to show them how to overcome these things. It is the great theme of the New Testament; but you find it also in the Old Testament. Take the third and fourth Psalms, for instance. How perfectly they put it all. The great problem in life is, in a sense, how to lay oneself down to rest and to sleep. 'I laid me down and slept,' said the Psalmist. Anybody can lie down, but the question is can you sleep? The Psalmist describes himself surrounded by enemies and by difficulties and trials, and his mighty testimony is that in spite of that, because of his trust in the Lord, he both laid him down and slept, and he awaked safe and sound in the morning. Why? Because the Lord was with him and looking after him.

That is the theme of so much of the Bible in the Old Testament and in the New that it is obviously a subject of supreme importance. I sometimes feel that there is nothing perhaps which provides such a thorough test of our faith and of our whole Christian position as just this matter. It is one thing to say that you subscribe to the Christian faith, it is one thing, having read your Bible and abstracted its doctrine, to say: 'Yes, I believe all that, it is the faith by which I live'. But it is not always exactly the same thing to find that faith triumphant and victorious and maintaining you in a state of joy, when everything seems to have gone against you and well nigh driven you to despair. It is a subtle and delicate test of our position because it is such an essentially practical test. It is far removed from the realm of mere theory. You are *in* the position, you are *in* the situation, these things are happening to you, and the question is, what is your faith worth at that point? Does it differentiate you from people who have no faith? That is obviously something of very great importance not only for our peace and comfort but also, and especially at a time like this, from the whole standpoint of our Christian witness. People today tell us that they are realists and practical. They say that they are not interested in doctrine, and not interested to listen very much to what we say, but if they see a body of people who seem to have something that enables them to triumph over life, they become interested at once. This is so because they are unhappy, and frustrated and uncertain, and fearful. If, when in that condition themselves, they see people who seem to have peace and calm and quiet, then they are ready to look at them and to listen to them. So that from the standpoint of our own personal happiness and our maintenance of the joy of the Lord, and also from the standpoint of our witness and our testimony in these difficult days, it behoves us to consider very carefully what the apostle has to say in these masterly statements about the way to deal with the tyranny of circumstances and conditions.

The matter seems to divide itself up quite simply. First of all he tells us what we have to avoid. There are certain things we must avoid, says the apostle—'Be careful for nothing'. That is a negative injunction—something to avoid. Now let us be quite clear about the term 'careful'. 'Be careful for nothing', says the Authorized translation, but you will find another translation even better: 'Be anxious for nothing' or 'Be anxious about nothing'. 'Careful' means 'full of care'—that means anxiety, harassing care, nervous solicitude, tending to brood or to ponder over things. It is the same word as our Lord used in the Sermon on the Mount—you remember that section in the sixth chapter of Matthew: 'Take no thought . . .' It means do not be over-anxious, do not brood and ponder, do not meditate over-much upon, do not have this nervous solicitude about the thing. That is the meaning of the term.

It is important, in passing, that we should understand that the Bible would nowhere teach us not to make ordinary provision for life, or not to use common-sense. It does not encourage laziness. You will remember that Paul in writing to the church at Thessalonica said that 'if any would not work, neither should he eat'. 'Careful' here, therefore, does not refer to wise fore-thought, but must be interpreted as anxiety, this harassing, wearying, wearing care. That is the thing the apostle tells us we must avoid at all costs.

But you notice that he does not stop merely at that negative injunction. There is a very profound piece of Biblical psychology here. The apostle shows us how we tend to get into this state of nervous, morbid, brooding anxiety. You notice that he tells us it is all due to the activity of the heart and mind—'The peace of God which passeth all understanding shall keep your hearts and minds through Christ Jesus'. Very well, the trouble is in the heart and mind. It is the heart and the mind that tend to produce this state of anxiety, this morbid care and solicitude.

This, I say, is a profound piece of psychology, and I am emphasizing it because later on we shall see how vital it is in applying the apostle's remedy to ourselves, that we should grasp and understand his psychological explanation of the condition.

What Paul is saying in other words is that we can control many things in our lives and outside our lives, but we cannot control our hearts and minds. 'This condition of anxiety,' says Paul, 'is something which is in a sense outside your own control, it happens apart from you and in spite of you'. And how true that is to experience. Recall any occasion when you were in this condition of anxiety. Remember how it could not be controlled. You were lying awake and you would have given the whole world if you could only sleep. But your mind would not let you sleep, your heart would not let you sleep. The heart and the mind are outside our control. We would give the whole world if we could but stop the heart and the mind from going on working, from revolving and thinking and so keeping us awake. Here is profound psychology indeed, and the apostle does not hesitate to use it. Here, once more, we come across the wonderful realism of the Scriptures, their utter absolute honesty, their recognition of man as he is. So the apostle tells us that in this way the heart and the mind, or if you prefer it, the depth of one's being, tends to produce this state of anxiety. Here the 'heart' does not only mean the seat of emotions, it means the very central part of one's personality. The 'mind' can be translated, if you like, by the term thought. We have all, alas, experienced this condition and we know exactly what the apostle means. The heart has feelings and emotions. If a dear one is taken ill how the heart begins to work! Your concern, your very love for the person, is the cause of the anxiety. If you thought nothing of the person you would not be anxious. There you see where the heart and the affections come in. Not only that, the imagination! What a prolific cause of anxiety is the imagination. You are confronted with a situation, but if it were merely that, you would probably be able to lie down and go to sleep. But the imagination comes in and you begin to think: 'What if this or that should happen? Everything is fairly under control tonight, but what if by tomorrow morning the temperature should be up, or what if this condition should arise and lead to that?' You go on thinking for hours, agitated by these imaginations. Thus your heart keeps you awake.

Or then, not so much in the realm of imagination but more in the realm of the mind and of pure thought, you find yourself beginning to consider possibilities and you put up positions and deal with them and analyse them and you say: 'If that should take place we shall have to make this arrangement, or we shall

have to do that'. You see how it works. The heart and the mind
are in control. We are the victims of thoughts; in this condition
of anxiety we are the victims; it is the heart and the mind, these
powers that are within us and which are outside our control that
are mastering us and tyrannizing over us. The apostle tells us
that this is something which at all costs we must avoid. I need
not dwell upon the reason for that. I think we must all know it
from experience. In this state of anxiety we spend the whole of
our time reasoning and arguing and chasing imaginations. And
in that state we are useless. We do not want to speak to other
people. We may appear to be listening to them as they speak in
conversation, but our mind is chasing these possibilities. And so,
alas, our testimony is useless. We are of no value to others and
above all we lose the joy of the Lord.

But let us hurry to the second principle. What have we to do
in order to avoid that inner .turmoil? What does the apostle
teach us here?

This is where we come to that which is peculiarly and specifically Christian. If I do nothing else I trust that I shall be
enabled to show you the eternal difference between the Christian
way of dealing with anxiety and the psychological way or the
common-sense way. Some of my friends seem to feel that I am
rather hard on psychology but let me indulge in a little apologia.
Psychology, I believe, is one of the most subtle dangers in connection with the Christian faith. People sometimes think that
they are being sustained by the Christian faith when what they
have is merely a psychological mechanism in operation; and it
breaks down in a real crisis. We do not preach psychology, we
preach the Christian faith.

Let me show you, then, the difference between the Christian
way of dealing with anxiety and this other method. What does
the apostle tell us to do when we are threatened by anxiety?
He does not just say: 'Stop worrying'. That is what common-
sense and psychology say: 'Stop worrying, pull yourself together'.
The apostle does not say that for the good reason that to tell a
person in that condition to stop worrying is useless. Incidentally
it is also bad psychology. That is what is called repression. If
you happen to be a strong-willed person you can hold these
things from the conscious mind with the result that they then go
on working in the unconscious mind and that is what is called
repression. That condition is even worse than anxiety itself.

But not only that, it is so idle to tell the average person to stop worrying—that is why I say Paul's 'psychology' is so important. It is the very thing they cannot do. They would like to, but they cannot. It is like telling a hopeless drunkard to stop drinking. He cannot, because he is helpless in the grip of this lust and passion. In the same way the Bible does not say: 'Do not worry, it may never happen'. This is a popular psychological slogan and people think it is very wonderful—'Why worry, it may never happen'—but if anyone says that to me when I am in this state, my reaction is: 'Yes, but it *may* happen. That is my problem. What if it does happen? That is the essence of my problem, so it does not help me to say it may never happen.

The third negative is this. People tend to say to those wretched people who are anxious and worried: 'You must not worry, it is wrong to worry, and all the worry in the world will not make any difference'. Now that is perfectly true, it is sound common-sense. The psychologists in their turn say: 'Do not waste your energy. The fact that you are worrying is not going to affect the position at all'. 'Ah, yes,' I say, 'that is all right, that is perfectly true; but, you know, it does not get at the source of my trouble for this good reason. I am concerned with what *may* happen. I agree when you put it to me that worrying is not going to affect the position, but the position remains and it is the position that is causing me this anxiety. What you say is perfectly true but it does not deal with my particular situation'. In other words all these methods fail to deal with the situation because they never realize the power of what Paul calls 'the heart' and 'the mind'—these things that grip us. That is why none of the psychology and common-sense methods are finally of any use.

What then does the apostle say? He puts his remedy in the form of a positive injunction. 'Let your requests be made known unto God.' That is the answer. But now, here, it is of vital importance that we should know precisely and in detail how to deal with this. The apostle says: 'Let your requests be made known unto God'. 'Alas!' says many a sufferer, 'I have tried, I have prayed; but I have not found the peace you speak of. I have not had an answer. It is no use telling me to pray.' Fortunately for us the apostle realized that also, and he has given us particular instructions for the carrying out of his injunction. 'Be careful for nothing, but in everything by prayer and supplication with thanksgiving, let your requests be made known unto

God.' Is the apostle just tumbling out one word after another, or is he speaking advisedly? I can show you that he is indeed speaking advisedly as he shows us how to let our requests be made known unto God.

How are we to do that? First he tells us to pray. He differentiates between prayer and supplication and thanksgiving. What does he mean by prayer? This is the most general term and it means worship and adoration. If you have problems that seem insoluble, if you are liable to become anxious and overburdened, and somebody tells you to pray, do not rush to God with your petition. That is not the way. Before you make your requests known unto God, pray, worship, adore. Come into the presence of God and for the time being forget your problems. Do not start with them. Just realize that you are face to face with God. In this word 'prayer' the idea of being face to face is inherent in the very word itself. You come into the presence of God and you realize the presence and you recollect the presence—that is the first step always. Even before you make your requests known unto God you realize that you are face to face with God, that you are in His presence and you pour out your heart in adoration. That is the beginning.

But following prayer comes supplication. Now we are moving on. Having worshipped God because God is God, having offered this general worship and adoration, we come now to the particular, and the apostle here encourages us to make our supplications. He tells us that we can take particular things to God, that petition is a legitimate part of prayer. So we bring our petitions, the particular things that are now concerning us.

We are now coming nearer to letting our requests be made known. But wait, there is still one other thing—'by prayer and supplication, with thanksgiving'. That is one of the most vital of all these terms. And it is just here that so many of us go astray when we are in this condition with which the apostle is dealing. I trust it is unnecessary that I should digress to point out that in connection with these steps the apostle was not merely interested in liturgical forms. What a tragedy that people should take an interest in the form of worship in a mere liturgical sense. That is not what the apostle is concerned about. He is not interested in formality, he is interested in worship, and thanksgiving is absolutely essential for this reason. If, while we pray to God, we have a grudge against Him in our hearts, we have no right to expect that the peace of God will keep our heart and our mind. If we go on our knees feeling that God is against us, we may as well get up and go out. No, we must approach Him 'with thanksgiving'. There must be no doubt as to the goodness of God in our heart. There must be no question or query; we must have positive reasons for thanking God. We have our problems and troubles but there on our knees we must ask ourselves: 'What can I thank God for?' We have to do that deliberately and it is something that we can do. We must remind ourselves of it. We must say: 'I may be in trouble at the moment, but I can thank God for my salvation and that He has sent His Son to die on the Cross for me and for my sins. There is a terrible problem facing me, I know, but He has done that for me. I thank God that He sent His Son, our Lord Jesus Christ, into the world. I will thank Him for bearing my sins in His own body on the tree, I will thank Him for rising again for my justification. I will pour out my heart in thanksgiving for that. I will thank Him for the many blessings I have received in the past'. We must just work out with our mind and with all our energy the reasons for thanking and praising God. We must remind ourselves that He is our Father, that He loves us so much that the very hairs of our head are all numbered. And when we have reminded ourselves of these things we must pour out our heart in thanksgiving. We must be in the right relationship to God. We must realize the truth concerning Him. Therefore we must come into His presence with a loving, praising, worshipping, adoration and confident faith and then make our requests known unto Him. The prayer that Paul advocates, in other words, is not a desperate cry in the dark, not some frantic appeal to God without any real thought. No, no, we first realize and recollect that we are worshipping a blessed, glorious God. We worship first and then we make our requests known.

Let me hurry on to the third great principle, and that is the gracious promise of God to all who do this. We have seen what we have to do, we have been instructed as to how we are to deal with it, and now comes the gracious promise to those who do what the apostle has just been telling us. This is, of course, the best of all, but we must learn how to look at it. Have you noticed the promise, have you noticed its character, have you noticed that it does not even mention the things that are worrying you? That is the peculiar thing about the Christian method of dealing

with anxiety. 'In all things,' says the apostle—these things that
are worrying—make your requests known and God will banish
and remove them all?' But Paul does not say that. He does not
mention them, he just says nothing about them. To me that is
one of the most thrilling things about the Christian life. The glory
of the gospel is this, that it is concerned about us and not about
our circumstances. The final triumph of the gospel is seen in
this, that whatever our circumstances, we ourselves can be put
right and maintained. It does not mention our condition, it
does not talk about these things that are harassing and per-
plexing, it does not say a single word about them. They may or
they may not happen, I do not know. Paul does not say that the
thing feared is not going to take place, he says that we shall be
kept whether it happens or whether it does not happen. Thank
God, that is the victory. I am taken above circumstances, I am
triumphant in spite of them.

That is the great principle. We all tend to be tyrannized by
circumstances because we depend upon them, and we would like
them to be governed and controlled, but that is not the way in
which the Scripture deals with the situation. What the apostle
says is this: 'Make your requests known unto God, and the peace
of God which passeth all understanding shall keep your hearts
and minds'. He will keep you absolutely safe from these things
which are keeping you awake and preventing your sleep. They
will be kept outside, and you will be kept in peace in spite of
them.

Again I would point out that never does the apostle say that if
we pray, our prayer in and of itself will make us feel better. It is a
disgraceful thing that people should pray for that reason. That
is the psychologists' use of prayer. They tell us that if we are
in trouble it will do us good to pray—very good psychology,
thoroughly bad Christianity. Prayer is not auto-suggestion.

Neither does he say: 'Pray, because while you are praying you
will not be thinking about that problem, and therefore you will
have temporary relief'. Again good psychology but bad Christianity.

Neither does he say: 'If you fill your mind with thoughts of
God and Christ these thoughts will push out the other things'.
Once more good psychology but nothing to do with Christianity.

Neither does he say, and I say this advisedly: 'Pray, because
prayer changes things'. No, it does not. Prayer does not 'change

things'. That is not what the apostle says, that is again psychology and has nothing to do with the gospel at all. What the apostle says is this: 'You pray and make your requests known unto God, and God will do something'. It is not your prayer that is going to do it, it is not you who are going to do it, but God. 'The peace of God that passeth all understanding'—He, through it all, 'will keep your hearts and minds in Christ Jesus'.

I must say a word about that expression 'keeping' your hearts and minds. It means garrisoning, guarding—a number of words can be used. It conjures up a picture. What will happen is that this peace of God will walk round the ramparts and towers of our life. We are inside, and the activities of the heart and mind are producing those stresses and anxieties and strains from the outside. But the peace of God will keep them all out and we ourselves inside will be at perfect peace. It is God that does it. It is not ourselves, it is not prayer, it is not some psychological mechanism. We make our requests known unto God, and God does that for us and keeps us in perfect peace.

What shall we say of this phrase: 'The peace of God that passeth all understanding'? You cannot understand this peace, you cannot imagine it, you cannot even believe it in a sense, and yet it is happening and you are experiencing it and enjoying it. It is God's peace that is in Christ Jesus. What does he mean by that? He is telling us that this peace of God works by presenting the Lord Jesus Christ to us and reminding us about Him. To put it in terms of the argument of the Epistle to the Romans: 'If while we were enemies we were reconciled to God by the death of His Son much more being reconciled, we shall be saved by His life' (Romans 5. 10). 'All things work together for good to them that love God, to them who are called according to His purpose.' 'He that spared not His own Son but delivered Him up for us all how shall He not with Him also freely give us all things' (Romans 8. 28, 32). 'I am persuaded that neither death, nor life, nor angels, nor principalities, nor powers, nor things present, nor things to come, nor height, nor depth, nor any other creature, shall be able to separate us from the love of God which is in Christ Jesus our Lord' (Romans 8. 38, 39). The argument is that if God has done that supreme thing for us in the death of His Son upon the Cross He cannot forsake us now, He cannot leave us half-way, as it were. So the peace of God that passeth all understanding keeps our hearts and minds through, or in,

Christ Jesus. In that way God guarantees our peace and our freedom from anxiety.

I end with just a word on the last principle, which is the all inclusiveness of the promise. 'In nothing be careful'—'be careful for nothing, but in all things'. It does not matter what they are, there is no limit in it. Beloved Christian, whatever it is that is tending to get you down, tending to make you a victim of this anxiety, this morbid care, harassing and spoiling your Christian life and witness, whatever it is, let it be known unto God in that way, and if you do so it is absolutely guaranteed that the peace of God which passeth all understanding shall guard, keep, garrison your heart and mind. That mighty turmoil of heart and mind within you will not affect you. Like the Psalmist you will lay yourself down and you will sleep, you will know this perfect peace. Do you know this, have you got this peace? Is this another bit of theory or does it actually happen? I assert that nearly two thousand years of Christian history—the story of the Christian Church—proclaim that this is a fact. Read the stories of the saints and the martyrs and the Confessors. Why, you get the same evidence in contemporary stories. Recently I read of an experience told by John George Carpenter, until a few years ago the General of the Salvation Army. He tells how he and his wife had to part with their daughter, a lovely girl, of whom they were so fond and proud and who had dedicated her young life to foreign mission work in the East. Suddenly she was taken ill with typhoid fever. Of course, they began to pray, but John Carpenter and Mrs. Carpenter somehow felt, although they could not explain it, that they could not pray for that child's recovery. They went on praying but their prayer was—'Thou canst heal her if Thou wilt'—they could not positively ask God to heal her, only—'Thou canst if Thou wilt'. They could get no further. They went on like that for six weeks and then this beautiful girl died. The very morning she died John Carpenter said to Mrs. Carpenter: 'You know, I am aware of a strange and curious calm within', and Mrs. Carpenter replied and said, 'I feel exactly the same'. And she said to him: 'This must be the peace of God'. And it was the peace of God. It was the peace of God keeping the heart and mind quiet in the sense that they could not upset the person. There they were, they had made their request known in the right way, and to their amazement and astonishment—they were almost chiding themselves because of it

—this amazing calm and peace had come to them. They could not understand it, and that was the only explanation—'it must be the peace of God'. It was. Thank God for it. You and I cannot explain these things, they overpower us; but He is Almighty. With prayer and supplication and thanksgiving, therefore, let your requests be made known unto Him, and He, through His peace in Christ, will keep your heart and mind at rest and in peace.

BUT I rejoiced in the Lord greatly, that now at the last your care of me hath flourished again; wherein ye were also careful, but ye lacked opportunity. Not that I speak in respect of want: for I have learned, in whatsoever state I am, therewith to be content. I know both how to be abased, and I know how to abound: every where and in all things I am instructed both to be full and to be hungry, both to abound and to suffer need.

Philippians 4. 10-12

XX

LEARNING TO BE CONTENT

WE have in the words of Philippians 4. 10-12 one of those portions of Scripture which always makes me feel that there is a sense in which the only right and proper thing to do after reading them is to pronounce the benediction! One trembles at the very approach to such exalted noble words, recalling as they do one of the high-water marks in the Christian experience of this mighty apostle to the Gentiles. Yet it is our business, though we approach them thus with fear and trembling, to try to analyse and expound them. With the end of the ninth verse in this chapter the apostle has reached the end of the particular exhortations which he was anxious to address to the members of the church at Philippi. He has really finished with his doctrine, but he still cannot close the letter. There is one other thing he must do, and that is he must express his profound gratitude to the members of the church at Philippi for the personal gift which they had sent to him, while held in prison in Rome, by the hand of their friend and brother Epaphroditus.

That, in a sense, is really the reason why Paul was writing the letter at all. The Philippian Church had sent him some gift. We are not told what it was, whether it was in money or in kind, but they had sent him some gift by their emissary Epaphroditus. Epaphroditus is now going back to them, and Paul sends the letter with him; and having finished with his doctrine, he wants to thank them for this expression of their love and solicitude for him in his suffering and his imprisonment. That is what he proceeds to do in these ten verses running from verse 10 to verse 20. There is nothing, I always feel, about this great Epistle, which is more interesting than to observe in detail the way in which the apostle does everything, and the way in which he offers his thanks to the members of the church at Philippi is full of instruction and of interest. It is quite clear that this question of thanking the members of the church at Philippi for their gift and for their kindness presented the apostle with a problem. You would have thought that there could surely be no problem in thanking people who have been kind and generous, and yet to Paul it is obviously a problem. It takes him ten verses to do this thing. You often find him dealing with a mighty doctrine in a verse or two, but when it comes to just thanking the members of the church at Philippi for their goodness and kindness it takes him ten verses. You notice also he goes on repeating himself. 'Not that I speak in respect of want', and later on, 'Not because I desire a gift'. There is a kind of argument and he seems to find it difficult to find the right words.

Paul's trouble was something like this. He was very anxious to thank the church at Philippi for their kindness. But at the same time he was equally anxious, if not more anxious, to show them that he had not been waiting impatiently for, or expecting, this expression of their kindness, and still more that he was in no sense dependent upon their goodness and generosity. In that way he finds himself confronted with a problem. He has to do these two things at one and the same time; he has to express his thanks to the members of the church at Philippi, and yet he has to do it in a way which will not in any sense detract or derogate from the reality of his experience as a Christian man, dependent upon God. That is why it takes him ten verses to do this. It was the problem of a Christian gentleman, sensitive to the feelings of others, trying to reconcile these two things. And what a great gentleman this apostle was, how concerned about the feelings of others. As a gentleman he is anxious to express his profound gratitude and to let them know that their kindness really did move him very deeply, and yet he is concerned on the other hand to make it abundantly clear to them that he had not been spending his time wondering why they had not thought of his needs, suffering because they had not sent him something there in prison, wondering why the churches had not sent supplies for his relief. He wanted to make it perfectly clear that that had never been his condition at all, and what we have in these ten verses is the apostle's method of resolving that particular problem.

Now the thing we have to grasp about Christian truth is that it is something that governs the whole of our life. The Christian gospel dominates the entire life of the Christian. It controls his thinking, as we see in verse 8, it controls his action as we see in verse 9. And now, in these ten verses, we see how a Christian, even in such a matter as returning thanks for a kindness, does so in a way which is different from the way and manner of a person that is not a Christian. The Christian cannot do anything, not even in a matter like this, except in a truly Christian manner. So here, the apostle, at one and the same time, shows his indebtedness to his friends, but his still greater indebtedness to the Lord. Paul was jealous always for the reputation of the Lord, and he was afraid that in thanking the Philippians for their gift he might somehow give the impression that the Lord was not sufficient for him apart from them. He must keep that first. He loves these Philippians very dearly and he is profoundly grateful to them. But he loves his Lord still more, and he is afraid lest in thanking them he might somehow give even a suspicion of a suggestion that the Lord was not sufficient for him, or that he had been depending upon the Philippians in an ultimate sense.

So he sets out in this mighty passage, with its staggering and astounding affirmations, to show the primacy of the Lord and the all-sufficiency of the Lord, while at the same time he shows his gratitude and his indebtedness and his love towards the Philippians for this manifestation of their personal care and solicitude for him. The real essence of the matter is found in verses 11 and 12. Here we have the doctrine—'Not that I speak in respect of want: for I have learned in whatsoever state I am, therewith to be content. I know both how to be abased and how to abound; everywhere and in all things I am instructed both to be full and to be hungry, both to abound, and to suffer need'.

We must now look at this great doctrine which Paul announces in this way. There are two big principles here. The first of course is the condition at which the apostle had arrived. The second is the way in which he had arrived at that condition. They constitute the subject matter of this tremendous statement.

Let us first look at the condition to which the apostle had attained. He describes it by the word that is translated here as 'content'—'I have learned in whatsoever state I am, therewith to be "content".' But it is important that we should get at the exact and precise meaning of this word. The word 'content' does not fully explain it; it really means that he is 'self-sufficient', independent of circumstances or conditions or surroundings, 'having sufficiency in one's self'. That is the real meaning of this word which is translated 'content'. 'I have learned in whatsoever state I am to be self-sufficient, independent of circumstances, independent of surroundings, independent of conditions.' The affirmation made by the apostle is that he has arrived at a state in which he can say quite honestly and truthfully that he is independent of his position, his circumstances, his surroundings and of everything that is happening to him. Now that that was no mere rhetorical statement on the part of the apostle is made very clear in the records that we have of this man and of his life in different parts of the New Testament. There is, for instance, an interesting example of it in the sixteenth chapter of the Book of the Acts of the Apostles describing the occasion of Paul's first visit to Philippi where the recipients of this letter lived. You remember how he and Silas were arrested and beaten and thrown into prison with their feet made fast in the stocks. Their physical conditions could not very well have been worse, yet so little effect did that have upon Paul and Silas that 'at midnight Paul and Silas prayed and sang praises unto God' (Acts 16. 25). Independent of circumstances, 'content in whatsoever state I am', to be self-satisfied, independent of surroundings. That is what you find also in the famous passage in the Second Epistle to the Corinthians, chapter twelve, where Paul tells us how he learned to be independent of 'the thorn in the flesh', self-sufficient in spite of it. You remember also how he exhorts Timothy to take hold of this principle by saying: 'Godliness with contentment is great gain' (1 Timothy 6. 6). There is nothing like it, he says in effect, if you have that you have everything. Paul had become an old man by then and he writes to the young man Timothy and says: The first thing you have to learn is to be independent of circumstances and conditions—'Godliness with contentment'. These are but a few of many like illustrations to which we might call attention.

The teaching of the New Testament, however, not only affirms that this was true of Paul, it makes it very plain and clear that it is a condition into which we should all as Christian people enter. You remember how our Lord makes this point in the sixth chapter of the Gospel according to St. Matthew—'Take no heed for the morrow', be not over-anxious and worried about food, and clothing and things of that kind. That is the glorious, mighty independence of what is happening to us, that we should all know and experience. It is self-sufficiency in the good sense.

But it is most important that we should have a clear understanding in our minds as to what this means. The word 'content' tends to provoke certain misunderstandings of what the apostle is teaching. You can so interpret this statement by Paul as more or less to justify the charge that is brought against the Christian gospel that it is nothing but 'the opium of the people'. It is characteristic of this particular generation in which we live to find a tendency on the part of large numbers of people to feel that the Christian gospel has been a hindrance to the forward march of mankind, that it has been a drag on progress, that it has been nothing but 'the dope of the people'. They say that it is a doctrine which has taught people to put up with all kinds of conditions whatever they may be, and however disgraceful and unjust. There has been a violent political reaction against the gospel of Jesus Christ because people have so misinterpreted this kind of text as to put it in this way:

'The rich man in his castle,
The poor man at his gate,
God made them, high or lowly,
And order'd their estate'.

Now that is just rubbish and a blank denial of what the apostle teaches here. Yet how often has it been interpreted like that. It is a matter of great regret that one who could have written the hymn 'There is a green hill far away' should have been guilty of such a violation of the teaching of the Bible—'The rich man in his castle, the poor man at his gate'. Were men meant to be like that and to stay like that for ever? The Bible never teaches that; it does not say that man should be content to remain in poverty, that he should never endeavour to 'better' himself. There is nothing in the Bible that disputes the proposition that all men are equal in the sight of God and that all are entitled to equality of opportunity. Grievous harm has been done to the Church of Christ because a statement such as this in our text has been misinterpreted in that way.

Neither does it mean mere indifference to circumstances. That is but the negative resignation of a pagan stoicism, and far removed from the Christian position. What, then, does it mean? To put it positively, what the apostle says here is that he is not mastered or controlled by circumstances. By all means if you can improve your circumstances by fair and legitimate means, do so; but if you cannot, and if you have to remain in a trying and difficult position, do not be mastered by it, do not let it get you down, do not let it control you, do not let it determine your misery or your joy. 'You', says the apostle, 'must come into the state in which, whatever your conditions, you are not controlled by them.' That is what he affirms of himself. 'Whatever my condition or circumstance,' he says in effect, 'I am in control. I am master of the situation, I am not mastered by the situation, I am free, I am at liberty, I do not depend for my happiness upon what is happening to me. My life, my happiness, my joy and my experience are independent of the things that are going on round about me, and even of the things that may be happening to me.' I would remind you again that Paul was actually in prison, probably chained to a soldier on his right and another on his left when he uttered these words, yet even while in that actual condition, he can say that he is independent of his circumstances. 'My life,' says Paul, 'is not controlled and determined by what is happening to me; I am in a state and condition in which I rise right above them. These things are not the determining factors in my life and experience.'

Now that is his claim, and he was most anxious to emphasize the fact that it is an all-inclusive claim. Observe again his actual words. Having made the general statement he now amplifies it: 'I know both how to be abased and how to abound, everywhere and in all things I am instructed'—again he goes back to it—'both to be full and to be hungry, both to abound and to suffer need'. He was anxious to make the all-inclusiveness of his claim perfectly clear. Let me put the opposites in series. He knows how to be abased, he knows how to be hungry and to suffer need; on the other hand he knows how to abound, how to be full and to have plenty. It would be interesting to discuss the relative difficulty of these two things. Which is the more difficult, to be abased or to abound without losing the contented mind? I do not know whether we can ever answer the question. They are both extremely difficult and one is as difficult as the other. Can I be abased without feeling a sense of grudge, or without being worried, or without being anxious? Can I suffer the need of food and clothing, can I be abased in my profession or office or work, can I somehow or another be put down and still remain in spirit exactly as I was before! What a difficult thing this is, to take a second place, to be hurt, to be insulted, to see others suffering in the same way, to suffer physical need or pain—to know how to be abased, how to be hungry, how to suffer need in some respect. One of the greatest tasks in life is to discover how to suffer any or all of those things without feeling a sense of grudge, without complaint or annoyance or bitterness of spirit, to discover how not to be worried or anxious. Paul tells us that he has learned how to do that. He had experienced every kind of trial and tribulation and yet he is unaffected by them.

Then take the other side. 'I know how to abound,' says Paul, 'I know how "to be full", I know how to enjoy plenty.' What a difficult thing this is. How difficult it is for the wealthy person not to feel complete independence of God. When we are rich and can arrange and manipulate everything, we tend to forget God. Most of us remember Him when we are down. When we are in need we begin to pray, but, when we have everything we need, how easy it is to forget God. I leave it to you to decide which is the more difficult. What Paul says is that in either of these positions he is perfectly free. Poverty does not get him down, riches do not carry him away and make him lose his hold. He says that he is not dependent upon either, that he is self-sufficient in this sense, that his life is not controlled by these things, that he is what he is apart from them. Whether he is 'to abound' or to 'suffer need' it does not matter.

But he is not content with that, he goes still further and says: 'In all things, everywhere' which means in everything and in all things—every single thing in detail, all things together. Now Paul divides it up like this quite deliberately. He wants to say that there is no limit to what he can do in this respect—'In every single particular thing I am like that'. Then he adds: 'Now I will put them together—in all things, whatever may happen to me, I am self-sufficient, I am not dependent upon them, my life and happiness and joy are not determined or controlled by them'.

That, according to the apostle, is the way to live, that is Christian living. It is good for us to face this mighty statement. We are living in days and times of uncertainty, and it may well be that the first and the greatest lesson we all may have to learn is to know how to live without allowing circumstances to affect our inner peace and joy. And yet perhaps there was never a time in the history of the world when it was so difficult to learn this lesson as it is today. The whole of life is so organized at the present time as to make it almost impossible to live this self-sufficient Christian life. Even in a natural sense we are all so dependent on the things that are being done for us and to us and around and about us, that it has become most difficult to live our own lives. We switch on the wireless or the television and gradually become dependent upon them, and it is the same with our newspapers, our cinemas, our entertainments. The world is organizing life for us in every respect and we are becoming dependent upon it. There was a good illustration of that in the early days of the last war when the blackout regulations were first imposed upon us. We used to hear of something which was described as the 'boredom of the blackout'. People found it almost impossible to spend a succession of nights in their own homes doing nothing. They had become dependent on the cinema, the theatre and various other forms of entertainment, and when these things were suddenly cut off they did not know what to do with themselves—'the boredom of the blackout'. That is the very antithesis of what Paul is describing here. But increasingly it is becoming the tendency in the life of man today; increasingly we are becoming dependent upon what others are doing for us. It is the very reverse of what Paul is teaching here.

This, alas, is not only true of the world in general, it is becoming true also of Christian people in particular. I would suggest that one of the greatest dangers confronting us in a spiritual sense is that of becoming dependent upon meetings. There is developing a kind of 'meetings mania' and there are Christian people who seem to be always at meetings. Now meetings are undoubtedly of great value. Let nobody misunderstand me and imagine that I am saying that you should only go to a place of worship on a Sunday. Meetings are good and excellent, but let us beware lest we become so dependent upon meetings that one day when we find ourselves ill and laid upon our bed we do not know what to do with ourselves. We can become too dependent even on Christian meetings—even on a Christian atmosphere. A man was discussing with me the other day what is referred to as the 'leakage' that takes place among the members of certain Christian organizations mainly concerned with young people. There is a very real problem here. While they are in the atmosphere of the Christian organization these young people are keen and interested, but in a few years' time they have become lost to the Church. What is the cause of the leakage? Very frequently it is that they have become too dependent upon a particular fellowship, so that when they go out into the world, or move to another district where they are no longer surrounded by all this Christian fellowship, they suddenly flag and fall. That is the kind of thing against which the apostle is warning us. We must beware of the danger of resting on props even in Christian service and witness. The apostle therefore exhorts us to get into that state in which we shall be independent of what is happening round and about us even in these things. We must cultivate this glorious self-sufficiency.

Professor Whitehead uttered a great truth when he said in his definition of religion that 'Religion is what a man does with his own solitude'. You and I, in the last analysis, are what we are when we are alone. I confess that in a sense it is easier for me to preach from a pulpit than it is to sit alone in my study; it is probably easier for most people to enjoy the presence of our Lord in the company of other Christians than when alone. Paul would have us enjoy what he himself was enjoying. He had a love for the Lord that rendered him independent of all that was happening, or that might happen, to him—in everything, in all things, wherever he might be, whatever was happening, he was content. Abased or abounding, in need or plenty, it did not matter, he had this life, this hidden life with Christ.

Let us consider briefly the second matter which we find here, namely, how the apostle reached this condition. Here again he makes a very interesting statement. You notice that he says: 'I have learned', or better, 'I have come to learn'. I thank God that Paul said that. Paul was not always like this any more than any one of us. He had 'come to learn'. He has another interesting word also. He says: 'Everywhere and in all things I am "instructed" both to be full and to be hungry'. The authorities are all agreed here in saying that what he really says is, 'I have been initiated', 'let into the secret', 'let into the mystery'.

Paul says that he has come to learn how to be in this condition. Now there are many intimations in the New Testament that this was particularly difficult for him. Paul was sensitive, proud by nature, and, in addition, he was an intensely active being. Nothing could be more galling for such a man than to lie in prison. He had been brought up as a Roman citizen, but here he is enduring bondage, not spending his life among great intellectual people, but among slaves. How does he manage it? 'Ah,' he says, 'I have come to learn, I have been let into the secret, I have been let into the mystery.'

How did he come to learn? Let me try to answer that question. In the first place it was by sheer experience. I need only direct your attention to the Second Epistle to the Corinthians, chapter twelve and especially verses 9 and 10 about 'the thorn in the flesh'. Paul did not like it. He struggled against it; three times he prayed that it might be removed. But it was not removed. He could not reconcile himself to it. He was impatient, he was anxious to go on preaching, and this thorn in the flesh was keeping him down. But then he was taught the lesson: 'My grace is sufficient for thee'. He came to a place of understanding as the result of sheer experience of the dealing of God with him. He had to learn, and experience teaches us all. Some of us are very slow to learn, but God in His kindness may send us an illness, sometimes He even strikes us down—anything to teach us this great lesson and to bring us to this great position.

But it was not to be experience alone. Paul had come to learn this great truth by working out a great argument. Let me give you some of the steps of the argument which you can work out for yourself. I think that the apostle's logic was something like this. He said to himself:

1. Conditions are always changing, therefore I must obviously not be dependent upon conditions.

2. What matters supremely and vitally is my soul and my relationship to God—that is the first thing.

3. God is concerned about me as my Father, and nothing happens to me apart from God. Even the very hairs of my head are all numbered. I must never forget that.

4. God's will and God's ways are a great mystery, but I know that whatever He wills or permits is of necessity for my good.

5. Every situation in life is the unfolding of some manifestation of God's love and goodness. Therefore my business is to look for this peculiar manifestation of God's goodness and kindness and to be prepared for surprises and blessings because 'His ways are not my ways, neither His thoughts my thoughts'. What, for example, is the great lesson that Paul learned in the matter of the thorn in the flesh? It is that: 'When I am weak then am I strong'. Paul was taught through physical weakness this manifestation of God's grace.

6. I must regard circumstances and conditions, not in and of themselves therefore, but as a part of God's dealings with me in the work of perfecting my soul and bringing me to final perfection.

7. Whatever my conditions may be at this present moment

they are only temporary, they are only passing, and they can never rob me of the joy and the glory that ultimately await me with Christ.

I suggest that Paul had reasoned and argued it out like that. He had faced conditions and circumstances in the light of the Christian truth and the Christian Gospel, and had worked out these steps and stages. And having done so he says: 'Let anything you can think of happen to me, I remain exactly where I was. Whatever may happen to me, I am left unmoved'.

The big principle that emerges clearly is that he had learned to find his pleasure and his satisfaction in Christ and always in Christ. That is the positive aspect of this matter. We must learn to depend upon Him and in order to do that we must learn to know Him, we must learn to have communion with Him, we must learn to find our pleasure in Him. Let me put it plainly—the danger with some of us is to spend far too much of our time even in reading about Him. The day may come, indeed will come, when we shall not be able to read. Then comes the test. Will you still be happy? Do you know Him so well that though you become deaf or blind this fount will still be open? Do you know Him so well that you can talk to Him and listen to Him and enjoy Him always? Will all be well because you have always been so dependent upon your relationship to Him that nothing else really matters! That was the apostle's condition. His intimacy with Christ was so deep and so great that he had become independent of everything else.

Finally, I believe that what helped him most to learn this lesson was his looking at the great and perfect example of Christ Himself. 'Looking unto Jesus . . . who for the joy that was set before Him endured the Cross, despising the shame' (Hebrews 12. 1-4). Paul 'looked unto Him' and saw Him and His perfect example. And he applied it to his own life. 'While we look, not at the things which are seen, but at the things which are not seen: for the things which are seen are temporal, but the things which are not seen are eternal' (2 Corinthians 4. 17, 18).

'I have come to learn in whatsoever state I am therein to be self-sufficient and independent of circumstances.'

Christian people, can you say that, do you know that state? Let this become first with us, let this become our ambition, let us strain every nerve and do everything we can to get into this blessed state. Life may force it upon us, but even if circumstances do not, the time is bound to come, soon or late, when earth and every earthly scene will pass away, and in that final isolation of the soul we shall be alone, facing death and eternity. The greatest thing in life is to be able to say with Christ Himself at that hour: 'And yet I am not alone because the Father is with me' (John 16. 32).

May God in His infinite grace enable us all to learn this great and vital lesson, and to this end let us offer frequently that prayer of Augustus Toplady:

> 'While I draw this fleeting breath
> When mine eyes shall close in death,
> When I soar through tracts unknown
> See Thee on Thy Judgment Throne,
> Rock of Ages cleft for me
> Let me hide myself in Thee'.

I can do all things through Christ which strengtheneth me.

Philippians 4. 13

XXI

THE FINAL CURE

HERE we are confronted by one of those staggering statements which are to be found in such profusion in the Epistles of this great and mighty apostle to the Gentiles.

There is nothing more misleading when one reads the letters of the Apostle Paul than to assume that when he has really finished the business which he set out to do, he has at the same time finished saying great and mighty things. We should always keep an eye on the postscripts of this apostle. You never know when he is going to throw in a gem. Anywhere, everywhere, in the introduction to his letters, in the postscripts to his letters, there is generally some amazing insight into the Truth or some profound revelation of doctrine.

We are here, in a sense, looking at the postscript to this letter. The apostle has finished the business at the end of verse 9 and he is now just offering his personal thanks to the members of the Church at Philippi for their goodness to him personally, for the gift which they had sent. But, as we have already seen, the apostle could not do that without being involved at once in doctrine. Anxious as he is to thank them, he is still more anxious to show them, and to show to others, that his sufficiency was in Christ, and that whether he is remembered or forgotten by men, he is always complete in the Lord. And it is in that connection that we come to this thirteenth verse.

I say that this is a staggering statement—'I can do all things through Christ which strengtheneth me'. It is a statement that is characterized at one and the same time by a sense of triumph and by humility. He sounds at first as if he were boasting, and yet when you look at his statement again you will find that it is one of the most glorious and striking tributes that he has ever paid anywhere to his Lord and Master. It is one of those paradoxical statements in which this apostle seems to have delighted; indeed, it is the simple truth to say that Christian Truth is always essentially paradoxical. It at one and the same time exhorts us to rejoice, to make our boast, and yet to be humble and to be lowly. And there is no contradiction, because the boast of the Christian is not in himself but in the Lord.

Paul was very fond of saying that. Take, for instance, the statement: 'God forbid that I should glory save in the Cross of our Lord Jesus Christ', or again: 'He that glorieth let him glory in the Lord'. There is the exhortation on the one hand for us to be boasting; yes, but always boasting in Him.

Now this statement belongs to that particular category and perhaps the best way for us to approach it is to give an alternative translation. The Authorized Version is in a sense quite correct, but it does not really bring out the particular shade of meaning the apostle was anxious to convey. It says: 'I can do all things through Christ which strengtheneth me'. But I suggest that a better translation would be: 'I am strong for all things in the One who constantly infuses strength into me'. That gives the exact meaning—'I am strong or made strong, for all things in the One who constantly infuses strength into me'. The authorities are agreed that the word 'Christ' should not appear in this text, and we need not boggle at that. Paul actually put it like that— 'I am strong for all things in the One (Christ) who constantly infuses strength into me'. What the apostle is really saying is not so much that he can do certain things himself, as that he is enabled to do certain things, indeed all things, by this One who infuses His strength into him. In other words we have in this verse the ultimate and the final explanation of what Paul has been saying in the preceding verses. There, you remember, he says—'I have learned in whatsoever state I am, therein (or therewith) to be content. I know both how to be abased and I know how to abound, everywhere and in all things I am instructed both to be full and to be hungry, both to abound and to suffer need'. We have seen that there the apostle is saying that he has come to learn. He was not always able to do this. Paul had had to learn how to be content in every state, how to be self-sufficient, how to be independent of circumstances and surroundings. He had had to learn, indeed he goes on to say that he had been 'initiated' into the secret of how to do this. That is the meaning of 'I have been instructed', and we have seen some of the ways in which the apostle had been led. We have seen that he had come to this knowledge by experience, by logical reasoning out of his Christian faith and by cultivating a personal intimate knowledge of the Lord, looking to Him and His glorious example.

But it is here in this thirteenth verse that we have the ultimate explanation. The real secret, says Paul, which I have discovered is that I am made strong for all things in the One who constantly is infusing strength into me. That is his final explanation. Now I need scarcely remind you that that is the point to which the apostle always returns. Paul never works out an argument without coming back to it. That is the point to which he always brings every argument and discussion, everything always ends in Christ and with Christ. He is the final point, He is the explanation of Paul's living and his whole outlook upon life. That is the doctrine which he commends to us here. In other words he is telling us that Christ is all-sufficient for every circumstance, for every eventuality and for every possibility. And, of course, in saying that, he is introducing us to what in many ways we may describe as the cardinal New Testament doctrine. The Christian life after all is a life, it is a power, it is an activity. That is the thing we so constantly tend to forget. It is not just a philosophy, it is not just a point of view, it is not just a teaching that we take up and try to put into practice. It is all that, but it is something infinitely more. The very essence of the Christian life, according to the New Testament teaching everywhere, is that it is a mighty power that enters into us; it is a life, if you like, that is pulsating in us. It is an activity, and an activity on the part of God.

The apostle has already been emphasizing that, in several places in this very Epistle. Let me remind you of some of them. In the first chapter he says that he is 'confident of this very thing, that He which hath begun a good work in you will perform it until the day of Jesus Christ' (verse 6). 'I want you,' says Paul, 'to think of yourselves as Christians in that way. You are the people in whom God has started to work; God has entered into you, God is working in you.' That is what Christians really are. They are not just men who have taken up a certain theory and are trying to practise it; it is God doing something in them and through them. Or listen again in the second chapter, verses 12 and 13: 'Work out your own salvation with fear and trembling. For it is God that worketh in you both to will and to do of His good pleasure'. It is of His own good pleasure that God is working in us both to will and to do—our highest thoughts, our noblest aspirations, our every righteous inclination is from and of God, is something that is brought into being in us by God Himself. It is God's activity and not merely our activity, and that is why Paul tells us in the third chapter verse 10 that his supreme ambition in life was: 'That I might know Him, and the power of His resurrection. . . .' All along he is interested in this question of the power and of the life.

You find him saying exactly the same thing in other Epistles. What is Paul's great prayer for the Ephesians? He prays that they might know 'the exceeding greatness of His power to usward who believe, according to the working of His mighty power, which He wrought in Christ, when He raised Him from the dead' (chapter 1. 19, 20). He goes on in chapter 2. 10 to say that we are 'His workmanship created anew in Christ Jesus'. You remember also the great statement at the end of the third chapter: 'He is able to do exceeding abundantly above all that we ask or think, according to the power that worketh in us'. Now, that is typical and characteristic New Testament doctrine, and if we have not grasped it we are surely missing one of the most glorious things about the Christian life and position. The Christian, essentially, is a man who has received a new life. We come back again to what I am never tired of quoting, namely, John Wesley's favourite definition of a Christian. He found it in that book by Henry Scougal, a Scotsman who lived in the seventeenth century, and in the very title—'The life of God in the souls of men'. That is what makes a Christian. The Christian is not just a good, decent, moral man; the life of God has entered into him, there is an energy, a power, a life in him and it is that that makes him peculiarly and specifically Christian, and that is exactly what Paul is telling us here.

Let me begin by putting this negatively. The apostle is not telling us in this great verse that he has become a Stoic. He is not saying that as the result of much self-culture, he has developed an indifference to the world and its surroundings, and that as a result of discipline he has at last been able to see that he can do all things or bear all things because of this culture. It is not that. Let me remind you that the Stoic could do that. Stoicism was not only a theory, it was in fact a way of life for many people. Read the lives of some of the Stoics and you will find that as a result of this outlook they had developed a kind of passive indifference to what might happen in the world. In the same way you may have heard or read of the Indian fakirs, men who have so developed the power of the mind that they can control their physical bodies, and by concentration on mind culture can develop this kind of immunity or indifference to what may be happening to them and round and about them. It is also the great principle which characterizes many Eastern religions such as Hinduism and Buddhism. All those religions are basically religions which are designed to help people to die to circumstances and surroundings, and to develop an indifference to the world that is round and about them, to go through this life and world unaffected by circumstances. Now the point I want to make is that the apostle is not teaching some such doctrine. Paul is not telling us that he has become like the Eastern mystics, he is not saying that he has developed this stoical philosophy to such a point that nothing can affect him.

Why am I concerned about this negative emphasis? The reason which compels me to do so is that all such teaching is really hopeless, all those religions are finally pessimistic. Stoicism, in the last analysis, was profound pessimism. It really came to this, that this world is hopeless, that nothing can do any good, that the thing you have to do therefore is to get through life as best you can and just refuse to let yourself be hurt by it. The Eastern religions are, of course, entirely pessimistic. They regard matter in itself as evil, they regard the flesh as essentially evil; everything, they say, is evil, and the only thing to do is to get through life with a minimum of pain and to hope that in some subsequent reincarnation you will be rid of it altogether and at last be absorbed and lost for ever in the absolute and the eternal, and cease to be as a separate personality.

Now that is the very antithesis of the Christian Gospel which is not negative but essentially positive. It does not regard matter as essentially evil nor the world as essentially evil in and of itself in a material sense. But we reject the negative view *in toto* supremely for this reason, that it fails to give the glory and the honour to the Lord Jesus Christ. That is the thing about which Paul is most concerned. Paul wants us to see that his victory is based upon his association with Christ. In other words, we come back to our original definition once more—to be a Christian is not only to believe the teaching of Christ and to practise it; it is not only to try to follow the pattern and example of Christ; it is to be so vitally related to Christ that His life and His power are working in us. It is to be 'in Christ', it is for Christ to be in us. Now these are New Testament terms—'in Christ', 'Christ in you the hope of glory'. They are found everywhere in these New Testament Epistles.

In other words, we can put our doctrine in this form. What Paul is saying here is that Christ infuses so much strength and power into him that he is strong and able for all things. He is not left to himself, he is not struggling alone and vainly against these mighty odds. It is a great power from Christ Himself which is entering, and has entered, into his life, and it is there as a dynamo, as an energy and strength. 'In this,' says Paul, 'I am able for anything.'

Now this is surely one of the most glorious statements he ever made. Here is a man in prison, a man who has already suffered a great deal in his life, a man who knows what it is to be disappointed in so many ways—persecuted, treated with derision and scorn, even disappointed sometimes, as he tells us in the first chapter, in his fellow workers, there in prison in conditions calculated to produce dejection in the stoutest heart, facing perhaps a cruel martyrdom—yet he is able to send out this mighty challenge. 'I am able to stand, to bear all things in the One who is constantly infusing strength into me.'

I am anxious to put this doctrine in this form at the present time. There are those who feel that at a time like this, it is the business of the Christian preacher and the Christian Church constantly to be making comments on the general situation. There are many people who say: 'Are you dealing only with matters of personal experience while the world is as it is? Is it not remote from life? Have you not read your newspaper or even heard the report on the wireless? Don't you see the whole state of the world? Why don't you make some pronouncement on the world situation or on the state of the nations!' My simple answer to such talk is this. What I, or a number of preachers, or the entire Christian Church, may say about the whole situation will probably not affect it at all. The Church has been talking about politics and the economic situation for many years but with no noticeable effect. That is not the business of Christian preaching. The business of Christian preaching is to put this to the people: In this uncertain world, where we have already experienced two world wars within a quarter of a century, and where we may have to face yet another and things that are even worse, here is the question—How are you going to face it all, how can you meet it all? For me to give my views on international politics will not help anybody; but thank God there is something I can do. I can tell you of something, I can tell you of a way which, if you but practise and follow it, will enable you, with the Apostle Paul to say: 'I am strong, I am able for anything that may happen to me, whether it be peace or war, whether it be freedom or slavery, whether it be the kind of life we have known for so long or whether it be entirely different, I am ready for it'. It does not mean, I must repeat, a passive, negative acquiescence in that which is wrong. Not at all—but it does mean that whatever may come, you are ready for it.

Are we able to speak the language of St. Paul? We have already known certain tests and trials, and more may well be coming. Can we say with this man that we have such strength and power that whatever may come we are ready for it? The apostle had power that enabled him to bear anything that might happen. How are we to obtain this power?

There is a great deal of confusion concerning this, and all I want to do is to try to lessen that confusion.

There are many people who spend the whole of their lives in trying to obtain this power, and yet they never seem to have it. They say: 'I meet other Christians who have this, but I never seem to get it'. Or, 'I would give the whole world if I could only get this power into my life. How can I get this power?' They spend their life trying to obtain it and yet they never do. Why is this? I think the main trouble is due to a failure on their part to recognize and to realize the right respective positions of the 'I' and the 'Him' or the 'One' who is mentioned by the apostle. 'I can do all things', or 'I am able for all things through the One who is constantly infusing strength into me', or, to put it in the Authorized Version, 'I can do all things through Christ which strengtheneth me'. Now there is the crux of the whole matter— the right relationship and the correct balance between 'I' and 'Christ'.

There is a great deal of confusion at this point. The first cause of confusion is to emphasize the 'I' only. In a sense I have already dealt with that. It is what the Stoic does, it is what the Hindu or the Buddhist does, it is what all these people who go in for 'mind culture' are constantly doing. And we have seen that this is inadequate. But perhaps the final reason for its inadequacy is that it is a type of teaching that is possible only for people who have a strong will power and who have time to cultivate this will power. Indeed, I agree entirely with what · Mr. G. K. Chesterton said was his main objection to the simple life, namely, that you have to be a millionaire in order to live it. You need the time, and if you are a working man you have neither the leisure nor the opportunity—you have to be a millionaire before you can live the simple life. Is it not exactly the same, or indeed more so, with this other teaching? If you happen to be born a highly intellectual person and have the time and the leisure, you can give your days and your weeks to concentration and to the culture of the mind and spirit. That is no gospel for the person who has not the leisure nor the energy, and especially not for those who have not the intelligence. We must not over-emphasize the 'I'.

That is one error, but there is another which is at the other extreme. As there are some who over-emphasize the 'I' there are those who tend to obliterate the 'I'. Let me put it in terms of something which I read this very week in a religious journal. This is their definition of a Christian.

The Christian, said that article, is:

'A mind through which Christ thinks,
A voice through which Christ speaks,
A heart through which Christ loves,
A hand through which Christ helps'.

My reply to that in terms of my text is—Nonsense. And it is not only nonsense but a travesty of Christian teaching. If the Christian is a mind through which Christ thinks, a voice through which Christ speaks, a heart through which Christ loves and a hand through which Christ helps, where is the 'I'? The 'I' has vanished, the 'I' has been obliterated, the 'I' is no longer present and in existence. The teaching represented by that quotation is that the Christian is a man whose personality has gone out of existence, while Christ is using his various powers and faculties. Not using him but using his voice, using his mind, using his heart, using his hand. But that is not what Paul says. Paul says: 'I can do all things through Christ which strengtheneth me'. Or listen to him elsewhere. You remember what he says in the second chapter of the Epistle to the Galatians: 'I live, yet not I, but Christ liveth in me'. Is there in these verses an obliteration of the 'I'? 'I live, yet not I, but Christ liveth in me. And the life

I now live in the flesh, I live by the faith of the Son of God who loved me and gave Himself for me.' The 'I' is still there.

We must, therefore, if we are to be just to this doctrine, safeguard the true position. The Christian life is not a life that I live myself and by my own power; neither is it a life in which I am obliterated and Christ does all. No, 'I can do all things through Christ'. I wonder if I can best put this by telling you of how an old preacher, famous in the last century, once put it when preaching on this very text. Those old preachers used sometimes to preach in a dramatic way. They would have a kind of dialogue with the apostle in the pulpit. So this old preacher began to preach on this text in this way: 'I can do all things through Christ which strengtheneth me.' 'Wait a minute, Paul, what did I hear you say?' 'I can do all things.' 'Paul, surely that is boasting, surely you are just claiming for yourself that you are a super-man?' 'No, no, I can do all things.' Well, the old preacher kept up the dialogue. He questioned Paul and quoted every statement made by Paul in which he says that he is the least of all saints, etc. 'You are generally so humble, Paul, but now you say "I can do all things", haven't you started boasting?' And then at last Paul says: 'I can do all things through Christ'. 'Oh, I am sorry,' said the old preacher, 'I beg your pardon, Paul, I did not realize there were two of you.' Now I think that puts it perfectly. 'I can do all things through Christ.' 'There are two of you.' Not I only, not Christ only, I and Christ, Christ and I, two of us.

Very well, then, let us put the doctrine like this. What is the right way to approach this question of power? How can I get this power which Paul tells us was being infused into him and which made him strong and able to stand and bear all things? May I suggest an analogy? I do so with hesitancy and trepidation because no analogy is perfect in this matter, and yet to use one can help us to arrive at the truth. The vital matter in this connection is the matter of the approach, or if you prefer a military term, the strategy. Never is the strategy of 'the indirect approach' more important than it is here. You know that in military strategy you do not always go straight at the objective. Sometimes you may appear to be going in the opposite direction but you come back. That is the strategy of the indirect approach. Now that is the strategy that is needed here.

Let me put it, then, in terms of an illustration. This question of power in the Christian life is like the question of health physical health. There are many people in this world who spend most of their lives in seeking health. They spend their time and money going round from Spa to Spa, from treatment to treatment, from physician to physician. They are seeking health. Whenever you meet them they begin at once to talk about their health. The big thing in their lives is this question of health and yet they are never well. What is the matter? Sometimes the trouble is due to the fact that they forget first principles, and the whole explanation of the state they are in, is that they eat too much, or take too little exercise. They are living an unnatural life, and because they eat too much they produce certain acids and these acids produce conditions that call for treatment. They have to be told to eat less or to exercise more, or whatever it may chance to be. Their problem would never have arisen were it not that they had forgotten the first principles, the fundamental rules of life and living. Because of this they develop an unnatural situation and a condition that needs treatment. Now I suggest that that is analogous to this whole subject of power in one's life as a Christian. Health is something that results from right living. Health cannot be obtained directly or immediately or in and of itself. There is a sense in which I am prepared to say that a man should not think of his health as such at all. Health is the result of right living, and I say exactly the same thing about this question of power in our Christian lives.

Or let me use another illustration. Take this question of preaching. No subject is discussed more often than power in preaching. 'Oh, that I might have power in preaching', says the preacher and he goes on his knees and prays for power. I think that that may be quite wrong. It certainly is if it is the only thing that the preacher does. The way to have power is to prepare your message carefully. Study the Word of God, think it out, analyse it, put it in order, do your utmost. That is the message God is most likely to bless—the indirect approach rather than the direct. It is exactly the same in this matter of power and ability to live the Christian life. In addition to our prayer for power and ability we must obey certain primary rules and laws.

I can therefore summarise the teaching like this. The secret of power is to discover and to learn from the New Testament what is possible for us in Christ. What I have to do is to go to Christ. I must spend my time with Him, I must meditate upon Him, I must get to know Him. That was Paul's ambition—'that I might know Him'. I must maintain my contact and communion with Christ and I must concentrate on knowing Him.

What else? I must do exactly what He tells me. I must avoid things that would hamper. To use my illustration, I must not eat too much, I must not get into an atmosphere that is bad for me, I must not expose myself to chills if I want to be well. In the same way, if we do not keep the spiritual rules we may pray endlessly for power but we shall never get it. There are no short cuts in the Christian life. If in the midst of persecution we want to feel as Paul felt, we must live as Paul lived. I must do what He tells me, both to do and not to do. I must read the Bible, I must exercise, I must practise the Christian life, I must live the Christian life in all its fullness. In other words I must implement what Paul has been teaching in verses eight and nine. This, as I understand it, is the New Testament doctrine of abiding in Christ. Now the word 'abiding' makes people become sentimental. They think of abiding as something passive and clinging, but to abide in Christ is to do what He tells you, positively, and to pray without ceasing. Abiding is a tremendously active thing.

'Well,' says the apostle, 'if you do all that He will infuse His strength into you.' What a wonderful idea. This is a kind of spiritual blood transfusion—that is what Paul is teaching here. Here is a patient who has lost much blood for some reason or another. He is faint and gasping for breath. It is no use giving him drugs because he has not enough blood to absorb them and use them. The man is anaemic. The only thing you can do for him is to give him a blood transfusion, infuse blood into him. That is what Paul tells us the Lord Jesus Christ was doing for him. 'I find I am very feeble,' says Paul, 'my energy seems to flag and sometimes I feel I have no life blood in me at all. But, you know, because of this relationship, I find He infuses it into me. He knows my every state and condition, He knows exactly what I need. Oh, how much He gives me! He says, "My grace is sufficient for thee", and so I can say, "when I am weak then I am strong". Sometimes I am conscious of great power; there are other times when I expect nothing, but He gives everything.'

That is the romance of the Christian life. Nowhere does one experience it more than in a Christian pulpit. There is certainly romance in preaching. I often say that the most romantic place on earth is the pulpit. I ascend the pulpit stairs Sunday after Sunday; I never know what is going to happen. I confess that sometimes for various reasons I come expecting nothing; but suddenly the power is given. At other times I think I have a great deal because of my preparation; but, alas, I find there is no power in it. Thank God it is like that. I do my utmost, but He controls the supply and the power, He infuses it. He is the heavenly physician and He knows every variation in my condition. He sees my complexion, He feels my pulse. He knows my inadequate preaching, He knows everything. 'That is it,' says Paul, 'and therefore I am able for all things through the One who is constantly infusing strength into me.'

That, then, is the prescription. Do not agonize in prayer beseeching Him for power. Do what He has told you to do. Live the Christian life. Pray, and meditate upon Him. Spend time with Him and ask Him to manifest Himself to you. And as long as you do that you can leave the rest to Him. He will give you strength—'as thy days so shall thy strength be'. He knows us better than we know ourselves, and according to our need so will be our supply. Do that and you will be able to say with the apostle: 'I am able (made strong) for all things through the One who is constantly infusing strength into me'.

Printed at the Press of the Publishers.